Lecture Notes of the Institute for Computer Sciences, Social Informatics and Telecommunications Engineering

More information about this series at http://www.springer.com/series/8197

Octavian Fratu · Nicolae Militaru
Simona Halunga (Eds.)

Future Access Enablers for Ubiquitous and Intelligent Infrastructures

Third International Conference, FABULOUS 2017
Bucharest, Romania, October 12–14, 2017
Proceedings

 Springer

Editors
Octavian Fratu
Politehnica University of Bucharest
Bucharest
Romania

Simona Halunga
University Polytechnica of Bucharest
Bucharest
Romania

Nicolae Militaru
University Polytechnica of Bucharest
Bucharest
Romania

ISSN 1867-8211   ISSN 1867-822X (electronic)
Lecture Notes of the Institute for Computer Sciences, Social Informatics
and Telecommunications Engineering
ISBN 978-3-319-92212-6   ISBN 978-3-319-92213-3   (eBook)
https://doi.org/10.1007/978-3-319-92213-3

Library of Congress Control Number: 2018944406

Printed on acid-free paper

This Springer imprint is published by the registered company Springer International Publishing AG
part of Springer Nature
The registered company address is: Gewerbestrasse 11, 6330 Cham, Switzerland

Preface

After the prestigious EAI scientific events in Ohrid, Republic of Macedonia, and in Belgrade, Republic of Serbia, the Third EAI International Conference on Future Access Enablers of Ubiquitous and Intelligent Infrastructures (Fabulous 2017) was held in Bucharest, Romania, hosted by the Politehnica University of Bucharest. The conference succeeded in providing an excellent international platform for prominent researchers from academia and industry, innovators and entrepreneurs, to share their knowledge and their latest results in the broad areas of future wireless networks, ambient and assisted living, and smart infrastructures.

The main topics of Fabulous 2017 included future access networks, the Internet of Things and smart city/smart environment applications, communications and computing infrastructures, security aspects in communications and data processing, and signal processing and multimedia. Three special sessions – "Computational Modeling and Invited Papers," "Multimedia Security and Forensics," and "Optoelectronic Devices and Applications Thereof in the Communications Domain" – completed the technical program. With two invited papers, six keynote speeches, and 39 regular papers, Fabulous 2017 hosted high-quality technical presentations from young researchers and, also, from well-known specialists from academia and industry who have shaped the field of wireless communications.

The two invited papers were presented by two young female researchers, Elena Diana Șandru and Ana Neacșu, PhD and MSc students, respectively, from the Politehnica University of Bucharest.

The six keynote speeches were presented by Prof. Ramjee Prasad (Aalborg University, Denmark), Prof. Nenad Filipovic (University of Kragujevac, Serbia), Dr. Marius Iordache (Orange, Romania), Prof. Hana Bogucka (Poznan University of Technology, Poland), Dr. Onoriu Brădeanu (Vodafone, Romania), and Thomas Wrede (SES, Luxembourg).

Fabulous 2017 was co-sponsored by Orange Romania and SES Luxembourg. The latter company also sponsored the participation of young researchers in the conference, based on the reviewers' evaluation. The "Innovative Cybersecurity Public Private Partnership" round table, chaired by Prof. Iulian Martin from the National Defense University Carol I and sponsored by Safetech Innovation SRL and Beia Consult International SRL, were received by participants with great interest. The Best Paper Award of the conference was granted to the paper "Prediction of Coronary Plaque Progression Using a Data-Driven the Approach" having as first author Bojana Andjelkovic Cirkovic, a young researcher from University of Kragujevac, Serbia.

We would like to show our appreciation for the effort, constant support, and guidance of the Fabulous 2017 conference manager, Katarina Antalova (EAI) and of the Steering Committee members, Imrich Chlamtac, Liljana Gavrilovska, and Alberto Leon-Garcia. Our thanks also go to the Organizing Committee, and especially to the Technical Program Committee, led by Prof. Simona Halunga, whose effort materialized in a high-quality technical program. We are also grateful to the local Organizing Committee co-chairs, Dr. Carmen Voicu and Dr. Ioana Manuela Marcu, for theirs sustained effort in organizing and supporting the conference.

Last but not least, the success of the Fabulous 2017 EAI conference is also due to the high quality of the participants, researchers from academia and industry, whose contributions – included in this volume – have proven to be very valuable. It is our opinion that Fabulous 2017 provided opportunities for the delegates to exchanges their ideas, to find mutual scientific interests, and thus, to foster future research relations.

May 2015

Octavian Fratu
Nicolae Militaru

Organization

Steering Committee

Imrich Chlamtac	EAI/Create-Net and University of Trento, Italy
Liljana Gavrilovska	Ss. Cyril and Methodius University in Skopje, Macedonia
Alberto Leon-Garcia	University of Toronto, Canada

Organizing Committee

General Chairs

Octavian Fratu	Politehnica University of Bucharest, Romania
Liljana Gavrilovska	Ss. Cyril and Methodius University, Skopje, Macedonia

Technical Program Committee Chair

Simona Halunga	Politehnica University of Bucharest, Romania

Web Chair

Alexandru Vulpe	Politehnica University of Bucharest, Romania

Publicity and Social Media Chairs

Albena Mihovska	Aalborg University, Denmark
Cristian Negrescu	Politehnica University of Bucharest, Romania

Workshop Chairs

Corneliu Burileanu	Politehnica University of Bucharest, Romania
Pavlos Lazaridis	University of Huddersfield, UK

Sponsorship and Exhibits Chair

Eduard Cristian Popovici	Politehnica University of Bucharest, Romania

Publications Chair

Nicolae Militaru	Politehnica University of Bucharest, Romania

Posters and PhD Track Chairs

Răzvan Tamaş	Constanta Maritime University, Romania
Alexandru Martian	Politehnica University of Bucharest, Romania

Local Chairs

Carmen Voicu   Politehnica University of Bucharest, Romania
Ioana Manuela Marcu   Politehnica University of Bucharest, Romania

Secretariat

Madalina Berceanu   Politehnica University of Bucharest, Romania
Ana-Maria Claudia   Politehnica University of Bucharest, Romania
  Dragulinescu

Conference Manager

Katarina Antalova   European Alliance for Innovation

Technical Program Committee

Anđelković-Ćirković Bojana	University of Kragujevac, Serbia
Atanasovski Vladimir	Ss. Cyril and Methodius University in Skopje, Macedonia
Bota Vasile	Technical University of Cluj, Romania
Boucouvalas Anthony	University of the Peloponnese, Greece
Brădeanu Onoriu	Vodafone, Romania
Burileanu Dragos	University Politehnica of Bucharest, Romania
Chiper Doru Florin	Gheorghe Asachi Technical University of Iaşi, Romania
Croitoru Victor	University Politehnica of Bucharest, Romania
Enaki Nicolae	Academy of Sciences of Moldova
Feieş Valentin	University Politehnica of Bucharest, Romania
Filipović Nenad	University of Kragujevac, Serbia
Halunga Simona	University Politehnica of Bucharest, Romania
Marghescu Ion	University Politehnica of Bucharest, Romania
Ionescu Bogdan	University Politehnica of Bucharest, Romania
Isailović Velibor	University of Kragujevac, Serbia
Khwandah Sinan	Brunel University London, UK
Latkoski Pero	Ss. Cyril and Methodius University in Skopje, Macedonia
Lazaridis Pavlos	University of Huddersfield
Manea Adrian	University Politehnica of Bucharest, Romania
Marcu Ioana	University Politehnica of Bucharest, Romania
Mihovska Albena	Aarhus University, Denmark
Militaru Nicolae	University Politehnica of Bucharest, Romania
Nikolić Dalibor	University of Kragujevac, Serbia
Paleologu Constantin	University Politehnica of Bucharest, Romania
Pejanović-Đurišić Milica	University of Montenegro
Petrescu Teodor	University Politehnica of Bucharest, Romania
Popovici Eduard Cristian	University Politehnica of Bucharest, Romania
Poulkov Vladimir	Technical University of Sofia, Bulgaria
Preda Radu Ovidiu	University Politehnica of Bucharest, Romania
Radusinović Igor	University of Montenegro

Contents

Session on Multimedia Security and Forensics

**Session on Optoelectronic Devices and Applications thereof
in Communications Domain**

Session on Computational Modeling

Fabulous Main Track

A Hybrid Testbed for Secure Internet-of-Things

Ştefan-Ciprian Arseni[✉], Alexandru Vulpe[✉], Simona Halunga, and Octavian Fratu

Telecommunications Department, University Politehnica of Bucharest, 1-3 Iuliu Maniu Blvd., 061071 Bucharest, Romania
{stefan.arseni, alex.vulpe}@radio.pub.ro, {shalunga, ofratu}@elcom.pub.ro

Abstract. The need for insertion of technology in everyday tasks has brought an increase in new methodologies and concepts used to accomplish such objectives. By trying to make technology an enabler for an increasing number of personal or work-related activities, we allow devices to collect data about our way of being, that, if not properly protected and used, can prove a vulnerability for our personal security. This is why new means of securing information, even by the tiniest or low-resource devices, need to be implemented and, in many cases, they take the form of cryptographic algorithms, classic or lightweight. Assessing these algorithms can sometimes become difficult, depending on the targeted system or on the environment where the device will be deployed. To address this issue and help developers, in this paper we present a hybrid testbed, comprised of three hardware architectures, that will ensure a general environment in which users can test their security solutions, in order to have an idea of what changes need to be made to provide optimal performances.

Keywords: Internet-of-Things · Security · Hybrid testbed
Software middleware · Hardware architectures

1 Introduction

Ever since the industrial revolution, humanity has been searching for methods of creating better technologies that can improve the way humans not only interact with the environment, but also how they make use of the resources provided. Recent years have brought a new technological revolution, in terms of miniaturization of devices and their embedment in all layers of society. Earlier proposed concepts, such as Internet of Things [1, 2], Cloud Computing [3, 4] or Deep Learning [5, 6], have become today's trending technologies, being in a continuous process of development [7] and integration [8–10]. Yet, this fast pace that is characteristic to any recent offer-demand pair in nowadays' economy [11, 12] introduces also some vulnerabilities regarding mainly the security aspects [13, 14]. Focusing on the Internet of Things (IoT) concept [15, 16], the embedment of sensors or smart devices in the environment [17] surrounding us sets new thresholds that need to be passed before any data is captured, processed and/or transmitted to a sink device or to a Cloud service.

© ICST Institute for Computer Sciences, Social Informatics and Telecommunications Engineering 2018
O. Fratu et al. (Eds.): FABULOUS 2017, LNICST 241, pp. 3–8, 2018.
https://doi.org/10.1007/978-3-319-92213-3_1

Addressing the need of security in transmitting information has been generally made by using cryptographic algorithms to encrypt the data that needs to be sent. These cryptographic algorithms have different key features that make them reliable under certain conditions or in specific environments. The miniaturization of devices brought a problem for security, given that classic cryptographic algorithms require a certain amount of resources to function with an acceptable performance. The constraint resources of a sensor or embedded device lead to the introduction of a new branch of cryptographic algorithms, namely lightweight cryptographic algorithms that give a reasonable degree of security, without requiring too many resources [18–20].

Being a relatively new study domain, when compared to classic cryptography, lightweight cryptographic algorithms can, sometimes, prove to be difficult to implement or create, thus requiring a strict phase of testing in which any minor vulnerability or performance drop can be resolved. The hybrid testbed presented in this article was first introduced in [21] and it addresses the problem of testing the implementations of lightweight cryptography, by giving developers a unified platform to conduct their tests on. This testbed is comprised of three different types of hardware architectures, so that the behavior of the implementation on specific environments can be observed. The access to these hardware architectures is done through a middleware that acts as a unique point-of-entrance, enabling developers to write their implementation once and test it simultaneously or consecutively, on each one of the three base architectures. This paper continues the testbed presentation initiated in the previously mentioned paper, by adding information regarding the middleware layer of the testbed, on how it makes use of the hardware architectures and how it enables users to interact with the testbed.

The present paper is organized as follows. Section 2 gives an overview of the proposed testbed, while in Sect. 3 we focus on the software layer of the testbed and give a description of the method of interfacing users with the middleware. In Sect. 4, some conclusions are drawn.

2 Overview of the Testbed

In scientific literature, multiple papers, [22–26], have presented the benefits given by the hardware implementations of cryptographic algorithms as compared to the software counterparts. By integrating in our testbed an SDSoC (Software Defined System-On-a-Chip) that contains also a number of logical gates that can be programmed, we enable users to test their implementation in this type of environment also. The other two hardware architectures of the testbed allow only a software implementation of an algorithm.

In order for users to interact with these hardware architectures, they need to interact with the middleware layer of the testbed. This layer is composed of two sub- layers: one consisting of the drivers or APIs (Application Programming Interface), required to communicate with the hardware layer, and one consisting of the integrator APIs which developers will use and integrate in their implementations.

The main architecture of the testbed, with an emphasis on the hardware layer, was presented in papers [21, 27] and Fig. 1 depicts its high-level design. The current paper continues the description through an initial validation of the middleware layer, emphasizing on the connection of it with the hardware layer and the means that users can access its functions.

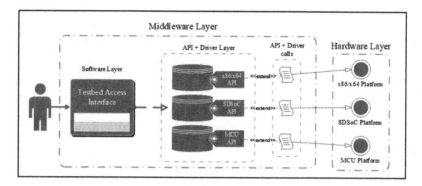

Fig. 1. Main architecture of testbed

3 Middleware Layer of the Testbed

As described in [27], the main challenge is to create a unified access point for all three hardware systems, while maintaining control over the operating characteristics that represent criteria when assessing an algorithm. In order to achieve this point of integration the platforms were customized to support a self-contained operating environment, either under the form of an operating system or a scheduler-service, as will be described in the remaining part of the section.

Each one of the hardware architectures presents its own methods of interaction that are made available to a user or developer. Figure 2 presents an overview of forming and receiving, by the corresponding architecture, the API and driver calls, shown in Fig. 1. The UI (User Interface) is the component that sends calls to the middleware and customizes the task sent to each one of the hardware elements, as follows:

- For the standard x64 processor that can run also x86 applications, a simple task dispatcher is implemented as a service that waits for the user to send a task to be executed. The task represents an algorithm implementation that is done by the user and sent through the testbed UI. After the completion of the task, collected metrics are parsed and sent to the UI to give the user a performance view of its implementation or algorithm.
- The SDSoC architecture is comprised of two hardware elements that can be used either separately or as a whole. In our proposed testbed, these elements are used as one, by establishing the required communication bridge between them. The FPGA (Field Programmable Gate Array) element contains some defined cryptographic functions, such as permutation, standard AES (Advanced Encryption Standard) S-Boxes or substitutions, which can increase the performance of an algorithm. The implementation in FPGA was taken into consideration given a few performance tests made between a hardware and software implementation of the same algorithm,

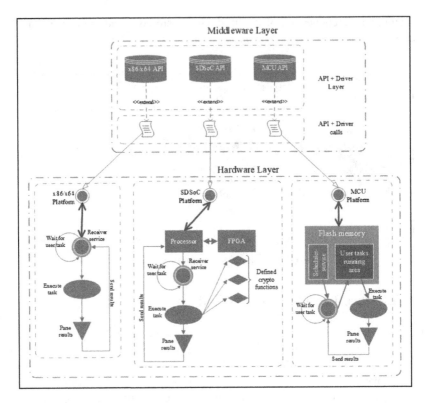

Fig. 2. Hardware layer customization

tests that were briefly presented in [27]. The second element, the processor, is the point in which the dispatcher service resides and the task is mainly being executed. After the successful completion of the task, results are parsed and transmitted to the UI.

- The third hardware element takes advantage of the possibility of dynamically writing an application into the Flash memory that can be executed afterwards. Implemented as a bootloader, the scheduling-service waits for a task to be deployed through the UI. After receiving a task, the service writes it into the Flash at a separate address and launches it into execution. In this case, the service will return in the waiting state, but will not have the functionality of parsing and sending the results. This functionality will reside in the task itself and will be attached to the user code at deployment.

After terminating all the deployed tasks, the UI will act also as a collector of data from the underlying dispatcher-services, by formatting and grouping the data and presenting it to the user as performance metrics.

4 Conclusions

The paper introduces a part of the elements that the proposed hybrid testbed contains, with a focus on the software layer and on method of interaction between users and it. Given that this testbed will enable simultaneous testing on three different hardware architectures, it can prove to be an important factor in the process of large-scale integration of the IoT concept. An initial validation of the proposed testbed has been made with high-level tests, through which observations were made on how the testbed can be completely integrated and how multiple functionalities can be developed for users.

Acknowledgments. This work was supported by University "Politehnica" of Bucharest, through the "Excellence Research Grants" Program, UPB – GEX, Identifier: UPB–EXCE-LENTA–2016, project "Platform for Studying Security in IoT", contract number 96/2016 (PaSS-IoT) and by a grant of the Ministry of Innovation and Research, UEFISCDI, project number 5 Sol/2017 within PNCDI III and partially funded by UEFISCDI Romania under grant no. 60BG/2016 "Intelligent communications system based on integrated infrastructure, with dynamic display and alerting - SICIAD".

References

1. Wortmann, F., Flüchter, K.: Internet of Things - technology and value added. Bus. Inf. Syst. Eng. **57**(3), 221–224 (2015)
2. Gubbia, J., Buyyab, R., Marusica, S., Palaniswamihuang, M.: Internet of Things (IoT): a vision, architectural elements, and future directions. Future Gener. Comput. Syst. **29**(7), 1645–1660 (2013)
3. Qian, L., Luo, Z., Du, Y., Guo, L.: Cloud computing: an overview, cloud computing. In: Proceedings of The First International Conference CloudCom 2009, Beijing, China, 1–4 December 2009, pp. 626–631 (2009)
4. Buyyaa, R., Yeoa, C.S., Venugopala, S., Broberga, J., Brandic, I.: Cloud computing and emerging IT platforms: vision, hype, and reality for delivering computing as the 5th utility. Future Gener. Comput. Syst. **25**(6), 599–616 (2009)
5. Schmidhuber, J.: Deep learning in neural networks: an overview. Neural Netw. **61**, 85–117 (2015)
6. LeCun, Y., Bengio, Y., Hinton, G.: Deep learning. Nature **521**(7553), 436–444 (2015). https://doi.org/10.1038/nature14539
7. Miorandia, D., Sicarib, S., De Pellegrinia, F., Chlamtaca, I.: Internet of Things: vision, applications and research challenges. Ad Hoc Netw. **10**(7), 1497–1516 (2012)
8. Botta, A., Donato, W., Persico, V., Pescapé, A.: Integration of cloud computing and Internet of Things: a survey. Future Gener. Comput. Syst. **56**, 684–700 (2016)
9. Lane, N.D., Bhattacharya, S., Georgiev, P., Forlivesi, C., Kawsar, F.: An early resource characterization of deep learning on wearables, Smartphones and Internet-of-Things devices. In: Proceedings of the 2015 International Workshop on Internet of Things Towards Applications, 01 November 2015, Seoul, South Korea (2015). https://doi.org/10.1145/2820975.2820980

10. Ma, X., Yu, H., Wang, Y., Wang, Y.: Large-scale transportation network congestion evolution prediction using deep learning theory. PLoS ONE **10**(3), e0119044 (2015). https://doi.org/10.1371/journal.pone.0119044
11. Porter, M.E., Heppelmann, J.E.: How smart, connected products are transforming competition. Harvard Bus. Rev. **92**(11), 64–88 (2014)
12. Weber, R.H.: Internet of Things – new security and privacy challenges. Comput. Law Secur. Rev. **26**(1), 23–30 (2010)
13. Subashini, S., Kavitha, V.: A survey on security issues in service delivery models of cloud computing. J. Netw. Comput. Appl. **34**(1), 1–11 (2011)
14. Zissis, D., Lekkas, D.: Addressing cloud computing security issues. Future Gener. Comput. Syst. **28**(3), 583–592 (2012)
15. Sicaria, S., Rizzardia, A., Griecob, L.A., Coen-Porisini, A.: Security, privacy and trust in Internet of Things: the road ahead. Comput. Netw. **76**, 146–164 (2015)
16. Yana, Z., Zhangc, P., Vasilakos, A.V.: A survey on trust management for Internet of Things. J. Netw. Comput. Appl. **42**, 120–134 (2014)
17. Romana, R., Zhoua, J., Lopezb, J.: On the features and challenges of security and privacy in distributed Internet of Things. Comput. Netw. **57**(10), 2266–2279 (2013)
18. Poschmann, A.Y.: Lightweight cryptography: cryptographic engineering for a pervasive world. Ph.D. thesis (2009)
19. Masanobu, K., Moriai, S.: Lightweight cryptography for the Internet of Things. Sony Corporation (2008). https://pdfs.semanticscholar.org/9595/b5b8db9777d5795625886418d38864f78bb3.pdf
20. Manifavas, C., Hatzivasilis, G., Fysarakis, K., Rantos, K.: Lightweight cryptography for embedded systems – a comparative analysis. In: Garcia-Alfaro, J., Lioudakis, G., Cuppens-Boulahia, N., Foley, S., Fitzgerald, William M. (eds.) DPM/SETOP -2013. LNCS, vol. 8247, pp. 333–349. Springer, Heidelberg (2014). https://doi.org/10.1007/978-3-642-54568-9_21
21. Arseni, S., Miţoi, M., Vulpe, A.: PASS-IoT: a platform for studying security, privacy and trust in IoT. In: 11th International Conference on Communications (COMM 2016), Bucharest, Romania, 9–11 June 2016 (2016). ISBN: 978-1-4673-8196-3
22. Eisenbarth, T., Sandeep, K.: A survey of lightweight-cryptography implementations. IEEE Des. Test Comput. **24**(6), 222–533 (2007)
23. Panasayya, Y., Kaps, J.-P.: Lightweight cryptography for FPGAs. In: 2009 Proceedings of International Conference on Reconfigurable Computing and FPGAs, ReConFig 2009, pp. 225–230. IEEE (2009)
24. Cédric, H., Kamel, D., Regazzoni, F., Legat, J.-D., Flandre, D., Bol, D., Standaert, F.-X.: Harvesting the potential of nano-CMOS for lightweight cryptography: an ultra-low- voltage 65 nm AES coprocessor for passive RFID tags. J. Cryptograph. Eng. **1**(1), 79–86 (2011)
25. Aydin, A., Gulcan, E., Schaumont, P.: SIMON says: break area records of block ciphers on FPGAs. IEEE Embed. Syst. Lett. **6**(2), 37–40 (2014)
26. Vivek, V., Shila, D.M.: High throughput implementations of cryptography algorithms on GPU and FPGA. In: 2013 IEEE International Instrumentation and Measurement Technology Conference (I2MTC), pp. 723–727. IEEE (2013)
27. Vulpe, A., Arseni, Ş.-C., Marcu, I., Voicu, C., Fratu, O.: Building a unified middleware architecture for security in IoT. In: Rocha, Á., Correia, A.M., Adeli, H., Reis, L.P., Costanzo, S. (eds.) WorldCIST 2017. AISC, vol. 570, pp. 105–114. Springer, Cham (2017). https://doi.org/10.1007/978-3-319-56538-5_11

Considerations on Estimating the Minimal Level of Attenuation in TEMPEST Filtering for IT Equipments

Mircea Popescu[1]([⊠]), Răzvan Bărtuşică[1], Alexandru Boitan[1], Ioana Marcu[2], and Simona Halunga[2]

[1] The Special Telecommunications Service, Bucharest, Romania
mpopescu@sts.ro
[2] University Politehnica of Bucharest, Bucharest, Romania
imarcu@radio.pub.ro

Abstract. The main purpose of this research is to improve the security of critical computer systems with minimal costs. One of the main problems in such cases is the secondary emissions generated by electronic equipment that, sometimes, might contain confidential information stored inside a secured computer network. The implementation of a set of measures necessary to prevent information leakage through compromising emissions is generally expensive. This paper analyzes some minimal requirements that have to be fulfilled by the filtering devices in order to protect the existing commercial IT equipment against compromising emissions.

Keywords: Compromising emissions · TEMPEST · Electrical filter

1 Introduction

Protection against electromagnetic disturbances is becoming an increasingly important issue for all researchers that have to deal with critical information, such as banks, commerce and security, given that our daily activity becomes more dependent on computers and telecommunications. As they become more and more sophisticated, they tend to become less resistant to electromagnetic interferences.

Both filtering and shielding are designed to reduce the electromagnetic radiation, so these two operations can be seen as a synergy, each complementing the other. Thus it is important to understand that inappropriate filtering can easily increase the risk of radiated coupling and inappropriate shielding can lead to conductive coupling.

A proper design of the filters may prevent interferences from electrical wires inside or outside the protected area through metallic interfaces, reducing the conductive coupling, as well as the radial coupling to and from the cables. In TEMPEST protection [1] filters are used to prevent these interferences generated in computer equipment to propagate outward as compromising emissions transmitted through the power supply network.

A large number of research and studies in the area of compromising emissions in the interconnection lines of electrical equipment are under development, underlining

© ICST Institute for Computer Sciences, Social Informatics and Telecommunications Engineering 2018
O. Fratu et al. (Eds.): FABULOUS 2017, LNICST 241, pp. 9–15, 2018.
https://doi.org/10.1007/978-3-319-92213-3_2

the importance of the domain. In [1–3] the authors concentrated on evaluating and reducing the compromising radiations of LCD/TV sets, while in [4] a number of TEMPEST security testing models and countermeasures are illustrated. In [5] the authors presented the results obtained in reconstruction of laser printer information based on the leakages in the media of electromagnetic radiation, power and signal lines. A model and testing procedures for critical systems to severe electro-magnetic threats are given in [6] while in [7] the authors show a number of results related to efficiency of shielding for communication equipment under TEMPEST evaluation.

In this paper we estimate a minimum level of attenuation of an electrical filter installed on the supply line of commercial computer equipment, so that at the exit of the controllable zone the compromising signals generated by the equipment cannot be detected and intercepted by a hostile receiver. Based on the developed testbed the estimated value is then verified under worst case scenario.

The paper is organized as follows: Sect. 2 sets the theoretical basis for estimating the minimum attenuation value of an electric filter for TEMPEST protection of commercial computer; Sect. 3 illustrates by relevant laboratory tests the theoretical considerations presented in Sects. 2 and 4 contains the main conclusions drawn from tests in Sect. 3.

2 Estimation of the Minimum Attenuation Level for an Electrical Filter in TEMPEST Protection

To establish the minimum level of attenuation of the filter installed on the power line to ensure TEMPEST protection of an IT system, we assume the following: the target computer equipment is commercial type (COTS) and meets the electromagnetic disturbance requirements specified in European Standard EN 55022 [8]; the signal-to-noise ratio (*SNR*) received on the power line in the controllable space is limited to 1 (or 0 dB) to reduce the probability of detecting compromising emissions generated by computer equipment; the attacker has the ability to connect sensitive receivers directly to the building's power supply, communication cables or other metal structures near the target device as well as to receive and process compromising signals with low levels comparable to electrical noise; the electrical noise received by the interceptor on the power line is specific to the residential environment; the interceptor searches for broadband pulses in a quiet zone of the spectrum, with as little external interference as possible; it uses "notch" filters to suppress strong emissions from narrowband radio stations as well as strong signal processing techniques to extract the information carrier from the unwanted background noise.

The minimum filter attenuation level installed on the power line to reduce the probability of detecting and intercepting compromising emissions by a hostile receiver at the limit of controllable space can be determined by [1]

$$A_F \frac{U_B \cdot G_p}{U_{n,B} \cdot A_c \cdot f_r \cdot SNR}. \tag{1}$$

where *UB* is the maximum voltage of the conducted disturbances allowed by EN 55022 [8] received with equipment with the IF bandwidth *B*; *Gp* is the processing gain obtained by specific techniques (e.g. periodic mediation, correlations) for recovering the information from the compromising signal; *Un,B* is the root mean square of the background noise noticed by the IF receiver with the bandwidth *B*; *AF* is the attenuation of the electrical filter installed on the power line between the target equipment and the hostile receiver; *Ac* is the attenuation of the signal through the conductor network between the target equipment and the hostile receiver; *fr* is the noise figure of the interceptor receiver.

Rewriting (1) on a logarithmic scale

$$[A_F] = [U_B] + [G_p] - [U_{n,B}] - [A_c] - [f_r] - [SNR], \qquad (2)$$

where $[x] = 20lg\ (x)$ is the value of parameter x expressed in dB.

The noise and cable attenuation values in the above equations are random variables, which, in the absence of standardized data, might be modeled as a normal distribution with mean and variance evaluated statistically based on a large number of measurements in different environments. For other parameters, reasonable estimates must be made, based on the values used in most practical applications, such that the [SNR] should be below an acceptable level with a sufficient detection probability.

Different types of target signals are received on different frequency ranges and allow different processing gains. Thus all parameters must be estimated separately for the different types of signal of interest. In this paper we assume that the signals have the data rate equal to 5 MHz (e.g. the signal generated by the video card).

The EN 55022 EMC standard imposes that the maximum allowed voltage disturbances measured across a 50 Ω impedance in parallel with 50 μH should not exceed 46 dBμV in the frequency range 0.5 ÷ 5 MHz, respectively 50 dBμV in the frequency range 5 ÷ 30 MHz measured with a average detector having a resolution bandwidth of 9 kHz [8]. The compromising emissions of modern digital signals contains wideband impulses so the receiver passband has to be extended from 9 kHz (specified in EN 55022 standard) to 2 or 5 MHz. Hence, the received signal strength increases by 20lg (2 MHz/9 kHz) = 47 dB for signal with the bandwidth of 2 MHz, and 20lg (5 MHz/9 kHz) = 55 dB for signal with the bandwidth 5 MHz.

To determine the value of the electrical filter attenuation, [AF], the worst case scenario has been taken into consideration corresponding to the case in which the electronic equipment generates secondary emissions on the power line to the maximum allowed level. Applying this correction (i.e. for 5 MHz resolution bandwidth) we obtain the limits for the conducted emissions: [UB] = (46 + 55) = 101 dBμV, for RBW@5 MHz, in the frequency range 0.5 ÷ 5 MHz and [UB] = (50 + 55) = 105 dBμV for RBW@5 MHz in the frequency range 5 ÷ 30 MHz.

The eavesdropping receiver used for tests is a Rohde& Schwarz FSET 7 with IF bandwidths of 2 or 5 MHz and noise figure [fr] = 7 dB [7]. Using time domain averaging to increase the signal-to-noise ratio of a periodic signal [1] with *N* repetitions of a properly in phase aligned signal the processing gain can be calculated by

$$G_p = \sqrt{N} \text{ or } [G_p] = 10 \cdot \lg N \text{ (dB)}. \tag{3}$$

Assuming that the attacker applies signal processing techniques by mediating the received signal on $N = 10$ frames, the resulting processing gain is approximately 10 dB. The noise on the power supply is expected to be at least 30 dB above the thermal noise level [1, 9] which is 0 dBµV at $B = 5$ MHz. Therefore $[U_n,5] = 30$ dBµV might be a plausible value of the electrical noise received on the power line at $B = 5$ MHz. From experimental measurements the attenuation between two outlets in a building for the frequency range $1 \div 60$ MHz can be, on average, around 10 dB if the sockets are in the same circuit, and 40 dB if they are located in different circuits [1, 9]. From (3) there can be determined the minimum attenuation value, $[AF]$, for a low- pass filter in the HF/VHF frequency range installed on the power supply line of the computer system, so, at the building boundary, the compromising signals accidentally emissions transmitted on the power circuit from a COTS computer system cannot be detected by an attacker, is given by

$$[A_F] = 105 + 10 - 30 - 10 - 7 - 0 = 68 \text{ dB} \tag{4}$$

Thus we can conclude that a low-pass electrical filter with attenuation equal to 70 dB, evaluated for HF/VHF frequency range, provides adequate TEMPEST protections if all the COTS informatics equipment operated indoor comply with EN55022 limits.

3   Experimental Validations of the Results

In order to validate the theoretical aspects presented in Sect. 2, a series of tests and measurements were carried out in Special Telecommunications Service (STS) TEMPEST lab.

The first test aimed to detect compromising emissions generated by a commercial computer on the power line and recover the information contained in the received emissions. To achieve this, a test receiver Rohde& Schwarz FSET 7 with IF bandwidths of 5 MHz was used and a line impedance stabilization network (LISN) was installed on the supply line of the test equipment. The results, presented in Fig. 1a, show the level of the secondary emissions through the power line from a computer with an image displayed on the monitor (red trace) and without an image displayed on the monitor (green trace). From the spectral analysis a compromise emission around 25 MHz has been determined, which in this case contains the video signal from the video card. Using a dedicated software package for TEMPEST evaluation, the signals received at the 25.37 MHz frequency were filtered, correlated and the image displayed by the test computer monitor was restored, as shown in Fig. 1b.

The second test has been developed to validate the estimated value for the attenuation of the electrical filter obtained in Sect. 2. For this, the test configuration in Fig. 2a has been used, where PG is the pulse generator, RFG is the radiofrequency signal generator Rohde & Schwarz SMP04, ATT is the variable attenuator, REC is the TEMPEST test receiver, Rohde & Schwarz FSET7 and AQ&PC are the data

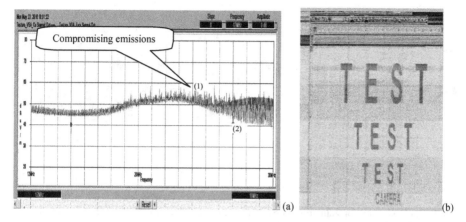

Fig. 1. (a) The comparative spectral analysis of the secondary emissions in power line by a computer using an image displayed on the monitor (trace 1) and no image displayed on the monitor (trace 2), and (b) recovered image processed from secondary emissions by a computer, from power line. (Color figure online)

acquisition board and processing computer. To simulate the compromising signal generated by an electronic device, we use a periodic radio pulse as reference signal, with the carrier frequency of 25 MHz, the modulating frequency of 5 MHz and the modulation index of 50%. The RF generator has been set for a signal level of 105 dBμV, which is the level corresponding to the EMC limit of the EN 55022 converted for the 5 MHz band. This reference emission obtained with the RF generator was injected into the power line of a computer using an absorbing clamp Rohde & Schwarz MDS21. The computer power cable with the length of 10 m was inserted into the LISN. The RF output from LISN was connected to a variable attenuator, used to simulate the attenuation introduced by an electrical filter interposed between the computer equipment and the hostile receiver. In the reception chain a test receiver (Rohde & Schwarz FSET 7) set on 5 MHz IF bandwidth was connected. The receiver video output was connected to the acquisition board and a computer for spectral analysis and data processing. The reference electrical signal injected onto the computer power line is shown in Fig. 2b.

Next, the variable attenuator was incrementally increased until the reference signal was covered by the power line radio frequency, so $[SNR] = 0$ dB was obtained. Thus, it has been concluded that for 65 dB attenuation, the electrical signal from the power line cannot be restored. From the comparative analysis between theoretical and practical results, it has been concluded that a 70 dB attenuation of the electrical filter installed on a computer's power line ensures the TEMPEST protection of the information system against leakage through secondary emissions.

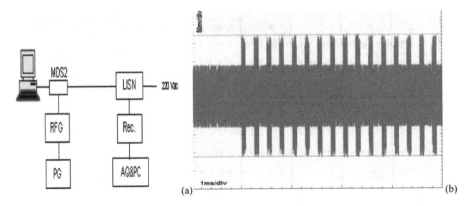

(a)   (b)

Fig. 2. (a) Test setup for validation of evaluation the minimum level of filter attenuation (b) the waveform of reference electrical signal

4   Conclusions

Based on the evaluations and tests performed we can conclude that, for commercial computer system installed in a residential environment, an electrical filter with an attenuation of 70 dB in the HF/VHF frequency range for conducted emissions, provide adequate TEMPEST protection against leakage of compromising emissions if the electrical equipment it complies to the EN 55022 limits. This value was achieved in the worst case scenario in which the IT equipment is of a commercial type, without TEMPEST protection measures (shielding, interconnection filtering, etc.), the distance between the source of the compromising emission and the hostile receiver was only 10 m, the electrical noise on the power line was only generated by the computer equipment because the entire test system was isolated by LISN from the power supply and the tests were carried out in the shielded room.

Whereas the technical measures to prevent information leakage through compromising emissions are generally expensive, this study is applicable in practice by the fact that recommends minimum technical requirements for security of emissions that can be implemented at low cost and with commercial resources.

Open issues that can be addressed in the future are oriented towards the study of the minimum attenuation for the electrical filters installed on the interconnection circuits of the information systems (data network, voice communications, etc.), as well as analyzing the compromising emissions conducted in the grounding circuit of a computer.

Acknowledgments. This work was supported by a grant of the Ministry of Innovation and Research, UEFISCDI, project number 5 Sol/2017 within PNCDI III.

References

1. Kuhn, M.G.: Compromising emanations: eavesdropping risks of computer displays. University of Cambridge Computer Laboratory, Technical report (2003)
2. Sekiguchi, H., Seto, S.: Measurement of computer RGB signals in conducted emission on power leads. Prog. Electromagnet. Res. C **7**, 51–64 (2009)
3. Kuhn, M.G.: Compromising emanations of LCD TV sets. In: Proceedings of the IEEE International Symposium on Electromagnetic Compatibility, pp. 931–936 (2011)
4. Jinming, L., Mao, J., Zhang, J.: The designing of TEMPEST security testing model. TELKOMNIKA Indonesian J. Electr. Eng. **2**, 866–871 (2014)
5. Ulaş, C., Aşık, U., Karadeniz, C.: Analysis and reconstruction of laser printer information leakages in the media of electromagnetic radiation, power, and signal lines. Comput. Secur. **58**, 250–267 (2016)
6. Christopoulos, C.: Electromagnetic Compatibility (EMC) in Challenging environments. In: Daras, N.J., Rassias, T.M. (eds.) Operations Research, Engineering, and Cyber Security. SOIA, vol. 113, pp. 95–115. Springer, Cham (2017). https://doi.org/10.1007/978-3-319-51500-7_5
7. Popescu, M., Bîndar, V., Crăciunescu, R., Fratu, O.: Estimate of minimum attenuation level for a TEMPEST shielded enclosure. In: Proceedings of COMM 2016, Bucharest (2016)
8. EN 55022 Standard: Information technology equipment - Radio disturbance characteristics-Limits and methods of measurement. European Committee for Standardization (1998)
9. Recommendation ITU-T K.84: Test methods and guide against information leaks through unintentional electromagnetic emissions. International Telecommunication Union (2011)

Innovative Platform for Resource Allocation in 5G M2M Systems

Alexandru Vulpe$^{(\boxtimes)}$, George Suciu, Simona Halunga, and Octavian Fratu

Telecommunications Department, University Politehnica of Bucharest,
Bucharest, Romania
{alex.vulpe,george.suciu}@radio.pub.ro, {shalunga,ofratu}@elcom.pub.ro

Abstract. One of the major drivers of cellular network evolution towards 5G systems is the communication between devices, also known as Machine-to-Machine (M2M) communications. M2M mobile connections will reach an estimated 3.2 billion devices and connections by 2020, which will pose a challenge as the state-of-the-art cellular and wireless networks were designed keeping in mind Human-to-Human (H2H) communication. A massive amount of M2M devices create overload problems with a significant impact on the radio access and core network of the cellular system leading to what are known as the problems of RAN overload and CN overload. The paper presents a proof-of-concept hardware implementation of novel resource allocation algorithms in 4G cellular communication systems. The proof-of-concept thus, will enable lab-scale analytical and experimental studies for validating theoretically developed algorithms with the focus being on validating the scheduling and admission control algorithms for M2M scenarios. The platform will be based on an LTE-A eNodeB implemented using a software defined radio (SDR) platform and a UE simulator that enables simulating a large number of UEs sharing the same spectrum. The platform will be complemented by field-programmable gate array (FPGA) devices that enable the hardware implementation of the analytically developed resource allocation algorithms.

Keywords: Wireless networks · Machine-to-Machine · 5G
Resource allocation

1 Introduction

Scheduling and resource allocation are essential components of wireless data systems and they tend to be a very complex problem [1,2]. This is because different variables have to be taken into account like the user radio conditions, the user's traffic pattern or the user Quality of Service (QoS) and the allocation of radio resources has to be optimized from the whole system point of view. Essentially, one has to decide when and how the available resources in a cell are assigned to each of the users, where the resources depend on the access method.

© ICST Institute for Computer Sciences, Social Informatics and Telecommunications Engineering 2018
O. Fratu et al. (Eds.): FABULOUS 2017, LNICST 241, pp. 16–24, 2018.
https://doi.org/10.1007/978-3-319-92213-3_3

For users in an LTE or LTE-Advanced system, the users are allocated Physical Resource Blocks (PRBs). This has led to a great deal of interest in the research community on scheduling and resource allocation algorithms [1].

However, most scheduling and admission control algorithms remain at the stage of theoretical development. There are few testbeds which have been developed for evaluating resource allocation. One such testbed has been developed by Toshiba in 2011 [3]. However, the authors used a pair of laptops to mimic Femto-UE communication, as the transmission was done via Wi-Fi cards. Another testbed for reconfigurable, multi-layered communication systems is ASGARD [4] which is a "software tool for the implementation of Cognitive Radio communication systems over Software Defined Radio equipment". Although the platform is modular and flexible, it lacks implementation of resource allocation algorithms and it is mostly software-based for higher layer protocols experimentation. It is, however, available for using under an open source license. OpenLTE [5] provides an open source implementation of the 3GPP LTE specifications suitable for implementing it on a Software-Defined Radio platform with GNU Radio [6] applications available.

Additionally, it is foreseen [7] that M2M mobile connections will reach more than 26 percent of total devices and connections by 2020. This poses a challenge as the state-of-the-art cellular and wireless networks were designed keeping in mind Human-to-Human communication. In the light of M2M scenarios, present-day mobile networks face challenges of [8, 9]:

- **variation of QoS requirements** as M2M devices have QoS requirements that vary depending on different purposes of data delivery;
- **different traffic patterns** as some M2M devices may transmit data at large time intervals (hours, months) while others may transmit data continuously.

Therefore, there will be the need to differentiate between M2M, M2H, H2H traffic in wireless cellular communications [10]. Researchers have been studying resource allocation (packet scheduling and admission control) algorithms for 4G (LTE-Advanced) wireless communication systems. In particular, the main author has developed a number of scheduling algorithms for carrier aggregation systems, using a convex optimization approach, that take into account the existence of multiple component carriers, and optimizes the allocation of radio resources in LTE-Advanced systems. The developed algorithms have been proven to outperform existing traditional scheduling algorithms. Also, we have developed novel admission control algorithms for 4G systems that, together with already developed scheduling algorithms, form the basis of new resource allocation algorithms. The algorithms take also into account the existence of different QoS requirements and are suitable candidates to be employed in next-generation cellular communication systems with different possible applications such as differentiating between M2M, H2H and M2H traffic. The results have been published in a number of papers [11–15] and part of the results therein constituted the main author's PhD thesis [16].

Starting from the developed scheduling and admission control algorithms and examples mentioned above, together with existing 3GPP standards, the paper proposes a proof-of-concept hardware implementation of the theoretically-developed scheduling and resource allocation algorithms. The proof-of-concept is to be designed to work in different scenarios such as different types of traffic and different types of devices in order to validate key performance indicators (KPIs) of the theoretical algorithms.

The present paper is organized as follows. Section 2 presents the resource allocation algorithms that form the basis of the proposed platform, while Sect. 3 presents a preliminary architecture for such a testbed. The impact the proposed platform would have is outlined in Sect. 4, while Sect. 5 draws the conclusions.

2   Resource Allocation Algorithms

LTE Rel. 10 specifies the aggregation of up to 5 LTE Rel. 8 carriers, also known as component carriers (CCs), in order to achieve an overall bandwidth of 100 MHz. The main author has proposed [11] an algorithm which enables the best user allocation over any number of CCs, with the objective of maximising the total user throughput, and maintaining QoS requirements. The algorithm is based on solving an optimisation problem for the best use of network resources. The following Profit Function is proposed in order to maximize the total throughput of the cell [13]:

$$\sum_{c=1}^{N_c} \sum_{u=1}^{N} w_{cu} x_{cu} \tag{1}$$

where x_{cu} is the allocation variable and wcu is a normalized metric. Also N_c is the number of configured component carriers (CCs) in the cell and N is the number of users attached to the cell. The allocation variable x_{cu} is defined as:

$$x_{cu} = \begin{cases} n, & \text{if } n \text{ PRBs are allocated to user } u \text{ on component carrier } c \\ 0, & \text{if no PRBs are allocated to user } u \text{ on component carrier } c \end{cases} \tag{2}$$

The normalized metric w_{cu} is defined as:

$$w_{cu} = \frac{T_u}{R_u} \tag{3}$$

where T_u is the current estimated throughput for user u and R_u is the average received throughput for user u.

Therefore, the values of x_{cu} that maximize the proposed profit function have to be found taking into account allocation and bandwidth constraints. This is called the Multi-Carrier Scheduling Algorithm (MCSA) algorithm. An enhanced version of the algorithm (called Enhanced MCSA - E-MCSA) was developed and presented in [13] taking into account a variable upper bound on the user allocation constraint. Because of this, an admission control algorithm had to be developed [13], otherwise, the optimization problem could have become unbounded or unfeasible.

The algorithms were validated in comparison with traditional scheduling algorithms (Round Robin, Proportional Fair) and in a scenario with different types of users (macro cell, femto cell, with QoS, without QoS) [16]. The *general conclusion* regarding the developed scheduling algorithms is that convex optimization used for resource allocation in a Carrier Aggregation system has better performances than existing state-of-the-art algorithms (as seen in Figs. 1 and 2). In particular, MCSA is more suited in a mixed scenario of both LTE and LTE-A users, but, if we consider that there are mainly QoS users that are LTE-Advanced capable, E-MCSA would be a better choice.

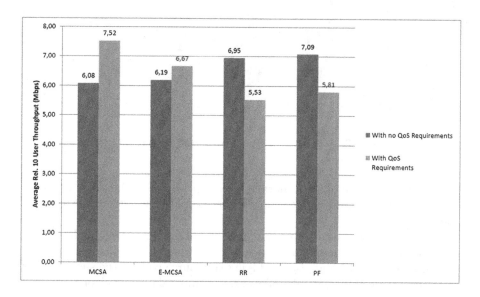

Fig. 1. Average Rel. 10 user throughput

With theoretical validation achieved, comes the next step and that is the physical implementation of the developed algorithms. Therefore a hardware and software architecture is needed in order to physically implement the algorithms.

3   Preliminary Architecture

We take a *bottom-up approach* in which the emphasis is laid on first, deriving the mathematical models for radio resource scheduling and admission control algorithms for massive M2M access in future 5G systems, then designing the software framework for validation through simulation and emulation. This is to be done by considering different approaches, for instance, applying the concepts of convex optimization, identifying constraints for M2M massive access and formulating a convex optimization problem for determining the radio resource

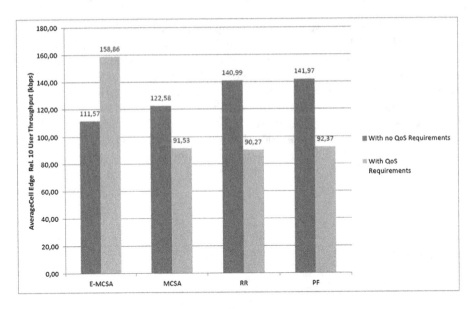

Fig. 2. Average Rel. 10 cell edge user throughput

allocation matrix in an M2M scenario. Other approaches can be taken into consideration such as clustering techniques, machine learning, game theory, or a combination thereof.

The work is then taken to developing a plugin for a network emulator able to handle M2M communications in an LTE network, based on existing standards such as NB-IoT[1] and also modifying the source code of the simulator for implementing the mathematical model of the resource allocation algorithms. The development of the resource allocation algorithms is to be done according also to the simulator/emulator constraints, and they will be evaluated and compared to existing state-of-the-art algorithms using the developed software framework. The need for an emulator is justified by the fact that there is physical equipment that is not readily available (Massive M2M gateway) and an emulator serves to connect simulated devices and network elements to existing physical infrastructure. Figure 3 illustrates a conceptual architecture of the experimental simulation/emulation platform to be developed.

The simulation platform has a two-fold purpose: first it should enable the validation of new resource allocation algorithms specifically designed for M2M therefore serving as a validation platform including also for other interested parties. Second, it should serve as the bridge for a physical implementation of the algorithms. The algorithms can be extensively tested before starting a physical implementation, therefore eliminating any limitations from the theoretical point of view.

---

[1] http://www.3gpp.org/news-events/3gpp-news/1785-nb_iot_complete.

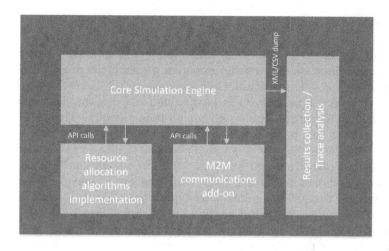

Fig. 3. Conceptual architecture of the experimental emulation platform

After emulation comes the physical implementation. This will be done, first, via hardware development of the LTE-Advanced Radio Access Network with an eNodeB implemented via OpenLTE and USRP B210 SDR platform and the UEs are emulated via an UE simulator that can emulate tens of UEs and is connected to an USRP N210 platform. The enhancement of the existing resource allocation algorithm will be done according to the identified hardware constraints, and they will be evaluated and compared to the original theoretical algorithms using the developed proof-of-concept. Figure 4 presents the envisioned proof-of-concept architecture.

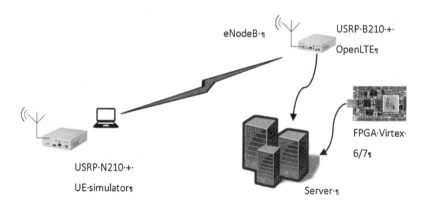

Fig. 4. Envisioned proof-of-concept architecture

4   Impact

Considering the rapid growth of the M2M data traffic in mobile networks and the continuous increase of the radio resources demand, the proposed proof-of-concept aims to provide solutions for efficient massive M2M access to the cellular network. Thus, it can be viewed as contributing to solving the challenges of the M2M paradigm in future wireless communication network. The M2M access will play a vital role in future 5G systems, both as an enabler of potential disruptive paradigms (Smart City) and as potential challenges that it might pose to the communication network services. Aside from traditional enhancements such as increased data rate and increased user and system energy efficiency, 5G will be required to provide minimal latency for critical services and to support massive M2M services, without degrading the Quality of Service of the so-called conventional services (voice, video streaming, web browsing etc.).

There are some major impacts of the proposed platform as follows:

- economic growth by enabling new applications to be developed that benefit from a richer awareness of the surrounding environment, enabling the concept of Smart City; these include applications ranging from e-Health to vehicle tracking and public safety;
- the development of technologies that are considered to be effective in 5G networks;
- the promotion and facilitation of new business models for operators by solving the challenges brought by the massive M2M ecosystem. Mobile operators and users may deploy a plethora of nodes that can connect to their network and have minimal impact on the human-originated data or voice traffic;
- improving the quality of life of the individuals by enabling the paradigms of smart home, connected home and smart city.

By designing, developing and validating new radio resource allocation algorithms for massive M2M communications, the envisioned platform is expected to promote future radio access technology and resource management methods that consider the key features of M2M networks that have massive connectivity, explosive traffic, various applications with diverse QoS and reliability features. As more and more devices become connected, the operators' networks will be subject to increasing overload, therefore hindering the Quality of Service of their human users, but also affecting the reliability of M2M devices. Thus the results obtained by using the proposed platform in the perspective of the future 5G communication networks can become a significant engine for network efficiency for mobile operators.

5   Conclusions

As presented throughout the article, the main objective of the proposed platform is to provide means of implementing resource allocation algorithms for massive M2M access.

The M2M paradigm will be a major pillar of the future 5G systems and numerous challenges related to it will occur. The proposed platform is to serve as a stepping stone towards more optimized massive M2M access.

Therefore, even though the proposed platform is not entirely implemented, based on results obtained from our preliminary analysis made and their innovation in specific areas, we can state that our proposed architecture will enable its users to create efficient M2M systems.

Acknowledgement. This work has been funded by University Politehnica of Bucharest, through the "Excellence Research Grants" Program, UPB - GEX. Identifier: UPB - EXCELENTA - 2016 project "Platform for Studying Security in IoT", contract number 96/2016 (PaSS-IoT) and by a grant of the Ministry of Innovation and Research, UEFISCDI, project number 5 Sol/2017 within PNCDI III and partially funded by UEFISCDI Romania under grant no. 60BG/2016 "Intelligent communications system based on integrated infrastructure, with dynamic display and alerting - SICIAD".

References

1. Dahlman, E., Parkvall, S., Skold, J.: 4G: LTE/LTE-Advanced for Mobile Broadband. Academic Press, Oxford (2011)
2. Song, G., Li, Y.: Utility-based resource allocation and scheduling in OFDM-based wireless broadband networks. IEEE Commun. Mag. **43**(12), 127–134 (2005)
3. Kulkarni, P., Gormus, S., Chin, W.H., Haines, R.J.: Distributed resource allocation in small cellular networks - test-bed experiments and results. In: 2011 7th International Wireless Communications and Mobile Computing Conference, Istanbul, pp. 1262–1267 (2011). https://doi.org/10.1109/IWCMC.2011.5982721
4. ASGARD - Platform for Cognitive Radio. http://blog.asgard.lab.es.aau.dk/what_is_asgard
5. OpenLTE. http://openlte.sourceforge.net/
6. GNU Radio. http://gnuradio.org/
7. Cisco Visual Networking Index: Global Mobile DataTraffic Forecast Update, 2016–2021. http://www.cisco.com/c/en/us/solutions/collateral/service-provider/visual-networking-index-vni/mobile-white-paper-c11-520862.pdf
8. Luigi, A., Antonio, I., Giacomo, M.: The Internet of Things: a survey. Int. J. Comput. Telecommun. Netw. **54**(15), 2787–2805 (2010)
9. Machina Research: M2M application characteristics and their implications for spectrum, Final Report (2014)
10. Song, G., Li, Y.: Utility-based resource allocation and scheduling in OFDM-based wireless broadband networks. IEEE Commun. Mag. **43**(12), 127–134 (2005). https://doi.org/10.1109/MCOM.2005.1561930
11. Vulpe, A., Fratu, O., Mihovska, A., Prasad, R.: Admission control and scheduling algorithm for multi-carrier systems. Wirel. Pers. Commun. **93**(3), 629–645 (2017). https://doi.org/10.1007/s11277-014-2218-9. ISSN: 0929-6212
12. Vulpe, A., Fratu, O., Halunga, S.: Downlink packet scheduling in LTE-advanced heterogeneous networks. Univ. Politehnica Bucharest Sci. Bull. Ser. C **77**(3), 85–94 (2015). ISSN: 2286-3540

13. Vulpe, A., Fratu, O., Mihovska, A., Prasad, R.: A multi-carrier scheduling algorithm for LTE-Advanced. In: 2013 15th International Symposium on Wireless Personal Multimedia Communications (WPMC), 24–28 June 2013, Atlantic City, USA, pp. 1–5 (2013). ISBN 978-87-92982-52-0

14. Vulpe, A., Fratu, O., Halunga, S.: QoS-aware downlink scheduling in multi-carrier communication systems. In: 2014 4th International Conference on Wireless Communication, Vehicular Technology, Information Theory and Aerospace and Electronic Systems Technology (Wireless VITAE), Aalborg, Denmark, 11–14 May 2014 (2014). https://doi.org/10.1109/VITAE.2014.6934495

15. Oproiu, M., Boldan, V., Vulpe, A., Marghescu, I.: Maximizing LTE network performance by using differential scheduling and carrier aggregation. In: Global Wireless Summit (GWS) 2016, Aarhus, Denmark, 27–30 November 2016 (2016, in press). http://www.riverpublishers.com/pdf/ebook/RP_GSW9788793609297.pdf

16. Vulpe, A.: Contributions to the optimization of radio access networks in 4th generation communication systems, Ph.D. thesis, University Politehnica of Bucharest (2014)

Implications of Network Resources and Topologies Over SDN System Performances

Bojan Velevski[1], Valentin Rakovic[2(✉)], and Liljana Gavrilovska[2]

[1] Makedonski Telekom, Skopje, Macedonia
bojan.velevski@telekom.mk
[2] Ss. Cyril and Methodius University in Skopje,
Rugjer Boskovic 18, Skopje, Macedonia
{valenitn,liljana}@feit.ukim.edu.mk

Abstract. The next generation communication networks are envisioned to be flexible, scalable, reliable and secure. Software Defined Networking introduces mechanisms to build and orchestrate efficient, flexible and adaptable networks. This is achieved by the separation of software and hardware functionalities in the network devices. This paper evaluates the overall Software Defined Networking performances with respect to the allocated network resources, i.e. different CPU's and bandwidth's allocations. The performance results clearly show that the overall system performances can be highly influenced by the network setup and chosen topology.

Keywords: SDN · Mininet · Network resources · CPU · Bandwith

1 Introduction

During the last decade, the rapid development of the communication technologies has resulted in significant increase of novel services and user's data demands. This has opened new challenges and issues that cannot be addressed by the conventional communications networks. For example, conventional IP based core networks are experiencing significant difficulties regarding manual configuration, management and optimization of network resources, enforcement of security policies - activities dependable on vendor OS upgrade, patch, release.

Recently, Software Defined Networking (SDN) [1] has drawn significant attention from both academia and industry as an auspicious technology capable to solve these issues. The core concept behind SDN is to separate the control plane from the forwarding plane, i.e. to separate the software from the hardware functionalities of the networking infrastructure, i.e. devices. This aspect facilitates on-the-fly and dynamic reconfiguration of the network and its underlying resources, such as *CPU power*, *link bandwidth*, *routing protocols*, etc. This reconfiguration is orchestrated by the SDN controller, which represents the Networking Operating System in the considered architecture. Currently, OpenFlow [2] is the most promising and exploited protocol that leverages the communication between the SDN controller and the networking devices. SDNs can leverage rapid deployment of new businesses, as well as swift and effective research and development.

© ICST Institute for Computer Sciences, Social Informatics and Telecommunications Engineering 2018
O. Fratu et al. (Eds.): FABULOUS 2017, LNICST 241, pp. 25–31, 2018.
https://doi.org/10.1007/978-3-319-92213-3_4

The industry and academia commonly exploit simulators, emulation platforms and prototype testbed, for developing and testing novel SDN related features. Testbeds offer the most accurate analysis for SDN experiments. However, the number of SDN related research activities performed on testbeds is scarce and limited [3–5]. Most of the current research is performed by exploiting the network emulator Mininet [6]. The research works commonly focus on SDN performance analysis based on different types of networking aspects, such as SDN controller algorithm and advantages over conventional networks [7, 8] routing protocols [9, 10], network anomaly detection and recovery [11] resource allocation [12], etc.

However, none of the ongoing research works, have evaluated the impact of the network resources and topology on the overall system performances. This paper specifically analyses different network resource allocations for different network topologies and scrutinizes their effect over the overall SDN performance.

The paper is structured as follows. Section 2 presents the generic scenario setup. It also elaborates on the SDN topologies used for the performance analysis. Section 3 provides the performance evaluation and analysis. Section 4 concludes the paper.

2   Scenario Setup and SDN Topologies

This section presents the scenario setup and the relevant SDN topologies used for the performance analysis. The main goal of the paper is to evaluate different SDN setups with respect to the allocated network resources, like *CPU* and *link bandwidth*, for a set of network topologies and analyze their impact on the overall system performance. The performance metrics of interest are, achieved *network throughput* and the *end-to-end jitter*. These metrics are chosen, since they clearly reflect the network capabilities and are crucial QoS parameters for *non-real-time* and *real-time* applications.

All observed SDN topologies are *Open-Flow* based that are designed in the Mininet emulator [6]. Mininet, by default supports a plethora of built-in network topologies which can be implemented using the available Mininet command-line options. Every SDN topology consists of a SDN controller, SDN switches and hosts. The paper, specifically focuses on three distinct SDN topologies, i.e. *Single*, *Linear* and *Tree* topology.

Single Topology. The topology is consisted of single Open-Flow (OF) switch connected with multiple hosts, Fig. 1a.

Linear Topology. The topology is consisted of predefined number of hosts and switches, where each host is connected to a specific switch. All switches serve the same number of hosts and are interconnected between each other on the same network depth, Fig. 1b.

Tree Topology. The topology is consisted of hosts and switches arranged in a tree fashion, where the hosts are always located at the end of the topology, i.e. leafs. The branches in the topology interconnect multiple switches and hosts according to the specific topological design. The network depth parameter is utilized to reflect the number of branches i.e. network levels, Fig. 1c.

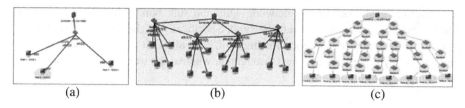

(a)   (b)   (c)

Fig. 1. SDN topologies: Single (a), Linear (b), Tree (c)

For the purpose of the performance analysis and comparison, all three topologies are assumed to incorporate the same number of hosts. Specifically, the network design and topological complexity is presented in Table 1.

Table 1. Parameters of the proposed OF topologies.

	Single topology	Linear topology	Tree topology
Number of OF controllers	1	1	1
Number of OF switches	1	4	31
Number of hosts	32	32	32

All of the SDN topologies utilize the same controller. The implemented controller is the Mininet built-in one, which employs L2 i.e. hub-like operation to all SDN switches.

3   Performance Analysis

This section, provides the performance analysis of the different network configurations presented in the previous section. The analysis is performed for both TCP and UDP flows, using the "iperf" tool and it is averaged over all of the different hosts in the network. All network topologies incorporate the same number of hosts, Table 1. The network configuration parameters of interest are given in Table 2.

Table 2. Network configuration parameters.

Parameters	Values
CPU (%)	10, 30, 50, 70, 90, 100
Bandwidth (Mbps)	10, 30, 50, 70, 90, 100

Figure 2a depicts the achieved network throughput versus the allocated CPU to network elements when streaming the TCP traffic. It is evident that the achieved network throughput increases when allocating lager portions of the available CPU resources. However, for the CPU allocation higher than 50%, the network throughput converges to a specific value for all three topologies. This is a result of the underlying transmission capabilities of the network. Different link bandwidths would result in different behavior of the achieved throughput. Specifically, higher link bandwidths will induce a throughput convergence for higher CPU values. It is also evident that the *single* topology achieves the highest throughput, whereas the tree topology achieves the lowest throughput.

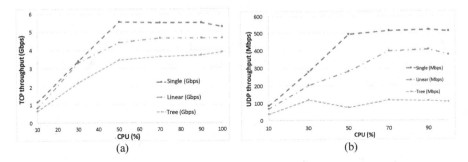

(a)   (b)

Fig. 2. Achieved network throughput vs CPU load: TCP traffic (a), UDP traffic (b), (Link Bandwidth = 100 Mbps)

Figure 2b depicts the achieved network throughput versus the allocated CPU to the network elements when streaming the UDP traffic. Similar conclusions hold as for Fig. 2a, i.e. the system throughput increases when allocating lager portions of the available CPU resources. It is also evident that the *single* topology achieves the highest throughput, and the three topology achieves the lowest throughput.

Figure 3 depicts the end-to-end jitter between two hosts in the network versus the allocated CPU to the network elements. It is evident that the allocated CPU resources have no impact on jitter for the single and linear topologies. However, for the tree topology the CPU allocation significantly impacts the network performances, due to its underlying complexity.

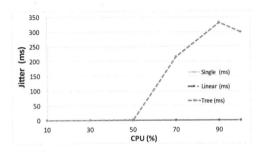

Fig. 3. End-to-end jitter vs CPU load (Link Bandwidth = 100 Mbps)

Figure 4a depicts the achieved network throughput versus the allocated bandwidth when streaming the TCP traffic. It is evident that the network throughput increases proportionally when increasing the allocated bandwidth. All three topologies have almost identical behavior.

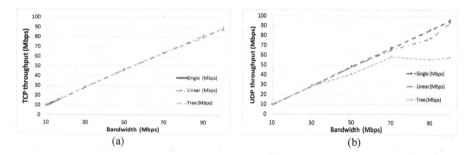

Fig. 4. Network throughput vs allocated bandwidth: TCP traffic (a), UDP traffic (b), (CPU Load = 50%)

Figure 4b depicts the achieved network throughput versus the allocated bandwidth when streaming the UDP traffic. It is also evident that for UDP traffic that increasing the bandwidth increases the overall system throughput. Similarly, to the previous figures, the single topology achieves the best performances, whereas the tree topology achieves the worst performances. It is also evident form the figure that the underlying transport protocol influences the system performances. Specifically, UDP results in lower achieved throughputs compared to TCP.

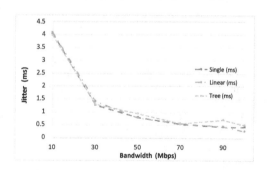

Fig. 5. End-to-end jitter vs allocated bandwidth (CPU Load = 70%)

Figure 5 depicts the end-to-end jitter between two hosts in the network versus allocated bandwidth on network links. It is evident that higher bandwidth allocations result in decreased end-to-end jitter in the network. The tree topology introduces the highest levels of jitter of all evaluated topologies, due to the high complexity. Specifically, the three topology introduces the highest number of hops, of all presented topologies, resulting in increased routing and processing delay. This delay significantly impacts the system performance, specially the end-to-end delay.

This section analyzes the SDN system performances for different network resource configurations, i.e. for differed CPU and bandwidth allocations for three different network topologies. The results clearly show that the network resources such as the CPU and the bandwidth as well as the network topology can play crucial role for achieving the optimal system performances.

4   Conclusions

Software Defined Networking represents a novel and auspicious technology that will pave the road for the next generation of communication networks. Most of the ongoing SDN related research is performed by exploiting the network emulator Mininet, as an accurate and low-cost option for evaluating and analyzing variety of networking related aspects.

This paper analyses the system performance of SDN networks with respect to the underlying network resources, i.e. for different CPU and bandwidth allocations at the networking elements. The Mininet based evaluation is performed for three different network topologies, (i.e. simple, linear and tree topology). The results show that the underlying network resources can have significant impact on the attained system performances. Specifically, higher bandwidth allocations facilitate improved system throughput and decreased end-to-end jitter for all types of networking topologies. Higher CPU allocation also results in significantly improved system throughput for all network topologies. However, the CPU allocation impacts the jitter performances only in very complex network topologies, i.e. network topologies with multiple depth layers. Future work will focus on evaluating the impact of additional network resources and topologies, as well as different types of SDN controllers.

References

1. Jackson, C.R., et al.: Demonstration of the benefits of sdn technology for all-optical data centre virtualisation. In: Optical Fiber Communication Conference 2017, Los Angeles, California United States (2017)
2. Robertazzi, T.: Introduction to Computer Networking: Software-Defined Networking. Springer, Germany (2017). https://doi.org/10.1007/978-3-319-53103-8
3. Chen, Q., et al.: An integrated framework for software defined networking, caching and computing. In: IEEE Network (2016)
4. Huo, R., et al.: Software defined networking, caching, and computing for green wireless networks. IEEE Commun. Mag. **11**, 185–193 (2016)
5. Huang, T., et al.: A survey on large-scale software defined networking (SDN) testbeds: approaches and challenges. IEEE Commun. Surv. Tutorials **12**(4), 531–550 (2017)
6. Mininet network emulator. http://mininet.org
7. Bholebawa, I., et al.: Performance analysis of proposed openflow-based network architecture using mininet. Wirel. Pers. Commun. **86**, 943–958 (2016)
8. Shivayogimath, C., et al.: Performance analysis of a software defined network using mininet. In: Artificial Intelligence and Evolutionary Computations in Engineering Systems, pp. 391–398 (2016)

9. Barrett, R., et al.: Dynamic traffic diversion in SDN: testbed vs mininet. In: Proceedings of 2017 International Conference on Computing, Networking and Communications (ICNC): Network Algorithms and Performance Evaluation. Silicon Valley, USA (2017)
10. Chai, R., et al.: Energy consumption optimization-based joint route selection and flow allocation algorithm for software-defined networking. Sci. China Inf. Sci. **60**(4), 040306 (2017)
11. Mauthe, A., et al.: Disaster-resilient communication networks: principles and best practices. In: Proceedings of 8th International Workshop on Resilient Networks Design and Modeling (2016)
12. Cao, B., et al.: Resource allocation in software defined wireless networks. IEEE Netw. **31**, 44–51 (2017)

A Preview on MIMO Systems in 5G New Radio

Razvan-Florentin Trifan$^{(\boxtimes)}$, Andrei-Alexandru Enescu, and Constantin Paleologu

POLITEHNICA University of Bucharest, Splaiul Independentei 313,
Bucharest, Romania
razvan-florentin.trifan@sdettib.pub.ro, aenescu@gmail.com,
pale@comm.pub.ro

Abstract. With 3GPP 5G new radio (NR), proposals are already being discussed. Although participants offer various suggestions for the first 5G standardization, common ideas can already be identified. The purpose of the paper is to anticipate, in the context of massive multiple input multiple output (MIMO) systems, the main directions the standard would focus on; for example, a unified transmission scheme, multi-level channel state information (CSI), and non-linear precoding (NLP). The latter, an alternative to linear precoding employed in Long Term Evolution (LTE), is analyzed in detail in the paper.

Keywords: 3GPP · NR · MIMO · CSI-RS · DM-RS · NLP · MRT
ZF · THP

1 Introduction

With the approval of the service requirements for the 5G [1], the work for the first 3GPP 5G New Radio (NR) release is now at full speed. To finalize a first version of the standard by March 2018, a major decision was taken in Radio Access Network (RAN) group on the 5G NR workplan (Fig. 1), to have an intermediate non-standalone (NSA) 5G NR mode for the enhanced Mobile Broadband (eMBB) use-case. For NSA-NR, the connection is anchored in Long Term Evolution LTE, while 5G NR carriers are used to boost data-rates and reduce latency. The Standalone (SA) 5G NR mode is estimated in September 2018.

Several scenarios require the support of very high data rates or traffic densities of the 5G system, as part of eMBB use case. They address different service areas, including massive gatherings, broadcast, residential, and high-speed vehicles. As such the focus on multiple input multiple output (MIMO) systems (with a higher number of antennas - massive) to deliver high data rate services, in an energy efficient way with a manageable implementation complexity, is still under full investigation in 5G NR.

When talking about the NR MIMO, the main concepts can be clustered in Unified transmission mode, DM-RS and CSI-RS based transmission schemes, and Non-linear precoding directions.

© ICST Institute for Computer Sciences, Social Informatics and Telecommunications Engineering 2018
O. Fratu et al. (Eds.): FABULOUS 2017, LNICST 241, pp. 32–38, 2018.
https://doi.org/10.1007/978-3-319-92213-3_5

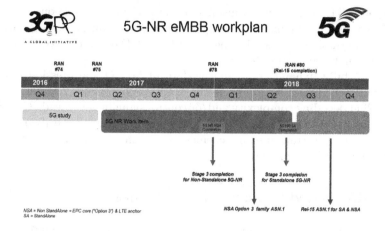

Fig. 1. 3GPP 5G NR workplan.

To address various MIMO proposal for 5G NR, the remainder of this paper is organized into the following sections. Section 2 describes the concepts and motivations behind using a unified MIMO transmission scheme for 5G NR. Section 3 addresses the possibility of using transmission schemes that only require channel estimation with demodulation reference signals (DM-RS) or channel state information reference signals (CSI-RS) in the context of massive number of antennas. Section 4 deals with a proposal of changing the precoding technique to a non-linear one, and as such to address use cases of ill-conditioned channels and correlated inter-user interference. Finally, Sect. 5 presents the research directions for the future work.

2   Unified Transmission Mode

In every release the downlink MIMO has evolved. Due to system design constraints and backward compatibility, each release added just a small enhancement on top of previous specifications. The motivation to design one single transmission mode is to simplify the system design and increase the flexibility to fit different application scenarios. Since the NR shall meet the requirement of diverse use cases and scenarios, one unified and scalable MIMO mode is required [2].

Avoiding of transmission mode handover for different scenarios, reducing standardization efforts, simplifying user equipment (UE) behaviors and related test cases, as well as providing performance benefits over legacy transmission mode, are reasons for designing one unified downlink MIMO framework. The main challenges of a unified transmission mode are the possibility to cover multiple legacy transmission schemes, the enabling transmission scheme switching, the use of DM-RS and setting up the relationship between transmission scheme and type of CSI report.

In legacy LTE system, one transmission mode corresponds to one transmission scheme, hence dynamic switching between some transmission schemes in different transmission modes, like open loop (OL)-MIMO and closed loop (CL)-MIMO), has not been supported.

Although fully dynamic switching within all MIMO transmission schemes may provide scheduling flexibility at the base station (BS) scheduler, it may increase blind decoding complexity and/or control signaling overhead. Therefore, to enable fast transmission scheme switching, it is necessary to specify one mode integrating multiple transmission schemes, to balance between the scheduling flexibility and receiver complexity.

3   DM-RS Based Transmission Schemes

There has been a proposal to design NR MIMO transmission schemes based on DM-RS for a more flexible transmitter design as well as minimizing always-on RS, like common (CRS) [3,4]. To some extent, it is beneficial to design all NR MIMO transmission schemes with DM-RS as it allows tailored DM-RS patterns for each MIMO transmission scheme and for each channel condition. On the other hand, the channel estimation performance is worse than a CRS.

DM-RS will enable the BS to apply different precoding operation transparent to the UE. It will be beneficial to support flexible transmission scheme utilization within one unified MIMO mode, as with DM-RS, UE will be aware of rank indication without additional identification to real signal transmission format. From UE point of view, it will simplify the receiver complexity.

There have been mainly two categories of DM-RS based transmission schemes discussed - transmit diversity and spatial multiplexing.

3.1   Transmit Diversity

DM-RS based transmit diversity is specifically designed for reliable transmission. DM-RS could be UE-specific or shared for transmit diversity. The DM-RS advantages include the use of non-precoded or beamformed DM-RS, both being transparent to UE, or adaptively adjusting beam width and beam direction of DM-RS coverage optimization.

3.2   Spatial Multiplexing

Among the techniques to improve spectral efficiency, the most known one is spatial multiplexing (SM), which includes OL/semi-OL SM scheme and CL spatial multiplexing scheme [5].

To facilitate various use cases such as a wide range of UE speeds, a two-tier precoding-based framework is proposed. Dynamic precoding is analogous to LTE CL MIMO, while semi-dynamic precoding is analogous to OL/semi-OL MIMO proposed in release 14 enhanced full duplex (eFD) MIMO [4].

Semi-dynamic Precoding. denotes a spatial multiplexing scheme that uses cyclic delay diversity or precoder/beam cycling to achieve SM and an extra spatial diversity gain. It is especially applicable when CSI quality is outdated at the base station (for instance, high UE speeds and poor cell isolation, which causes bursty inter-cell interference). In this case, it is more advantageous for the BS to transmit data through a group of directional beams since the UE can only indicate an approximate directional information. For this purpose, precoder (beam) cycling within a group of beams in frequency domain can be employed. This approximate directional information can be reported via Precoding Matrix Indicator (PMI) or other precoding-related feedback, which includes only long-term precoding information.

Dynamic Precoding. is the most effective scheme to improve spectral efficiency, essential to NR data channel transmission. It is applicable when accurate CSI is available at the base station. In this case, the base station can transmit data through a narrow directional beam since accurate directional information is available in the CSI report. This directional information can be reported via PMI or other precoding-related feedback, which includes both long-term and short-term precoding information. It is worth noting that long-term CSI is beneficial to reduce the channel spatial dimension for CL spatial multiplexing transmission, thereby reducing CSI-RS and reporting overhead for massive MIMO transmission in NR. Analogous to LTE, short-term precoding information can be reported as a wideband or sub-band CSI parameter. This facilitates frequency-selective precoding.

Unified CSI Reporting. In legacy LTE system, different transmission modes use a different CSI feedback mode. The NR MIMO operation needs to be more flexible, for example, one transmission mode could operate with multiple feedback modes corresponding to different transmission schemes.

Each CSI mode could corresponds to one channel quality indicator (CQI) hypothesis and one CSI feedback accuracy. In order to simplify the design, for an unified CSI report, different CSIs will share the same feedback framework, with specific parameters configuration. For example, depending on the use case, a UE may be configured to measure CSI of a broader (uncompressed) or narrower (compressed) propagating channel. OL transmission required robust CQI feedback and rough CSI acquisition.

A first CSI type, coverage CSI-RS is proposed, where each resource corresponds to a the static macro (coverage) beam. The use cases of coverage CSI-RS are the combination of use cases of release 13 non-precoded CSI-RS and cell-specific beamformed (BF)CSI-RS. In CL transmission, the UE zooms into a smaller part of the channel. As such, the BS can increase CSI-RS penetration by beamforming and generate CSI-RS with a much smaller number of ports. The second type of CSI-RS, analogous to release 13 UE-specific BF CSI-RS, is named UE-specific CSI-RS [6, 7].

4   Non-linear Precoding

Linear precoding (LP) scheme is a conventional approach to realize multi-user (MU) MIMO. Block diagonalization (BD) is a well-known technique to create prescribed nulls for UEs except for the target UE and to mitigate inter-user interference (IUI). BD works well in a spatially-uncorrelated scenario and simplifies receiver designs. However, by consuming degrees of freedom in MIMO systems to cancel interference, a tradeoff between interference mitigation and achievable spatial diversity arises. Moreover, IUI mitigation performance of LP degrades considerably in ill-conditioned or spatially-correlated channels, resulting limited throughput [8].

Figure 2 shows how the spatial correlation and imperfect CSI limits the downlink throughput performance of the linear precoded TDD systems, assuming 80% of resources used for downlink. In case of the imperfect CSI feedback, Additive White Gaussian Noise (AWGN) with –20dB power is added to CSI. The equations that model the simulated system can be found in [9].

Alternatively, non-linear precoding (NLP) achieves near-capacity and establishes robust links over MU-MIMO donwlink transmission even in spatially-correlated or ill-conditioned channels. On the other hand, thanks to interference removal at the transmitter (TX), NLP yields throughput gain even with imperfect CSI feedback [10].

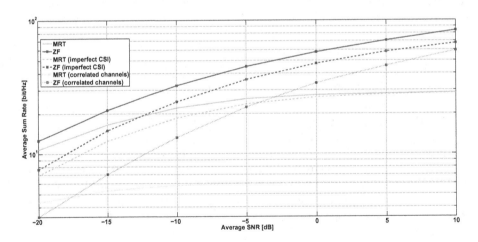

Fig. 2. MU-MIMO Maximum Ratio Transmitter (MRT) and Zero Forcing (ZF) linear precoders performance with 100 TX Antennas and 10 users.

In a typical NLP scheme, a combination of feedforward and feedback functionalities at TX is required, where the former is LP, and the latter is realized by IUI-precancellation (PC). Unitary matrix based LP can easily be realized by block triangulation (BT) [11,12]. Subsequently, NLP can be used to cancel IUI in the processed signal. Using a combination of LP and NLP spatial diversity, a IUI-free signal can be obtained simultaneously.

To realize low peak-to-average-power-ratio (PAPR) IUI cancellation at TX, a modulo operation is a well-known method to compress signal constellation at IUI-PC output. This configuration is generally known as Tomlinson-Harashima precoding (THP) [13,14].

5   Conclusion and Future Work

Although the two 5G NR directions are quite challenging, the non-linear precoding attracted particularly our attention. In the perspective of the massive MU-MIMO approach, the challenges would be to limit the computational burden as well as the overhead required for the channel estimation, in time division duplex (TDD) and frequency division duplex (FDD) systems, and CSI feedback (FDD).

To reduce the complexity of the precoding operations, hybrid non-linear precoding schemes, where non-linear IUI is canceled within the same group, are possible alternatives. How to optimize the user-grouping, to balance between performance loss and complexity reduction, requires further investigation.

In terms of reducing the CSI feedback and the overhead of the reference signals, it turns out that the performance of both LP and NLP schemes is affected by imperfect CSI estimation. This can be caused by rapid changing channel conditions, an insufficient resolution of reference signals or CSI feedback inaccuracy. Reducing the reference signals and feedback information is an essential approach in massive MIMO context.

The last aspect of NLP are the design of the reference signals used to estimate the channel in FDD [in TDD the BS estimates the channel trough reciprocity using the uplink sounding reference signals (SRS); both long and short term CSI can be obtained through SRS]. Although it was previously suggested to rely on DM-RS, as the precoding operation was transparent to the UE and interference for other UEs could have been estimated trough DM-RS assigned to different ports, it turns out that the NLP is not transparent for the UE. Using NLP signals, estimation of the channel or interference is not straightforward. Modulo operation is needed at the receiver for optimal demodulation of NLP signals, so the transmitter needs to signal the precoding type to UE.

References

1. 3GPP TS 22.261: Service requirements for the 5G system
2. Nokia: R1-1612845 Unified MIMO transmission mode for 5G new radio interface
3. InterDigital: R1-1612636 MIMO transmission scheme for NR
4. Samsung: R1-1612478 DMRS-based spatial multiplexing for DL NR MIMO
5. ZTE: R1-1611406 Discussion on DL MIMO transmission for NR
6. Samsung: R1-164015 DL MIMO framework for NR
7. Samsung: R1-164010 Discussions on CSI-RS design for NR

8. Mitsubishi Electric: R1-1610229, Perf. comparison of NLP schemes for MU-MIMO
9. Van Chien, T., Bjornson, E.: Massive MIMO Communications, pp. 77–116. ISBN 978-3-319-34206-1
10. Mitsubishi Electric: R1-1705816, MU-MIMO perf. evaluation of NLP schemes
11. Mitsubishi Electric: R1-164027, Design of massive MIMO for NR
12. Mitsubishi Electric: R1-1705817, Summary of analysis of NLP for NR
13. Fischer, R.F.H., Windpassinger, C., et al.: Space-time transmission using TH precoding. In: ITG Conference on Source and Channel Coding, pp. 139–147 (2002)
14. Sun, L., McKay, M.R.: TH precoding for MU-MIMO systems with quantized CSI feedback and user scheduling. IEEE Trans. Sig. Process. **62**(16), 4077–4090 (2014)

Compromising Electromagnetic Emanations of Wired USB Keyboards

Alexandru Boitan[1]($\boxtimes$), Razvan Bărtuşică[1], Simona Halunga[2], Mircea Popescu[1], and Iulian Ionuţă[1]

[1] The Special Telecommunications Service, Bucharest, Romania
boitanalexandru@yahoo.com, rbartusica@yahoo.com,
mpopescu@sts.ro
[2] University Politehnica of Bucharest, Bucharest, Romania
simona.halunga@upb.ro

Abstract. The TEMPEST methods and procedures focus on classified information carriers generated by any electronic devices through electromagnetic radiation. Any electromagnetic radiation-carrying information is called compromising emanation. In this paper we will exemplify the keystroke information recovery by receiving compromising emanations emitted by the USB keyboards and the possibility of automatic detection of compromising emanation by using the autocorrelation function as well as the risk assessment of information vulnerability.

Keywords: USB · Keyboard · TEMPEST · Compromising emanations

1 Introduction

We live in the era of digital communications, and no matter how traditional we are, we still have a personal computer or laptop, a smart phone or a tablet PC in our possession.

All electronic equipment emits electromagnetic radiations that can propagate in free space at considerable distances, in the order of meters or even tens of meters. This aspect has been known for decades and is being standardized by Electromagnetic Compatibility (EMC) rules and regulations [1]. A part of the electromagnetic signals emitted by electronic equipment consist in information carriers, meaning that, if they are received with specialized equipment, processed and analyzed by specialists, who possess the specific hardware and knowledge, they can partially or totally recover the information processed or manipulated by the targeted electronic equipment. These electromagnetic signals are known in the specialty TEMPEST regulations as compromising emanations (CE). The set of standardized methods and procedures necessary to protect against information leakage represent the Tempest standards. Like EMC, the TEMPEST domain has its own regulations which are in continuous updating process due to emerging technologies and the need for information security assurance. There are TEMPEST regulations both on EU and NATO level [2, 3]. The TEMPEST domain is a military-specific domain and it only applies to the protection of classified information. Therefore, all TEMPEST regulations are classified information also.

© ICST Institute for Computer Sciences, Social Informatics and Telecommunications Engineering 2018
O. Fratu et al. (Eds.): FABULOUS 2017, LNICST 241, pp. 39–44, 2018.
https://doi.org/10.1007/978-3-319-92213-3_6

Recent research shown that the keyboard and its connection to the computer is one of the most critical points. In [4] the authors proposed a method to analyze the electromagnetic radiation from USB keyboard and, using signal processing algorithms, shown that the signal can be reconstructed, while in [5] an automatic control system for reception of the compromising emanations has been developed. In [6] the authors propose a method that jams the emanations and in [7] a number of general protection guidelines are proposed. In some of their previous work [8, 9] the authors have shown that the PS/2 keyboard uses a low-speed serial cable communication (10–15 kHz) is considered outdated and should not be used in the future. One can also use a virtual keyboard as an input method but this falls under the video signal display eavesdropping that was approached by Wim van Eck for the first time in 1985 [10].

We will focus our attention on the USB signal with the bit duration of 600 [ns] or 80 [ns], used by the USB keyboard communication as it is a more complex signal than the PS/2 communication with the bit duration of 100 μs, and, therefore harder to recover from the CE radiation but also because most of the keyboards currently used are USB type. In this work we will exemplify that the USB signal can be rebuild from CE signal at the bit level in laboratory conditions, which has not been achieved in the past, as well as the possibility of automatic detection of the compromising signal. We will also try to evaluate the level of risk of disclosing the information from the compromising signal radiated by USB keyboards.

This paper is organized on 5 sections: Sect. 2 presents the measurement configuration testbed, in Sect. 3 some examples of USB keyboard codes recovery are illustrated. In Sect. 4 a number of examples will be presented to highlight the difficulty of CE detection, while Sect. 5 contains the conclusions of this paper.

2 The Measurement Setup

In order to observe, evaluate and measure the reception of compromising signals coming from USB keyboards, the testbed described in Fig. 1 has been used. The measurements were performed in a semi-anechoic chamber and reception equipment is located outside the test room.

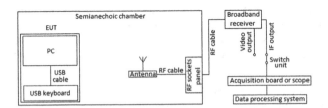

Fig. 1. Measurement setup

The TEMPEST laboratory measurements need much higher resolution bandwidth. However, the reception of compromising signals from the USB 1.0 and USB 1.1 keyboards can also be achieved with EMC receivers.

The CE detection tests were performed using a Rohde & Schwarz FSET 7 test receiver with 10 MHz resolution bandwidth (RBW) and a HL223 passive logperiodic antenna. For signal processing, we used an acquisition board with a sampling frequency of 125 MHz and 12-bit Resolution, controlled by a computer with a dedicated software package for TEMPEST evaluations.

The testing equipment (EUT) was a commercial Jujitsu Siemens desktop, CELSIUS W350 type, installed in normal working conditions, at a distance of 1 m from the receiving antenna (EMC test distance according to MIL461F standard).

3 CE from USB Keyboard Communication

In order to highlight the CE detection for USB 1.0 and USB 1.1 signals performed with the receiver system described above we used a Tektronix type DPO70804B.

If we monitor the USB bus through an oscilloscope and galvanic probing we will see two types of USB packets: synchronization and data packets. The data packet is illustrated in Fig. 2.

The USB communication uses Non Return to Zero Inverted (NRZI) encoding, in which "0" represents transition and "1" means no transition. All USB packets start with a synchronization field (SYNC), used by the receiver circuits to synchronize with the transmitter. The SYNC field is 8 bits long at low speed (USB 1.0) and full speed (USB 1.1) USB communications "11111100", where the last two bits indicate the end of the SYNC field, according to the USB standard [11].

Using the measurement setup described in Sect. 2, we were able to receive the Compromising Emanations (CE) generated by data packet, as shown in Fig. 3. As one can see, only the transitions are reflected in the compromising emanations.

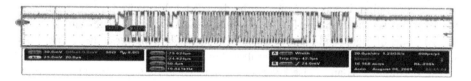

Fig. 2. USB data packet (by pressing the "c" key)

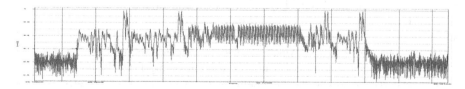

Fig. 3. CE from USB data packet (by pressing the "c" key)

From the comparative analysis of the USB waveforms captured galvanically with the oscilloscope and the accidentally radiated signals of the EUT and received by the measurement system it resulted that these types of signals can be intercepted by an attacker and the information can be compromised by restoring the data.

4 CE Propagation

To analyze the risk level of information leakage through the low speed USB (USB 1.0) we used CE generated by a desktop keyboard and we evaluated the maximum distance from which such signals can be detected under the most disadvantageous conditions for the targeted computer, namely a reduced ambient electromagnetic noise (provided by the semi-anechoic chamber) and the use of commercial equipment as equipment under test (EUT), without any TEMPEST protection measures (shielding, data lines filtering, power lines filtering etc.).

In some situations, the CE detection process is hampered due to the complexity of the electromagnetic waves propagation phenomenon, since it has a broadband spectrum and its different frequency components may propagate differently. In Fig. 4 is illustrated the most advantageous situation, in which the payload is received at a much higher level than the USB-specific packaging fields. However, the opposite might happen as well.

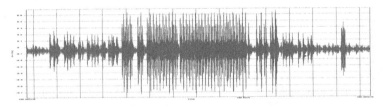

Fig. 4. CE from USB data packet ("m" keystroke)

For measurement and evaluation of CE the testbed described in Sect. 2 has been used. The "p" keystroke has been repeated with an operator's typed frequency. A compromising signal was received on the 212.3 [MHz] frequency, and, after filtering and time correlation, it was confirmed to be the USB 1.0 waveform corresponding to the "p" key, as illustrated in Fig. 5. We can observe the searched signal in the left-upper side of Fig. 5 and the data acquisition we are looking for at the top right. At the bottom of Fig. 5 we can see the result of the time correlation function.

The maximum CE and noise level were evaluated in time domain and the corresponding signal-to-noise ratio resulted to be 20.8 [dB]. To prevent detection and interception of this signal, the SNR ratio should be less or equal to 0 [dB], hence, in this setting, the received signal should be reduced by 20.8 [dB].

The CE can be reduced either by electromagnetic shielding of the computer system, or by increasing the separation distance between the target computer equipment and the minimum protection area from which an attacker can intercept the CE. The shielding effectiveness is larger than or equal to 20.8 [dB], resulting from the evaluation presented above. To determine the minimum radius of the TEMPEST protection area (around the IT system), the worst case scenario is assumed, where the attenuation of the building is 0 [dB] and the free space attenuation formula is used:

$$L_{bf} = 32.4 + 20 * \log\left(f_{[\text{MHz}]}\right) + 20 * \log\left(d_{[\text{Km}]}\right). \tag{1}$$

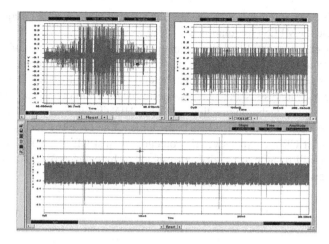

Fig. 5. CE time correlation ("p" keystroke)

Using this, it resulted a minimum distance of 11 meters for the TEMPEST protection area around the targeted computer system in order to prevent leakage of information through USB signals accidentally emitted by computer equipment. However, this value does is covering and does not represent a danger of compromising the information processed by the targeted electronic equipment because, in reality, the ambient radio noise is much higher than the one considered in the tests performed, and this falls within the TEMPEST minimum protection area according to the current TEMPEST regulations.

5 Conclusions

In this paper we presented several examples of CE recovery and demonstrated that it is possible to restore the keystroke information from the CE radiation of the USB keyboards. We also illustrated an example of time correlation process used for automatic detection of CE.

Since people are asked to be as open as possible in terms of working time, one may get to work on a computer not only in our office but also at home, in a car on the way to work or even outdoors, in green parks, at the playground of our children. This may be efficient from time optimization point of view, but may lead to significant flows with respect to security. One is not protected against security TEMPEST attacks when our workspace is located in free space or a car and not even if we're in an office but right next to the window. In fact, we are the least protected. The window offers small electromagnetic waves attenuation. It is very important how much a possible attacker can approach us without being visible and obviously what physical obstacles (distance in free space, perimeter delimitation fencing, vegetation, building elements, etc.) are between us and the attacker. Another important technical aspect is represented by fortuitous conductors leaving our workspace represented by any conductor that may provide an unintended propagation path for CE signals (water and gas pipes, wires, cables, and any metal building structure). They can override any propagation pattern, and in this case the estimation of the propagation can be unrealistic and it is necessary to make specific measurements to assess the site attenuation in a certain frequency range imposed by the TEMPEST regulations.

In this paper we exemplified the estimation of the maximum risk of information vulnerability from USB keyboard CE, which can be an important component of the risk analysis that is required during the implementation of the TEMPEST protection measures. Similar risk analysis should be also performed for the others CE signals corresponding to the latest technologies like USB 3.0, HDMI, Ethernet 1 GB/s, etc.

We can conclude that the TEMPEST phenomenon is complex and the methods of protection against CE are expensive. If protection against CE is needed, a TEMPEST security officer will be able to provide customized technical expertise, according to the equipment, location and the information classification level.

References

1. The Electromagnetic Compatibility Regulations (2016). http://www.legislation.gov.uk/uksi/2016/1091/pdfs/uksi_20161091_en.pdf. Accessed 20 Mar 2017
2. NATO Standard, SDIP-27/1: NATO TEMPEST Requirements and Evaluation Procedures (NATO CONFIDENTIAL), NATO Military Committee Communication and Information Systems Security and Evaluation Agency (SECAN) 2009
3. EU Standard, IASG 07-03: Information assurance security guidelines on EU TEMPEST requirements and evaluation procedures (EU CONFIDENTIAL), General Secretariat of the Council of the European Union (GSC) (2013)
4. Choi, H.J., Lee, H.S., Sim, D., Yook, J.G., Sim, K.: Reconstruction of leaked signal from USB keyboards. In: URSI Asia-Pacific Radio Science Conference (URSI AP-RASC), pp. 1281–1283. IEEE, August 2016
5. Sokolov, R.I., Abdullin, R.R., Dolmatov, D.A.: Development of synchronization system for signal reception and recovery from USB-keyboard compromising emanations. In: IEEE International Conference on Industrial Engineering, Applications and Manufacturing (ICIEAM), pp. 1–4, May 2016
6. Ahsan, M.A., Islam, S.R., Islam, M.A.: A countermeasure for compromising electromagnetic emanations of wired keyboards. In: 17th IEEE International Conference on Computer and Information Technology (ICCIT), 22 Dec 2014, pp. 241–244 (2014)
7. Zhou, C., Yu, Q., Wang, L.: Investigation of the risk of electromagnetic security on computer systems. Int. J. Comput. Electrical Eng. 4(1), 92 (2012)
8. Popescu, M., Bîndar, V., Crăciunescu, R., Fratu, O.: Estimate of minimum attenuation level for a TEMPEST shielded enclosure. In: 11th International Conference on Communications – COMM 2016, Politehnica University of Bucharest, Military Technical Academy, Bucharest, pp. 521–526 (2016)
9. Bîndar, V., Popescu, M., Crăciunescu, R.: Aspects of electromagnetic compatibility as a support for communication security based on TEMPEST evaluation. In: 10th International Conference on Communications - COMM 2014, Politehnica University of Bucharest, Military Technical Academy, Bucharest, pp. 529–532 (2014)
10. van Eck, W.: Electromagnetic radiation from video display units: an eavesdropping risk? Comput. Secur. 4(4), 269–286 (1985)
11. Universal Serial Bus Specification-USB 2.0: Released in 27 April 2000. http://www.usb.org/developers./docs/usb20_docs/#usb20spec/usb_20.pdf. Recommendation ITU-R P.525-2. https://www.itu.int/dms_pubrec/itu-r/rec/p/R-REC-P.525-3-201611-I!!PDF-E.pdf. Accessed 10 May 2017

Security Risk: Detection of Compromising Emanations Radiated or Conducted by Display Units

Răzvan Bărtuşică[1]([⊠]), Alexandru Boitan[1], Simona Halunga[2], Mircea Popescu[1], and Valerică Bindar[1,2]

[1] Special Telecommunication Service, 323A, Splaiul Independentei, 060044 Bucharest, Romania
rbartusica@yahoo.com, alexandruboitan@yahoo.com,
bavaly@yahoo.com, mpopescu@sts.ro
[2] Telecommunications Faculty, University Politehnica of Bucharest, Bd. Iuliu Maniu 1-3, 061071 Bucharest, Romania
simona.halunga@upb.ro

Abstract. In this paper we propose a method of detecting the propagation frequencies of compromising emanations in order to evaluate the risk of eavesdropping the display units. By modulating the video signal with an audio file, we have been able to detect the compromising emanations on the frequencies where the audition occurred. The level of those emanations is an important issue in the process of evaluating the security risk. The higher the level, the higher is the probability of detection and reconstruction of displayed information.

Keywords: Compromising emanation · Emission security · TEMPEST

1 Introduction

In our days, the effort of protecting sensitive information is a critical one. Any form of security incident that involves protected information has a negative impact on the organization that relies on them. Therefore, a series of protective measures, technical and procedural, are needed in order to ensure information security.

One of those measures is known as Emission Security (EMSEC) or Transient Electromagnetic Pulse Emanation Standard (TEMPEST), which represents a set of technical, organizational and procedural measures applied for analysis, investigation and decrease of compromising emissions generated by electronic or electromagnetic equipment processing information, with the purpose of preventing the processed information recovery. Possible sources of compromising emanations can be, but not limited to: power supplies, power amplifiers, microprocessors, internal circuits and wires, keyboards, printers, modems, scanners and display units. This technique had been introduced in early 60 s [1, 2] and has been developed ever since as newer devices appeared on the market. In [3, 4] a number of security limits for compromising emanations have been highlighted for different existing public standards and devices

© ICST Institute for Computer Sciences, Social Informatics and Telecommunications Engineering 2018
O. Fratu et al. (Eds.): FABULOUS 2017, LNICST 241, pp. 45–51, 2018.
https://doi.org/10.1007/978-3-319-92213-3_7

and types of attack. Numerous testbeds and methodologies had been developed [5, 6] to evaluate the electromagnetic leakage emanations in different setups and for critical systems, sensitive to electromagnetic threats [7–9, 14]. It has been shown [1, 5, 10, 11] that display units like LCD, LED and old CRT monitors are ones of the most susceptible to eavesdropping due to their mode of operation. Compromising emanations can be processed by averaging since the video signal is periodic with the frame rate, leading to a processing gain of [2]

$$G_P = 10 \log_{10}(N). \tag{1}$$

where N is the number of averages, and $N \geq 2$.

2 Compromising Emanation Generation

In this chapter we present the evaluation method, that implies generation of a video *.avi file, that will be repeatedly played and displayed on a LCD monitor. The video file is bearing audio information, encoded in form of horizontal lines, displayed by the frame rate setting of the LCD. Each frame has a number of horizontal lines which represent 256 bit grayscale coded audio samples. Thus, the compromising emanation will be found in radiofrequency spectrum as an amplitude modulation. Then, by AM demodulating, one can recover the audio file encoded in as a video signal.

2.1 Audio File Parameters

The first step is importing an audio file, which has a number of samples N_a and a sampling rate F_s [Hz]. The duration of audio signal is

$$D_a = N_a/F_s \ (s). \tag{2}$$

The samples will be grouped in clusters, corresponding to video display parameters.

2.2 Video Signal Parameters

The LCD has H_{px} horizontal pixels, V_{px} vertical pixels and S_r [Hz] screen refresh rate corresponding to the visible area. The duration of video signal represented by the *.avi file is equal to the duration of the audio file, namely

$$D_v = N_f/S_r \ (s). \tag{3}$$

Where N_f represents the number of frames in the video file.

2.3 Compromising Emanation Encoding

Each video frame contains a number of M audio samples, determined by

$$M = \frac{N_a}{N_f} = \frac{F_s}{S_r}. \tag{4}$$

Because LCD's pixel frequency is larger than the audio file sampling rate by an order of magnitude of 4, the only way to make an image audible is to decrease the pixel frequency by displaying one audio sample on several horizontal video lines. The number of horizontal video lines used to display an audio sample is given by

$$H_l = \frac{V_{px}}{M}. \tag{5}$$

where V_{px} is the number of video lines.

The final step is to convert the audio samples, represented by vector A into a raster-type video stream, represented by matrices, according to values above.

$$A = [a_1\, a_2\, a_3 \ldots a_M \ldots a_{N_a-1}\, a_{N_a}]. \tag{6}$$

The audio samples are 8-bit encoded in order to obtain 256 grayscale values in order to obtain a video frame, as follows

$$Frame\ \#1 \begin{bmatrix} a_1 & \cdots & a_1 \\ \cdots & & \\ a_M & \cdots & a_M \end{bmatrix}, \quad Frame\ \#2 \begin{bmatrix} a_{M+1} & \cdots & a_{M+1} \\ \cdots & & \\ a_{2M} & \cdots & a_{2M} \end{bmatrix},$$

$$Frame\ \#N_f \begin{bmatrix} a_{N_a-M} & \cdots & a_{N_a-M} \\ \cdots & & \\ a_{N_a} & \cdots & a_{N_a} \end{bmatrix}. \tag{7}$$

3 Method Validation and Information Recovery

In order to check the efficiency of the method, an experimental testbed has been built, consisting of:

- LCD monitor, as the equipment under test with screen resolution of 1024 by 768 pixels and a refresh rate of 60 Hz [15]
- Log-periodic antenna, for wideband reception
- Test receiver, with AM demodulation and intermediate frequency output
- Oscilloscope, connected to the IF output of the receiver, in order to visualize the waveform on the frequency where the compromising emanation is present
- Speakers, used for audio detection of compromising emanations during the frequency sweep performed by the test receiver.

The experimental setup block diagram is presented in Fig. 1. By sweeping the spectrum and using AF demodulation option on the test receiver, we were able to detect the frequencies where the compromising emanation was identified. The tests were performed under different conditions, using several LCDs at distances between 3 and 30 meters, in line of sight or obstructed by concrete walls.

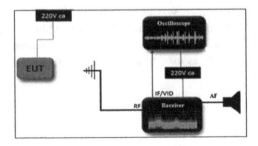

Fig. 1. The test setup used in the experiment. EUT represents different LCDs.

Next, to view the waveform and validate the method, we used the intermediate frequency output of the receiver connected to the scope input. We found that the waveforms visualized on the scope are correlated to the video frames displayed on the LCD, on those frequencies where the audition was possible.

The received frequency spectrum, presented in Fig. 2, contains several emissions, some of those being generated by the LCDs as spurious emissions. The compromising emanation of interest is marked in Fig. 2, at the frequency of 649.35 MHz.

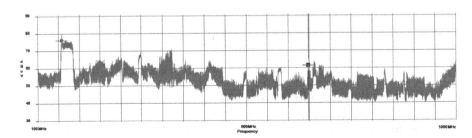

Fig. 2. Frequency spectrum. The marked frequency represents one detection.

Compromising emissions can be found on several frequencies, with different amplitude levels and audio quality. In this study the highest level and clearest audio recognition have been taken into consideration. On the other hand, different configurations of the testing scenario might lead to compromising emanations which are masked under the noise and interference, making it possible for the eavesdropper to recover information if he possesses a high quality receiver and strong signal processing capabilities.

One important parameter used for reducing the amount of received noise and increasing the frequency resolution is the resolution bandwidth, RBW. Thus the receiving sensitivity can be calculated as:

$$R_S = -174 + 10\log_{10}(RBW/Hz) + [NF]_{dBm} + [SNR]_{dBm} + [P_{att}]_{dBm} \quad (dBm). \quad (8)$$

where -174 is the thermal noise expressed in dBm, *RBW* is the bandpass filter of the receiver on the intermediate frequency path, *NF* is receiver noise figure, *SNR* is signal to noise ratio and P_{att} is the sum of antenna factor and cable loss, expressed in dB. By reducing RBW, the power of received noise decreases, compromising emanations can be separated from adjacent interferences making detection possible. Using a range of RBWs instead of a single one offers a higher confidence for our method.

The final step of validation is the visual correlation between displayed frames and received signal. To accomplish that we compared one video frame with corresponding waveform triggered on the oscilloscope. The amplitude and duration of each transition in oscilloscope waveform correspond with the intensity and thickness of displayed horizontal lines, as shown in Figs. 3 and 4.

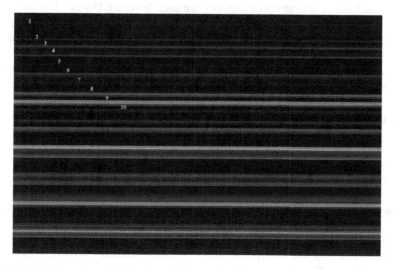

Fig. 3. Video frame displayed on the LCD. Audio samples are marked 1 to 10.

4 Conclusions

The method presented in this paper can be considered a fast solution for detecting compromising emanations from display units like LCD, LED and CRT monitors, using even a low cost wideband AM receiver.

The main advantage of this method is that it can be used in sites, to verify the conformity of installation process with emission security regulations, where display units operate as a part of a system and can't be moved or replaced by other display units. The disadvantage is that it is limited only to detection of compromising emanations and is not able to not measure their level, according to emission security regulations.

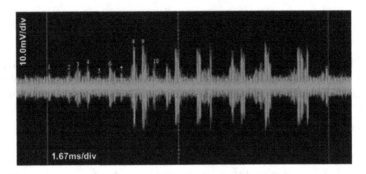

Fig. 4. Oscilloscope waveform. Detected audio samples are marked 1 to 10.

Information reconstruction by receiving and processing emissions generated by electronic equipment is a security risk and should be treated accordingly. The threat increases with the development of high performance Software Defined Radios that can be found on the market, which are becoming more affordable as the time passes.

Protective measures should be complex but also cost effective, starting with procedural measures which control operating conditions, software solutions like filtering displayed information and hardware measures like electromagnetic shielding and filtering [12, 13].

Acknowledgement. This work was supported by the grant of the Ministry of Innovation and Research, UEFISCDI, project number 5 Sol/2017 ToR-SIM within PNCDI III.

References

1. Kuhn, M.G.: Compromising emanations: eavesdropping risks of computer displays, Technical report (2003). http://www.cl.cam.ac.uk/TechReports/UCAM-CL-TR-577.pdf
2. Kuhn, M.G.: Security limits for compromising emanations. In: Rao, J.R., Sunar, B. (eds.) CHES 2005. LNCS, vol. 3659, pp. 265–279. Springer, Heidelberg (2005). https://doi.org/10.1007/11545262_20
3. Kuhn, M.G.: Eavesdropping attacks on computer displays. Inf. Secur. Summit, 24–25 (2006). Prague
4. Kuhn, M.G.: Compromising emanations of LCD TV sets. IEEE Trans. Electromagn. Compat. **55**, 564–570 (2013)
5. Katamreddy, S.: Experimental testbed for electromagnetic analysis doctoral dissertation. George Mason University (2016)
6. Kasmi, C., Esteves, J.L., Armstrong, K.: EMC/EMI and functional safety, methodology to characterize effects of interferences on devices. In: IEEE 2016 Asia-Pacific International Symposium on Electromagnetic Compatibility (APEMC), vol. 1, pp. 1178–1180 (2016)
7. Christopoulos, C.: Electromagnetic compatibility (EMC) in challenging environments. In: Daras, N.J., Rassias, T.M. (eds.) Operations Research, Engineering, and Cyber Security. SOIA, vol. 113, pp. 95–115. Springer, Cham (2017). https://doi.org/10.1007/978-3-319-51500-7_5

8. Jian, M., Jinming, L.: Information leakage from computer based on electromagnetic radiation. Control Intell. Syst. **43**(2) (2016)
9. Van Eck, W.: Electromagnetic radiation from video display units: an eavesdropping risk? Comput. Secur. **4**(4), 269–286 (1985)
10. Sekiguchi, H., Seto, S.: Measurement of radiated computer RGB signals. Prog. Electromagn. Res. C **7**, 1–12 (2009)
11. Bîndar, V., Popescu, M., Craciunescu, R.: Aspects of electromagnetic compatibility as a support for communication security based on TEMPEST evaluation. In: 2014 10th International Conference on Communications (COMM), Bucharest, pp. 1–4 (2014)
12. ITU-T K.84: test methods and guide against information leaks through unintentional electromagnetic emissions (2011)
13. ITU-T K.87: guide for the application of electromagnetic security requirements (2016)
14. https://www.sans.org/reading-room/whitepapers/privacy/introduction-tempest-981. Accessed Apr 2017
15. http://tinyvga.com/vga-timing. Accessed Apr 2017

LDPC Coding Used in Massive-MIMO Systems

Cela-Roberta Stanciu and Carmen Voicu[(✉)]

Telecommunication Department, University Politehnica of Bucharest,
Bucharest, Romania
carmen.voicu@radio.pub.ro

Abstract. This paper presents the importance of Massive-MIMO systems and the LDPC coding technique used to improve their performance. We will focus on LDPC coding used in the implementation of a Massive-MIMO system and the simulation results using Matlab. A comparison between the classical systems and the LDPC coded system will be made, in order to stress the improvements in particular cases. Starting with simple MIMO systems, the number of antennas at the receiver will be increased and the result will be discussed.

Keywords: Massive-MIMO · Channel coding · LDPC coding
Fading

1 Introduction

In the last years, requirements such as increasing the information capacity and throughput in order to support voice applications, video streaming, movies, games, etc., determined the need for increasing and improving the wireless equipment. The necessity of studying Massive-MIMO systems is that they are contained in wireless technologies such as LTE (Long Term Evolution), LTE-A (LTE Advanced), Wi-Fi and make a great point of interest in the future 5G [1, 2]. Regarding these topics, their users are interested in some important aspects like low energy consumption and high transfer rates, while the producers focus on serving as many users as possible without generating any congestion in the system.

In a Massive-MIMO system, a base station contains a large number of antennas (in the same place or spread along its action area) and it serves simultaneously a large number of users within the same time-frequency resource.

The information throughput can be defined as a product between the bandwidth and the spectral efficiency, so if we want to increase the throughput, we have to increase either the bandwidth or the spectral efficiency. The nowadays trend is to increase the last parameter and a very good method of doing this is by using a very large number of antennas for the transmitter and the receiver - which represents the study of Massive-MIMO systems [3].

© ICST Institute for Computer Sciences, Social Informatics and Telecommunications Engineering 2018
O. Fratu et al. (Eds.): FABULOUS 2017, LNICST 241, pp. 52–57, 2018.
https://doi.org/10.1007/978-3-319-92213-3_8

2 Massive-MIMO

MIMO (Multiple Input Multiple Output) represents a technology used in radio communications that uses multiple antennas both for the transmitter and for the receiver, for allowing multipath propagation and so the efficient use of the transmission path. Any system can be affected by fading, which seriously affects the signal-to-noise ratio.

Between the transmitter and the receiver, the signal may travel through various paths. By changing the position of the antennas, this path also changes. These paths can produce interferences, but the MIMO technology turns this fact into an advantage by offering robustness to the radio link by increasing the link capacity considering Shannon's law [4].

A MU-MIMO system (Multiuser-MIMO) it is a system where multiple users are simultaneously served by a base station having multiple antennas. Here, a gain is obtained by spatial multiplexing, even if each user has a single antenna [5].

In Massive-MIMO systems, a base station having hundreds of antennas serves ten or more users simultaneously, within the same time-frequency resource. The main advantages of Massive-MIMO are: high spectral efficiency and reliability; energetic efficiency; simplicity of signal processing; interference reducing [6].

It is important to know that these advantages cannot be accessed simultaneously, but according to the application they are used in. By increasing the number of antennas at the base station, the system performance should increase.

The performance of a Massive-MIMO system depends on the characteristics of the transmission and reception antennas but also on the environment where the signals propagate. Theoretically, Massive-MIMO works in a favorable environment, but, in reality, there are cases when the channel in not favorable, for instance the case when the number of paths is smaller than the number of mobile terminals or the case when channels coming from different users share the same path. A possible solution to this problem is placing the antennas of the base station so that they can coordinate a larger area [7].

3 LDPC Channel Coding

For coding Massive-MIMO systems, various techniques can be used, such as turbo codes, LDPC coding and polar coding. The desired channel capacity can be achieved using random codes.

LDPC (Low Density Parity Check) codes are error-correcting codes first used in 1960 at M.I.T. At the beginning, they were considered unpractical, which later turned out to be wrong. LDPC are useful in Massive-MIMO systems, as they have good performance regarding Shannon's limit, which is an important aspect to consider.

LDPC coding consists of creating the parity check matrix [8], H, which has r rows and n columns, which satisfy the relation: $k = n - r$. The element with the ij index is 1 if the j equation contains the i bit, so that the parity check matrix has a small number of ones, which is the reason that these codes are called *low density*. A regular LDPC code has the property that each code bit is contained in the same number of equations and each equation consists of the same number of code symbols.

For LDPC coding and decoding, a representation with graphs is used. The LDPC codes are linear codes obtained from sparse bipartite graphs having n nodes called message nodes and r nodes called check nodes. The property which makes the LDPC algorithms efficient is their sparsity, which means the fact that the occurrence of the 1 element is low. For decoding, LDPC uses message passing algorithms, which are iterative algorithms, being called so because at every iteration, messages are passed from message nodes to check nodes, and from check nodes back to message nodes [9].

For this article we choose to analyze the performance of LDPC in Massive-MIMO systems because the 3GPP standardization group is debating if the turbo code used in 4G should be replaced by the Low Density Parity Check (LDPC) or polar code in 5G. Thus, we are interested to study the performance obtained and the implementation complexity of a multiuser Massive-MIMO system using LDPC codes for the uplink case.

4   Performance of a Massive-MIMO System on the Uplink

For obtaining the following simulations, we started with a MIMO system with a 2×2 dimension (2 antennas for the transmitter, 2 antennas for the receiver), analyzing the case with 4 users, for which we have represented the bit error rate (BER) by changing the signal-to-noise ratio (SNR). The fading used has a Rayleigh distribution. We switched between BPSK and QPSK modulation and we used a MMSE detector (Minimum Mean Square Error).

By using BPSK modulation, for a high SNR value, the performance obtained is better than in the case of using QPSK modulation. The results are displayed in Figs. 1 and 2.

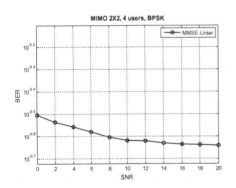
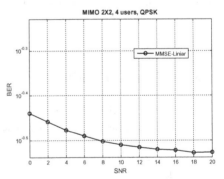

Fig. 1. MIMO system 2×2, 4 users, BPSK   **Fig. 2.** MIMO system 2×2, 4 users, QPSK

It can be noticed that for low SNR values, the performance obtained using BPSK and QPSK is similar: for a SNR = 2 dB, BER is about 0.29 for BPSK and 0.35 for QPSK. By increasing the SNR, for instance, for a SNR = 10 dB, BER = 0.24 for BPSK and BER = 0.31 for QPSK, so the system shows a better performance than the case of a low SNR. For a SNR = 18 dB, BER = 0.22 for BPSK and BER = 0.3 for QPSK.

By increasing the user number from 4 to 10, the performance is similar, as shown in Figs. 3 and 4. A better performance is obtained for high SNR and for BPSK modulation. For a SNR = 2 dB, BER = 0.3655 for BPSK and BER = 0.4055 for QPSK and for SNR = 16 dB, BER = 0.33 for BPSK and BER = 0.38 for QPSK.

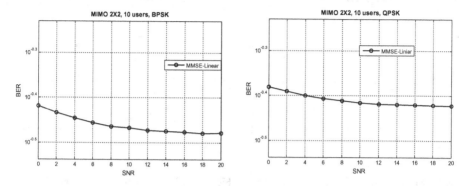

Fig. 3. MIMO system 2 × 2, 10 users, BPSK   **Fig. 4.** MIMO system 2 × 2, 10 users, QPSK

The most complex system implemented within this topic it is a system with 2 × . 1 dimension, serving 50 users simultaneously, as shown in Figs. 5 and 6. Here, the performance of using a large number of antennas can be noticed, as the BER decreases from the previous cases: for SNR = 6 dB, in case of BPSK, BER's value goes under 10^{-1}, while for QPSK, it is about 10^{-1}. When the SNR increases, the results are very good, BER = $5 \cdot 10^{-5}$ for BPSK and BER = 10^{-3} for QPSK, for SNR = 20 dB.

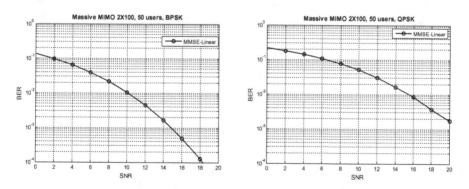

Fig. 5. Massive MIMO system 2 × 100, 50 users, BPSK   **Fig. 6.** Massive MIMO system 2 × 100, 50 users, QPSK

In order to analyze the results obtained for using LDPC coding within Massive-MIMO systems, we started with a MIMO system of 2 × 2 dimension which

serves 4 users simultaneously. Results are displayed in Figs. 7 and 8. Comparing
Figs. 7 and 8 with Figs. 1 and 2 respectively, we can see no improvements in the case
of the LDPC coded system and the results are similar for the two types of modulation:
BPSK and QPSK (for a SNR = 2 dB, BER = 0.4 for BPSK and BER = 0.36 for
QPSK, while for a SNR = 16 dB, BER = 0.34 for BPSK and BER = 0.32 for QPSK).

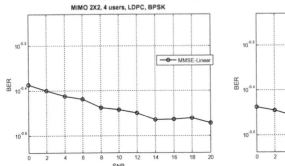
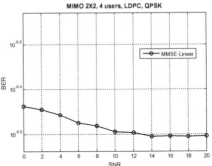

Fig. 7. MIMO system 2 × 2, 4 users, BPSK, LDPC coded

Fig. 8. MIMO system 2 × 2, 4 users, QPSK, LDPC coded

Further on, Figs. 9 and 10 depict the performance for a Massive-MIMO system,
LDPC coded, of dimension 2 × 100, serving 50 users simultaneously. This last case
shows the best improvements made by using multiple antennas for the receiver,
combined with LDPC coding, for which a BER of order of 10^{-6} for BPSK and 10^{-3} for
QPSK is obtained, which is a very good result to consider.

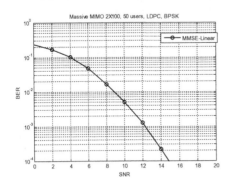
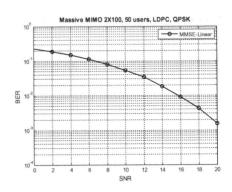

Fig. 9. Massive MIMO system 2 × 100, 50 users, BPSK, LDPC coded

Fig. 10. Massive MIMO system 2 × 100, 50 users, QPSK, LDPC coded

5   Conclusions

In this paper we analyzed the performance of a multiuser Massive MIMO system with LDPC code for the uplink case. We can highlight that the bit error rate decreases as the signal-to-noise ratio increases and has better values for BPSK modulation. BER has a tendency of rising as the number of served users increases. The performance is much better when using more antennas for the receiver, which explains why implementing Massive-MIMO systems in wireless communications. We consider that the results would have been even better if the coding of the source had been done, but we only performed the channel coding which, however, provides good results. Regarding the complexity of the system, which is growing according as the numbers of users and the numbers of antennas at the base station (BS) are increasing. Thus, there should be established a connection between the number of users and the number of BS antennas in order that the performance of the system to be the same for all users whatever is their position in the cell.

References

1. Arnott, R., Oketani, K., Prasad, N., Rangarajan, S., Wells, P.: Analysis and evaluation of a practical downlink multiuser MIMO scheduler over LTE advanced massive MIMO systems. In: 2016 50th Asilomar Conference on Signals, Systems and Computers, Pacific Grove, CA, pp. 188–192 (2016)
2. Pratschner, S., Schwarz, S., Rupp, M.: Single-user and multi-user MIMO channel estimation for LTE-Advanced uplink. In: 2017 IEEE International Conference on Communications (ICC), Paris, pp. 1–6 (2017)
3. Afzal, A., Feki, A., Debbah, M., Zaidi, S.A., Ghogho, M., McLernon, D.: Leveraging D2D communication to maximize the spectral efficiency of massive MIMO systems. In: 2017 15th International Symposium on Modeling and Optimization in Mobile, Ad Hoc, and Wireless Networks (WiOpt), Paris, France, pp. 1–6 (2017)
4. Jeong, Y., Trinh, D.P., Shin, H.: Cutset bounds on the capacity of MIMO relay channels. IEEE Access, PP(99), 1 (2017)
5. Suraweera, H.A., Ngo, H.Q., Duong, T.Q., Yuen, C., Larsson, E.G.: Multi-pair amplify-and-forward relaying with very large antenna arrays. In: Proceedings of the IEEE International Conference on Communications (ICC) (2013)
6. Hama, Y., Ochiai, H.: A low-complexity matched filter detector with parallel interference cancellation for massive MIMO systems. In: 2016 IEEE 12th International Conference on Wireless and Mobile Computing, Networking and Communications (WiMob), New York, NY, pp. 1–6 (2016)
7. Ngo, H.Q.: Massive MIMO: Fundamentals and System Designs. LiU-Tryck, Linköping (2015)
8. Gallager, R.G.: Low Density Parity-Check Codes. MIT Press, Cambridge (1963)
9. Sun, W.C., Wu, W.H., Yang, C.H., Ueng, Y.L.: An iterative detection and decoding receiver for LDPC-coded MIMO systems. IEEE Trans. Circ. Syst. I Regul. Pap. 62(10), 2512–2522 (2015)

Pesticide Telemetry Using Potentiostat

George Suciu[1,2(✉)], Alexandru Ganaside[1], Laurentiu Bezdedeanu[1],
Robert Coanca[1], Stefania Secu[1], Carmen Nădrag[1,2],
and Alexandru Marțian[2]

[1] BEIA Consult International, R&D Department, Bucharest, Romania
{george, alex. ganaside, laurentiu. bezdedeanu,
robert. coanca, stefania. secu, carmen. nadrag}@beia. ro
[2] University Politehnica of Bucharest, ETTI, Bucharest, Romania
martian@radio. pub. ro

Abstract. Even if the pesticides can cause different diseases, there are few methods to detect their influence and presence within the food products. However, it has been found a way to detect these harmful substances. The use of a potentiostat within a telemetry system can represent the solution to this problem. The potentiostat is an electronic device which can control a three electrode cell and run electroanalytical experiments. This paper aims to present methods and components of a telemetry system. It represents an experimental demonstrative model for immunobiosensor, composed of carbon nanomaterials/magnetic and antibodies serving for detecting the carbamate pesticides in horticultural products. In addition, a way of exploiting the properties of nanomaterials which could provide great platforms for the electronic/optic signals generator required for the development of a new generation of bio-detection devices will be presented.

Keywords: Pesticide · Telemetry · Potentiostat · Immunobiosensors

1 Introduction

Fruits and vegetables represent one of the most contaminated sources of food with pesticides that all of the people consume daily. Using pesticides represents a good method for eliminating plants diseases and most of the pests. Even so, the abuse of pesticides leads to endangering the health of those who consume the horticultural products. Moreover, these substances present low solubility and their decomposition takes a long time. This is why they are called persistent organic pollutants and their secondary effects can determine serious environmental and health diseases [1].

The scientific works which successfully implemented the electrochemical devices for detecting the pesticide residues come in the help of the population. The goal of these devices is to detect and monitor these solutions by using only few resources, sensitive and more practical instruments [2]. In laboratories, the electrochemical techniques are used to study the thermodynamics and kinetics processes of electrons and ions transfer in order to deduct the absorption phenomena that occurs on the electrode's surface and the possible reaction mechanisms in organic chemistry and biochemistry.

© ICST Institute for Computer Sciences, Social Informatics and Telecommunications Engineering 2018
O. Fratu et al. (Eds.): FABULOUS 2017, LNICST 241, pp. 58–63, 2018.
https://doi.org/10.1007/978-3-319-92213-3_9

In most of the voltammetric methods, an electrochemical cell consists of three electrodes [3]:

1. A working electrode at which the electrochemical reaction appears at the electron's transfer;
2. A reference electrode which is characterized by a constant potential in time;
3. An auxiliary electrode, where a counter reaction to the working electrode takes place in order to balance the total load all over the system.

These being said, when a voltage potential is applied to the working electrode interacting with a pesticide probe, the working electrode is getting oxidized or reduced, resulting in a concentration change on the electrode's surface. As consequence, this process causes the transfer towards the electrode and the appearance of an electric current. This current is recorded on a curve called voltammogram and it is directly proportional to the applied potential. Due to its dependency on the analyte's concentration, voltammetric methods can be applied for analytical purposes [4].

A biosensor represents an analytical device that turns a biological response into a quantifiable and processable signal. The composition of a typical biosensor used for pesticide detection consists of a bio-receptor, an electrochemical interface (electrode) to which the bioreceptor is connected and also an electronic system developed to turn the biological response of the electrode into a processable and measurable signal, as presented in Fig. 1. The steps of the analysis process are the following: when the working electrode gets in contact with a pesticide solution, an interaction between the bio receptor and pesticide solution appears. The basic tools necessary for an electro-chemistry experiment are an electrochemical cell and a voltamperometric analyzer, which consists of a potentiostat connected to a computer [5].

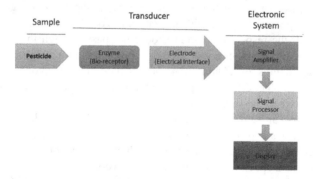

Fig. 1. Major components of a typical biosensor for pesticide detection

The rest of the paper is structured as follows: Sect. 2 presents the related work, Sect. 3 shows the methods of using the potentiostat for the telemetry system, while Sect. 4 presents the measurement results. Finally, Sect. 5 concludes the paper.

2 Related Work

In [6], a portable biosensor is used in order to detect the pesticide concentration. This biosensor makes use of screen-printed electrodes and it has the ability to determine the concentration of organophosphorus and carbamate pesticides. Developed in a laboratory, the biosensor uses a screen-printed electrode with 10 mU of immobilized AChE (Acetylcholinesterase) coupled to a potentiostat and a portable computer. The whole system has been evaluated and validated to be used for determining the neurotoxic pesticides in water samples and horticultural products.

In [7] an experimental solution for a potential point-of-use platform for multivariate analyses by presenting homemade potentiostat and smartphone is documented. This system combines high-performance detection with great simplicity, low-cost, portability, autonomy (6 h), and wireless communication device. The features presented proved efficiency in different assays by allowing the real-time accomplishment of the entire analytical measurement at remote places. The system is composed of a point-of-use platform used for detection of the electroanalytical in function of the diverse analyses and a portable, self-sustainable and free cabled platform system composed of a potentiostat and smartphone.

3 Potentiostat Measurement Methodology and Immunosensors

A potentiostat is an electronic device able to handle the voltage potential difference between a working and a reference electrode [8]. The reference electrode maintains a constant voltage with the reference to the electrode potential of hydrogen. However, when a current passes through the reference electrode, the electrode gets polarized, meaning that the potential varies with the current. To avoid this and to maintain a constant potential, the respective current should not pass through the reference electrode. This means that the potentiostat should be presented with a high input resistance of the order of GOhms to TOhms. Another method for the above problem is to implement a counter electrode [9], as presented in Fig. 2. In this case, a current must be forced to pass between the working and counter electrode.

Immunosensors can be defined as sensors that act on the principle that the response of a biological species exposed to contaminants will produce antibodies which can be measured [10]. They are based on the immunochemical reactions so that the antigen (Ag) is bounded to a specific antibody (Ab). For every antigen, determination corresponds the production of a particular (Ab), its purification and isolation. To increase the sensitivity of the immunosensors, the enzyme labels are coupled to (Ab) and (Ag) resulting in more chemical steps. It is worth mentioning that the immunosensors consist of two processes. The first process is called the molecular recognition process which determines the specific (Ag-Ab) binding reaction on the surface of the receptor while the second process is called the signal-transfer process which responds to the changes in an electrochemical parameter of the receptor. These changes are caused by the specific binding between (Ag-Ab) [2]. As resources, nanomaterials have already

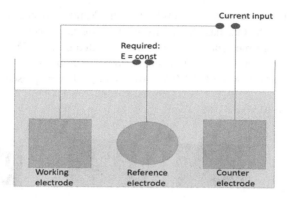

Fig. 2. Principle of a potential-controllable electrochemical cell

demonstrated their utilities for bio sensing applications in many technological domains. Nano-objects amazed with their increased performances in the sensitivity domain and accurate detections. One advantage of the nanomaterials is the high specific surface which enables the immobilization of an enhanced amount of bio receptor units. Nevertheless, a constant challenge reffers to the immobilization strategy or easier, the distinction which is used to conjugate intimately the bio-specific entity onto nanomaterials. Thus, immobilizing the pesticide sample represents one of the main factors in developing a reliable biosensor [11].

4   Measurement Results

In this section, the implementation of an experimental prototype model of imunobiosensor used for detecting carbamate pesticides in horticultural products is presented. In Fig. 3 is presented the schematic of the potentiostat.

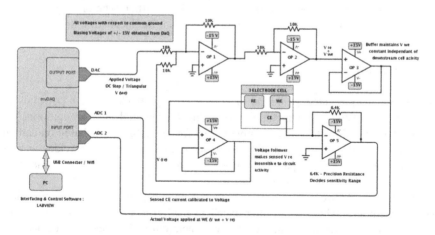

Fig. 3. The schematic diagram of the potentiostat

For measurements we used a NI myDAQ from National Instruments, which is a data acquisition device that has the ability to measure and analyze live signals, no matter the location or time. The potentiostat is connected on the ADC1, ADC2 inputs and DAC output of the myDAQ and the collected data can be easily visualized within the front panel interface of the LabVIEW environment [12], as presented in Fig. 4.

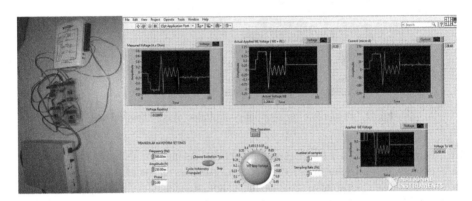

Fig. 4. Potentiostat - myDAQ connection and LabVIEW measurements front panel

The sensors connected to the potentiostat are a PAR Quantic Sensor which is used for the measurement of photosynthetic active radiation [13], a WET-2 sensor for measuring three vital soil properties: water content, electrical conductivity and temperature [14] and low cost and disposable Screen Printed Electrodes (SPE) [15].

Another set of sensors that can be used within CarbaDetect project are an SHT15 digital temperature and humidity sensor [16] – it is a unique capacitive sensor element that is used for measuring relative humidity while temperature is measured by a band-gap sensor and an ML8511 UV Sensor [17] which is equipped with an internal amplifier able to turn the photo-current into voltage depending on the UV intensity. Also, the graphical interface can be used for the manual input of some parameters like: pesticide type, antibody type, the protein, type of link, carbon type or magnetic link, fluorescent or not, ample label, concentration, dilution, the incubation time.

5   Conclusion

In this paper, we presented a solution for telemetry of pesticides using a potentiostat. The prototype is a compact analytic device designed for biomolecular recognition. We developed an experimental demonstrative model for imunobiosensor based on carbon nanomaterials/magnetic and antibodies for detection of carbamate pesticides in horticultural products. As compared to other existing systems, our solution is both cost-effective and easy to be implemented.

As future work, we envision to exploit the unique properties of nanomaterials (magnetic/carbonic) which could offer excellent platforms as electronic/optic signals generator necessary for the design of a new generation of bio detection devices. In addition to this, we aim to conduct various tests using different fruits and vegetables, under different conditions.

Acknowledgments. This work was supported by a grant of the Ministry of Innovation and Research, UEFISCDI, project number 5 Sol/2017 ToR-SIM within PNCDI III and partially funded by UEFISCDI Romania under grants CarbaDetect and EV-BAT projects, and by European Union's Horizon 2020 research and innovation program under grant agreement No. 643963 (SWITCH project).

References

1. Tietenberg, T., Lewis, L.: Environmental and Natural Resource Economics. Routledge, Abingdon (2016)
2. Mostafa, G.A.E.: Electrochemical biosensors for the detection of pesticides. Open Electrochem. J. **2**(1), 22–42 (2010)
3. Mirceski, V., Gulaboski, R., Lovric, M., Bogeski, I., Kappl, R., Hoth, M.: Square-wave voltammetry: a review on the recent progress. Electroanalysis **25**, 2411–2422 (2013)
4. Marcus, R.A.: On the theory of oxidation – reduction reactions involving electron transfer. v. comparison and properties of electrochemical and chemical rate constants. J. Phys. Chem. **67**(4), 853–857 (1963)
5. Tonle, K.I., Ngameni, E.: Voltammetric analysis of pesticides. In: Stoytcheva, M. (ed.) InTech (2011)
6. Hildebrandt, A., Bragos, R., Lacorte, S., Marty, J.L.: Performance of a portable biosensor for the analysis of organophosphorus and carbamate insecticides in water and food. Sens. Actuators B Chem. **133**(1), 195–201 (2008)
7. Giordano, G.F., et al.: Point-of-use electroanalytical platform based on homemade potentiostat and smartphone for multivariate data processing. Electrochim. Acta **219**, 170–177 (2016)
8. Potentiostat fundamentals. https://www.gamry.com/application-notes/instrumentation/potentiostat-fundamentals/. Accessed 12 June 2017
9. Rab, L.M., Munteanu, A.: Consideration and measurements regarding a didactic portable potentiostat. Bull. Transilvania Univ. Brasov **2**, 51 (2009)
10. Duffy, G., Moore, E.J.: Electrochemical immunosensors for food analysis: a review of recent developments. Anal. Lett. **50**(1), 1–32 (2016)
11. Holzinger, M., Le Goff, A., Cosnier, S.: Nanomaterials for biosensing applications: a review. Front. Chem. **2**, 63 (2014)
12. Suciu, G., Butca, C., Conu, R., Suciu, V., Hristea, G., Vochin, M., Todoran, G.: Rapid detection of pesticide residues based on telemetry platform. In 12th IEEE International Symposium on Electronics and Telecommunications (ISETC), pp. 95–98 (2016)
13. PQS1 – Senzor Cuantic PAR. http://st1.echipot.ro/files/Kipp-Zonen/Senzor-cuantic-PAR-PQS-1–Brosura.pdf. Accessed 12 June 2017
14. WET2 Sensor. http://st1.echipot.ro/files/Delta-T/Senzor-WET2—Brosura.pdf. Accessed 12 June 2017
15. Ahmed, M.U., Hossain, M.M., Savavieh, M., Wong, Y.L., Rahman, I.A., Zourob, M., Tamiya, E.: Toward the development of smart and low cost point-of-care biosensors based on screen printed electrodes. Crit. Rev. Biotechnol. **36**(3), 495–505 (2016)
16. Datasheet SHT1x. https://www.sparkfun.com/datasheets/Sensors/SHT1x_datasheet.pdf. Accessed 12 June 2017
17. ML8511. https://cdn.sparkfun.com/datasheets/Sensors/LightImaging/ML8511_3-8-13.pdf. Accessed 12 June 2017

5G Challenges, Requirements and Key Differentiating Characteristics from the Perspective of a Mobile Operator

Elena-Mădălina Oproiu[1,2(✉)], Catalin Costea[1],
Marius Nicuşor Nedelcu[1,2], Marius Iordache[1], and Ion Marghescu[2]

[1] Technology Department, Orange Romania, Bucharest, Romania
elena-madalina.oproiu@sdettib.pub.ro,
{catalin.costea,marius.nedelcu,
marius.iordache}@orange.com
[2] Telecommunications Department, University Politehnica of Bucharest,
Bucharest, Romania
marion@comm.pub.ro

Abstract. The present paper studies 5G challenges, requirements and key differentiating characteristics from the perspective of a Romanian mobile operator. The main contribution is that we created a vision about the use cases, physical and logical architecture needed to support these uses cases and other key differentiated factors, that the deployment of a future 5G network will bring in a mobile network. This global vision was made after studying and analyzing the results and publication of the most important research and industry projects on 5G, realized until now. Our main goal is to be prepared in 2020 to develop a commercial 5G network and this analysis was made to observe the main changes and the new requirements that this implementation will bring in our current mobile network.

Keywords: 5G · Mobile operator · Use case · Physical architecture
Logical architecture · Slice · Network functions virtualization (NFV)
Software-defined networking (SDN) · Orchestrator

1 Introduction

The fifth generation of mobile networks, 5G, represents one of the key topics in today's research, industry and standardization areas.

5G is the technology which will operate in the 2020–2030 decade. 5G is the future Internet including radio access as well as a convergent core network between fixed access and radio access. It is expected that 5G will deliver more than connectivity. Its innovative design, with a full software approach, will transform networks into one programmable and unified infrastructure integrating networking, computing and storage resources, paving the road to new business models.

5G represents more than an expansion of bandwidth capacity and expects to enable new business models, streamline the service delivery and support different vertical use

© ICST Institute for Computer Sciences, Social Informatics and Telecommunications Engineering 2018
O. Fratu et al. (Eds.): FABULOUS 2017, LNICST 241, pp. 64–70, 2018.
https://doi.org/10.1007/978-3-319-92213-3_10

cases. It is required to support actual and future diverse set of vertical industries and simplify their provisioning process that calls for new architectural frameworks.

A mobile operator will have to deploy orchestrator functions that will allocate appropriate computing and network resources to the services, targeting diverse and dedicated business driven logical networks.

The paper is organized as follows: Subsect. 1.1 presents the main challenges, requirements and key differentiating characteristics of a 5G network and Subsect. 1.2 presents 5G overall roadmap. In Sect. 2 we presented the 5G use cases and we summarized in Table 1 the user experience key performance indicators (KPI's) and system performance requirements for each of these use cases. The 5G architecture, who is formed by logical and physical architecture, needed to support these use cases is presented in Sect. 3. Finally, Sect. 4 draws the conclusions.

Table 1. User experience KPI's and system performance requirements

	Use case category	User Experience Data Rate	E2E Latency	Mobility	Connection Density	Traffic Density
Broadband access in dense area	Broadband access in dense areas	DL: 300 Mbps UL: 50 Mbps	10 ms	0-100 km/h	200-2500 /km2	DL: 750 Gbps / km2 UL: 125 Gbps / km2
	Indoor ultra-high broadband access	DL: 1 Gbps UL: 500 Mbps	10 ms	Pedestrian	75,000 / km2	DL: 15 Tbps/ km2 UL: 2 Tbps / km2
	Broadband access in a crowd	DL: 25 Mbps UL: 50 Mbps	10 ms	Pedestrian	150,000 / km2	DL: 3.75 Tbps/ km2 UL: 7.5 Tbps / km2
Broadband access everywhere	50+ Mbps everywhere	DL: 50 Mbps UL: 25 Mbps	10 ms	0-120 km/h	400 /km2 in suburban 100 / km2 in rural	DL: 20 Gbps / km2 in suburban UL: 10 Gbps / km2 in suburban DL: 5 Gbps / km2 in rural UL: 2.5 Gbps / km2 in rural
	Ultra-low cost broadband access	DL: 10 Mbps UL: 10 Mbps	50 ms	0-50 km/h	16 / km2	16 Mbps / km2
High user mobility	Mobile broadband in vehicles (cars, trains)	DL: 50 Mbps UL: 25 Mbps	10 ms	up to 500 km/h	2000 / km2 (500 active users per train x 4 trains, or 1 active user per car x 2000 cars)	DL: 100 Gbps / km2 (25 Gbps per train, 50 Mbps per car) UL: 50 Gbps / km2 (12.5 Gbps per train, 25 Mbps per car)
	Airplanes connectivity	DL: 15 Mbps/ user UL: 7.5 Mbps/ user	10 ms	up to 1000 km/h	60 airplanes per 18,000 km2	DL: 1.2 Gbps / plane UL: 600 Mbps / plane
Massive Internet of Things	Massive low-cost/long-range/low-power MTC	Low: 1-100 kbps	seconds to hours	0-500 km/h	Up to 200,000 / km2	Non critical
	Broadband MTC	See the requirements for the Broadband access in dense areas and 50+Mbps everywhere categories				
Extreme real time communication	Ultra-low latency	DL: 50 Mbps UL: 25 Mbps	<1 ms	Pedestrian	Not critical	Potentially high
Lifeline communication	Resilience and traffic surge	DL: 0.1-1 Mbps UL: 0.1-1 Mbps	not critical	0-120 km/h	10,000 / km2	Potentially high
Ultra-reliable communication	Ultra-high reliability & Ultra-low latency	DL: 50 kbps - 10 Mbps UL: few bps - 10 Mbps	1 ms	0-500 km/h	Not critical	Potentially high
	Ultra-high availability & reliability	DL: 10 Mbps UL: 10 Mbps	10 ms	0-500 km/h	Not critical	Potentially high
Broadcast like services	Broadcast like services	DL: Up to 200 Mbps UL: 500 kbps	<100 ms	0-500 km/h	Not relevant	Not relevant

1.1 Challenges, Requirements and Key Differentiating Characteristics

5G is the future Internet, accessible from any existing or future access technology and it will be the whole communication system of the 2020–2030 decade, at least, comprising new air interfaces, but also a new core network. The latter will leverage the convergence of telecom and IT in order to offer:

- an overall system architecture that permits any access technology to be connected to the core network, in particular new air interfaces defined in the future to address new needs;
- a dynamic configuration as a function of the requested applications to optimize the resource usage on a specific geographic area;
- a network operating system in charge of managing the global infrastructure;
- a facilitated fixed-mobile convergence [1].

A 5G network enhances the user experience by providing homogenous services over the coverage area by keeping a high throughput and a low latency communication, from static to high speed trains and from outdoor to deep indoor areas, assuring a seamless handover between any wireless access technology.

From a mobile operator perspective, the main 5G key requirements are: low power consumption and cost efficiency, higher capacity, higher spectrum efficiency and agility, integration of 3rd Generation Partnership Project Radio Access Technology (3GPP RATs) and non 3GPP RATs, ultra low latency, higher number of connected devices, seamless access to different wireless technologies, security and privacy of user`s data, resilience and robustness, flexibility and openness for future integrations, convergence between fixed and mobile verticals and ease of deployment and operation.

1.2 5G Overall Roadmap

The deployment plans in the following years, based on pre-standard technologies, are led by major mobile operators around the globe, including:

- Verizon - fixed wireless broadband using frequencies up to 28 GHz;
- TeliaSonera - signed a strategic partnership with Ericsson, intending to launch 5G services in Stockholm and Tallinn in 2018, including e-health and connected cars use cases;
- Korea Telecom (KT) and South Korean telecommunications (SKT) - partnership with Samsung and Nokia, respective with Ericsson, are planning to provide 5G services in 2018 at PyeongChang Winter Olympics;
- Orange Group - is leading the worldwide 5G tests and trials initiative, intending to be 5G ready for Euro 2020 in Belgium, Spain and Romania. On January 25th 2017, Orange and Ericsson have demonstrated a wireless 5G communication with peak rates beyond 14 Gbps [2].

As shown in Fig. 1, the first commercial 5G deployments are expected to start in 2020, this term being constrained by standards bodies` readiness and commercial equipment availability [2].

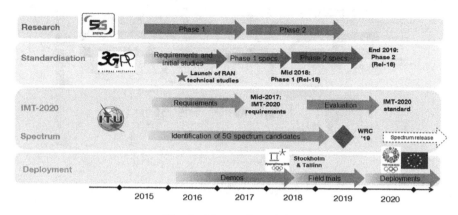

Fig. 1. 5G overall roadmap

2 Use Cases and Their Requirements

After analysis of most important research and industry projects (5GPPP, METIS I, METIS II, NGMN, ETSI, etc.), we found there are three main categories of use cases:

- massive broadband (xMBB) that delivers gigabytes of bandwidth on demand;
- massive machine-type communication (mMTC) that connects billions of sensors and machines;
- critical machine-type communication (uMTC) that allows immediate feedback with high reliability and enables for example remote control over robots and autonomous driving.

These three main categories could be further divided in eight families, each of them including some of use cases. This approach is very well presented in Next Generation Mobile Networks (NGMN) white paper [3]. We analyzed the main results of the 5G research projects and we decided that the NGMN presents and covers all the use cases. In the Table 1, we presented each family, its use cases and key requirements for each of these use case.

3 5G Architecture

5G infrastructure will consist in a collection of functions (the network slicing principle) that compose various logical architecture on top of a single physical architecture like in Fig. 2 [4].

3.1 5G Physical Architecture

We consider that in order to have an efficient 5G network on the radio network, it is necessary to integrate an additional layer of small cells into the existing macro-cellular radio access network (RAN). The new small cells layer can be implemented using the

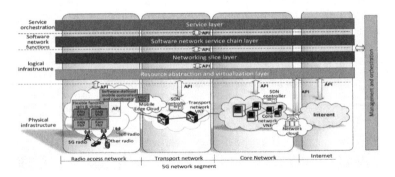

Fig. 2. 5G overall architecture

classic RAN distribution or the innovative cloud-RANs (C-RAN) solution in which small cells are deployed as remote radio heads (RRHs) connected to a centralized macro-cell via a front haul interface. Firstly, it is expected that new types of frequency bands such as micro and millimeter waves to be used. This will make the smaller cells even smaller and denser than in the current settings. As well, adopting massive MIMO (multiple input, multiple output) schemes will require more efficient interference management systems. This coordination of interferences must occur between systems (between macro and small cells e.g.) [4].

The transmission network will be deployed on fiber optic that can transport a large capacity (up to 100 Gb). There will be new segments of fiber and the existing ones will be adapted to support new requirements.

Core Network segment will be represented in majority of cases by VNF as we can observe from Fig. 2, thus running in virtual machines over standard x86 servers on cloud computing infrastructures orchestrated by a Virtual Infrastructure Manager. These VNFs have to be flexibly deployed by a VNF Manager in different data centers, with respect to the requirements regarding to latency, processing and storage capacity or available transport.

3.2   5G Logical Architecture

The 5G logical architecture will leverage the separation of hardware and software based on the programmability offered by SDN and NFV. In opposition to traditional network architecture where network functions are organized into logical entities, the 5G architecture will provide the flexibility to allow a per-slice basis grouping of network functions to logical entities and further the logical to physical architecture in accordance with ETSI (Telecommunication Standards Institute) NFV framework. When we talk about "network functions" in 5G, we will relate to computation and storage in all 5G network segments and the connectivity. With the ability to program the infrastructure, the control and data plane functions will be tailored according to the real-time network conditions and service needs, enabling scalability of both planes. In order to decoupling logical functionality from its physical realization, dedicated security mechanisms has always been required. One example can be access control mechanisms and encryption that are required to allow sensitive data to be stored or communicated on physically shared media such as radio links. In agreement with the decomposition of mobile network elements, the evolution towards 'cloudified' networks is envisioned that it will dramatically change the way mobile network functionality is deployed and geographically distributed. Insensitive to service- and slice-specific tailoring and chaining of network functions, and their flexible mapping to physical architecture, interoperability between vendors will require that some logical interfaces between network functions being standardized [4].

A network slice, namely "5G slice", supports the communication service of a particular connection type with a specific way of handling the control and user plane for this service. To this scope, a 5G slice is a collection of 5G network functions and specific radio access technology settings that are combined together for the specific use case. The slices don't contain the same functions, some functions that now seem essential for a mobile network might even be missing in some of the slices. The aim of a 5G slice is to provide just the traffic treatment required for the case and to avoid any other unnecessary functionality [3]. It will be enabled an end-to-end slice management across different planes, FCAPS (Fault, Configuration, Accounting, Performance and Security), that is missing in actual systems.

4 Conclusions

This paper presented, in a mobile operator vision, a brief description and the main challenges, requirements and key differentiating characteristics of a 5G network. We also analyzed the main future use cases, their requirements and the architecture that a mobile operator must to deploy to support these use cases. We consider that starting from different requirements of vertical use cases, 5G networks will rely on a larger spectrum portfolio compared with the previous generations. We think that besides re-farming the actual bands used in 2G, 3G and 4G networks, 5G will use low frequency bands to provide extended coverage and also high frequency bands to assure capacity and high user throughput.

Taking into account the aspects presented in this paper, we conclude that the spectrum characteristics, as well as the diverse use cases particularities, will require the ability to concurrently support multiple instances of differently parameterized network functions. The parameterization and the placement of these functions will depend on the deployment of the available hardware, the nature of the communication links and the required topology.

Acknowledgments. The authors are grateful to Alexandru Vulpe for the fruitful discussions that lead to this paper. This work has received funding from the European Union's Horizon 2020 research and innovation programme under grant agreement No. 761913; project SLICENET.

References

1. Graves, B., Lapszow, R. (eds.): NTG-Evolutions in Wireless Access Domain and Microwaves, p. 89, Orange intern doc
2. Orange Labs Networks (eds.): NTG-ED_Executive Document, p. 33, Orange intern doc
3. NGMN 5G White Paper. https://www.ngmn.org/uploads/media/NGMN_5G_White_Paper_V1_0.pdf. Accessed Feb 2017
4. 5G-PPP-5G–Arhitecture.   https://5g-ppp.eu/wp-content/uploads/2014/02/5G-PPP-5G-Architecture-WP-July-2016.pdf. Accessed June 2017

Microwave Microstrip Antenna Bio-Inspired from Dendritic Tree

Bogdan-Mihai Gavriloaia[1]([✉]), Marian Novac[2],
and Dragos-Nicolae Vizireanu[1]

[1] Politehnica University of Bucharest, Splaiul Independentei nr. 313, sector 6,
Bucharest, Romania
ggavriloaia@gmail.com
[2] University of Pitesti, Pitesti, Arges, Romania

Abstract. A new compact microstrip antenna technology for wireless sensor network is proposed in this paper. The shape of the planar microstrip line network is inspired by the dendritic tree of the natural neuron architecture given in free international neuron data bases. The major considerations of the bio-inspired antenna are compact size, multi resonant response, omnidirectional or directional pattering, beam scanning and frequency agility. The resonant frequencies, current distribution on the central strip, and radiation patterns are evaluated by simulation software tools. Several key parameters are discussed. The scope and future perspective of this paper are to develop new bio-inspired microwave antennas with tree structure having unequal and diversity spatial distribution of branches, small size and multi resonant operating capabilities.

Keywords: Dendritic tree · Microwave antenna · Microstrip lines
Radiation pattern · Electromagnetic field

1 Introduction

The number of the mobile communication systems has increased very much in the last few years. The main trend noticed in their technology was decreasing the weight and size. Therefore, new architectures have to be investigated in order to maintain the operational parameters and compatibility inside of an environment which has become more and more electromagnetic polluted. Small, compact, easy to integrate with the entire system, low profile, and omnidirectional radiation pattern in one plane are only few of the characteristics of wireless equipment [1]. The antenna, as part of the transmitting or receiving systems, could be realized as: wire, aperture, printed, array, and lens or reflector architectures.

The electric antenna characteristics as: operating frequency, input impedance, bandwidth, radiation pattern or directivity can be significant controlled by antenna topology. There is a large variety of antennas, many simulation software tools, and numerical optimization algorithms [2]. Even so the modern computer capabilities have been improved; the convergence to a desired radiation pattern by the phase and amplitude manipulation for smaller antennas is not always possible. There is a strong interdependence between the morphology and information processing capabilities of

O. Fratu et al. (Eds.): FABULOUS 2017, LNICST 241, pp. 71–76, 2018.
https://doi.org/10.1007/978-3-319-92213-3_11

systems [3, 4]. Perfection of biological systems has inspired scientists to achieve more models like of natural processes. The human brain is one of the most compact and complicated systems regarding understanding, control and production of the various activities. There are 10^{11} neurons in the 6 layers of the cortex, a density of 10^5 neurons/mm^3, and a synaptic density of 6 10^8/mm^3.

At the individual level, the morphology and behavior of neurons are similar for all species. Differentiation occurs at the level of their architecture or connectivity. Computational neuroscience attempts to explain the information communication by encoding and decoding, but the processes remain incomplete elucidated. In neuron, electrical signals propagates in a single direction, dendrites-soma-axon. A hypothesis of information encoding in peripheral neurons is that this process is made by firing rates or firing time. At the neurons from the central nervous system arguments are harder to prove, though some authors assert that the process of encoding is dependent on time and space [5]. In vivo measurements are difficult to be done because of the neuron real activity perturbation.

A multipolar neuron can integrate data from 200,000 neurons. In order to be able to process this vast amount of information it must be selective. The model has been proposed in order to explain or describe certain experimental observations relating to the selectivity of neurons or emphasizing the potentials evoked. It constitutes a simplified mathematical representation, can be biologically motivated and relies more on an abstraction of biological processes.

Taking in consideration that the neuron succeeds to manage a huge amount of information and has a compact spatial structure, a new antenna topology based on neuron morphology is proposed and investigated in this paper. The dendritic tree is modeled by a planar microstrip network. The bio-inspired model uses uniform strips and the resonance is given by the dendritic tree branches, but not the patch dimensions, as at the other printed antennas. Design of conventional microstrip antennas depends on the shape and size of the patches. The design and global capabilities of the patch antennas were published in [6]. The design of the proposed antenna is based on Maxwell's equations solving, and the multi-resonant response is argued and justifies the neuron selectivity that retrieves data from many neurons and can send them to different spatial areas. The resonant frequencies, radiation patterns and directivity are evaluated by simulation.

2 Material and Methods

The printed antennas are fabricated using photolithography techniques, most of them are microstrip lines on planar or non-planar surfaces, and are embedded in mobile devices, or on the surface of satellite, aircrafts, missiles, etc. Microstrip lines radiate the fringing electromagnetic field between strip and ground plane. Different shapes and dimensions are used for microstrip antennas having following common resonator shapes: circular, elliptical, rectangular, and triangular or ring. In the last years, their study has done important progress because of their important and useful capabilities: low volume, light in weight low cost, smaller in dimensions, easy of fabrication, provide linear or circular polarizations, multi-frequency operation, frequency agility, omnidirectional patterning, beam scanning, etc.

To investigate the microwave antenna with many branches, a neuron dendritic tree model with an archetypical multipolar morphology, P44-DEV192 available at the NeuroMorpho.org [7] was selected, Fig. 1a. The branch lengths have been changed from μm to mm. The dielectric substrate has electric permittivity of 4, 4 mm as height, and strips have 3 mm width. The entire structure is embedded within a sphere, Fig. 1b. The sphere outer boundary of 20 mm is a perfect match layer, an artificial medium that omnidirectional absorbs incident waves with virtually no reflection, simulating an infinite space [7]. The feed point, a coaxial line, was put in the soma area, and the microstrip lines were excited by continuous waves with different frequencies.

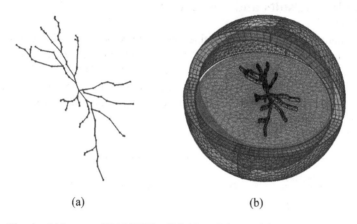

(a) (b)

Fig. 1. The dendritic tree of P44 DEV - 192 (a) and the modeled microstrip network (b)

The process of selective frequency response of dendritic tree was noticed by several authors [8, 9]. They modeled dendrites with the Rall's cable theory [4, 5] and analyzed the neurophysiological process at the mono-dimensional level of cell membrane. The investigation of proposed antenna model uses Maxwell's equations which allows assessment of dendrite topology, can prove the existence of potentials evoked and selective transmitting of data in different cortical areas. Solving the electromagnetic field equations inside the sphere was made with Finite Difference Frequency – Domain FDFD method that is used widely in microwave circuit analysis [6]. In the frequency domain, partial differential equations that govern electromagnetic phenomena are:

$$rot(E(r, \omega)) = -i\omega\mu H(r, \omega) - M(r, \omega) \tag{1.1}$$

$$rot(H(r, \omega)) = i\omega\epsilon E(r, \omega) + J(r, \omega) \tag{1.2}$$

where E and H are the electric and magnetic fields; M and J are the magnetic and electric current source densities; ε and μ are the electric permittivity and magnetic permeability and ω is angular frequency. A system of linear equations is obtained after finite difference approximation in the Cartesian coordinate system.

The maximum radiation efficiency takes place at resonant frequencies, when the electromagnetic waves have the highest amplitudes. Therefore, the resonant frequencies should be evaluated before. As a result, in the first step, the eigenvalues (resonant frequencies) and eigenvectors (electromagnetic field components) were evaluated from the linear system equation. It should be noted that these eigenvectors will only show own the electromagnetic field distribution along the microstrip lines.

In the second step, for each resonant frequency, the electromagnetic field generated by microstrip line network has computed inside of sphere.

3   Simulation Results and Discussion

A lot of resonant frequencies were obtained as eigenvectors by solving the Maxwell's equations in frequency domain. In Fig. 2 is shown the first 26 resonant frequencies. The first, fundamental, resonant frequency is at 0.3644 GHz. There is no relation between the first and the following resonant frequencies. This is because these resonant frequencies appear as the action of different branches. They have a specific spatial distribution and different lengths.

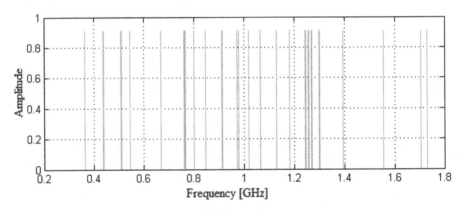

Fig. 2. The first 26 resonant frequencies for the simulated dendritic tree.

The field distribution in the plane situated at a half distance between central strip and ground plane is shown in Fig. 3. Figure 3a shows a suggestive image of the field distribution along the lines and around them, and b shows a 3D image of the field along the microstrip lines. Some lines are not excited and the maximum values are not the same at the other lines. This field distribution is the same as the voltage dipole distribution. This mode can be excited by the antenna feed point. Far field radiation is presented in Fig. 4. The antenna radiates electromagnetic energy in the microstrip plane, and the electric field is parallel to excited line axe.

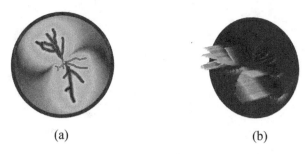

Fig. 3. Bi-dimensional (a) and tri-dimensional (b) field distribution for 0.3644 GHz

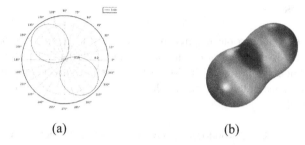

Fig. 4. Bi-dimensional (a) and tri-dimensional (b) radiation pattern for 0.3644 GHz

Up to 1.8 GHz, the radiation patterns look like the dipole pattern. Different lines or combination of them are excited. There is only one difference: the maximum radiation direction is moved in accordance to the direction of excited lines.

At the frequency of 1.8 GHz, the field distribution along the microstrip lines changes dramatically as it shown in Fig. 5a and b. More than one maximum value appears along line combination. As a result, the radiation pattern becomes larger, with more picks. The electromagnetic field appears in a plane perpendicular to the dielectric plane, as well, Fig. 6b.

Fig. 5. Bi-dimensional (a) and tri-dimensional (b) field distribution for at 1.8 GHz

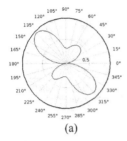
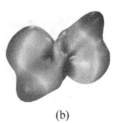

(a)   (b)

Fig. 6. Bi-dimensional (a) and tri-dimensional (b) radiation pattern at 1.8 GHz

4   Conclusions

The new microstrip antenna bio-inspired by a real neuritis architecture have success-fully demonstrated diversity in radiation patterns and multiband characteristics.

Neural field model is described by Maxwell's differential equations and emphases the role and importance of the dendrite topological structure for information processing at the neuron level.

Acknowledgments. SES, the world-leading operator of ASTRA satellites, is offering their support for the presentation and the publication of this paper.

References

1. Ayman, E., Mohamed, E., Mahmoud, S.: Design, Deployment and Performance of 4G-LTE Networks: A Practical Approach. Wiley-Blackwell, Hoboken (2014)
2. Gaurav, S., Alam, S.: 4G LTE technology. Int. J. Netw. Parallel Comput. **2**, 110–117 (2014)
3. Aage, N., Mortensen, N.A., Sigmund, M.O.: Topology optimization of metallic devices for microwave applications. Int. J. Numer. Methods Eng. **83**, 228–248 (2010)
4. Terao, T.: Computing interior eigenvalues of nonsymmetrical matrices: application to three-dimensional metamaterial composites. Phys. Rev. E **2**, 1–6 (2010)
5. Shyroki, D.M.: Modeling of sloped interfaces on a Yee grid. IEEE Trans. Antennas Propag. **59**, 3290–3295 (2011)
6. Bejan, A.: Shape and Structure, from Engineering to Nature. Cambridge University Press, Cambridge (2000)
7. Ascoli, G.A., Donohue, D.E., Halavi, M.: NeuroMorpho.Org: a central resource for neuronal morphologies. J. Neurosci. **27**, 9247–9251 (2007)
8. Rotstein, H.G., Nadim, F.: Frequency preference in two-dimensional neural models: a linear analysis of the interaction between resonant and amplifying currents. J. Comput. Neurosci. **37**, 9–28 (2014)
9. Lau, T., Zochowski, M.: The resonance frequency shift, pattern formation, and dynamical network reorganization via sub-threshold input. PLoS ONE **6**, 1–6 (2011)

Smart Pharma: Towards Efficient Healthcare Ecosystem

Sadia Anwar[1,2(✉)], Bhawani S. Chowdhry[2], and Ramjee Prasad[1,2]

[1] Department of Business Development and Technology, Aarhus University, Herning, Denmark
{sadia, ramjee}@btech.au.dk
[2] Mehran University of Engineering and Technology, Jamshoro, Pakistan
c.bhawani@ieee.org

Abstract. New innovative health related technologies will help people to empower them by making more aware of their health-related problems, early prevention and precaution of diseases. The technologies will be providing a platform for various disciplines of science to collaborate and solve problems people are facing. This paper proposes a smart pharma approach to empower the physician-patient relationship by utilizing new technological tools. Furthermore, a generic framework for efficient healthcare ecosystem is proposed to realize the smart pharma approach.

Keywords: Smart pharma · Patient empowerment · Digital metamorphosis
Beyond-the-pill concept · Telemedicine

1 Introduction

Digital metamorphosis and innovative transition of technologies have put pharmaceutical industries to think beyond the pill concept. New trends in technology will most likely disrupt prevailing existing models of pharmaceutical industries. There is a need of behavioral change from this prevalent model to more future oriented approach. Modern technologies are in process to empower common people to be more concerned about their lives. This calls for a smart pharma approach, which should be patient-oriented rather than focusing the market and maintaining competition with the existing brands and medications. It is not necessary to have a complete shift from the existing pharmaceutical models, as it may create financial burden to individual pharmaceutical industries. Therefore, a smart approach is required to make smart pharma and proactive business models. The smart approach will be able to cope and predict the upcoming disruption, and will provide suggestions for adaptation and changes in the existing models. Welfare technologies such as health care system and medical devices are facing a new era of innovations. This continuous transition will set a new platform for futuristic health care system.

O. Fratu et al. (Eds.): FABULOUS 2017, LNICST 241, pp. 77–82, 2018.
https://doi.org/10.1007/978-3-319-92213-3_12

1.1   New Trends in Health Care Technology

World Health Organization (WHO) has given us the definition of patient empowerment. It is the power and control, which makes patients to have a better control on their health-related decision making. The empowered and proactive patients have good understanding of latest method of treatment and medication therapy. There are some recent technology trends which have a potential to disrupt existing health care industry. For example, wearable smart devices have made easier for people to use various sensors with ability to continuously check and predict their health status. Toxicological information about different chemicals, metals is easily accessible today by using mobile apps related to drug-drug interaction, drug-food interaction and different medication with their chemical names. Moreover, a number of mobile apps can suggest over the counter drugs, their side effects and synergistic effects with different ingredients. Genetic engineering is another area, which is already disrupting the pharmaceutical industry as there are many companies provide data to people about their genes. People can now easily get familiar about their genetics, metabolic defects and acceptance to different diseases. Moreover, 3D printing is transforming manufacturing industry and already making a huge impact on electronic to airline industries. The 3D printers are being adopted in pharmaceutical industry and will make on demand and targeted drugs. This will also give a chance to new innovators and small companies to come and practice their ideas. Apricia pharmaceuticals has already approved a 3D printed drug called Spritam, which is being used in epilepsy. Generic name of this medication is Levetiracetam and it is available in market with different drug delivery systems [1].

This paper outlines open issues that must be addressed to develop a smart pharma (patient-oriented pharma) in opposite to existing market-oriented approach. The organization of this paper is as follows. Section 2 discusses the existing model of relationship between pharma and consumers. Section 3 presents the proposed the framework for the efficient healthcare considering a smart pharma concept. The concluding remarks are provided in Sect. 4.

2   Description of Old Model and Traditional Relationship Between Pharma and Consumers

Methods utilized by major pharmaceutical companies to sell medicinal products to physicians are mostly by the medical representatives. The medical representatives visit physicians periodically and introduce newly developed products. This usually includes the description of indications for the particular disease or symptoms.

Pharmaceutical companies invest quite a lot in their marketing area rather than developing a new drug entity and research. The budget summary of promotional activity for prescription medication has been given in the US congressional budget office in 2007. This describe about the amount of money pharmaceutical companies spent in their promotional activities which is around 29.5 billion US$.

Consumer digest described this amount as 28 billion US$ in 2008 and 50% of this amount has been given to physician a part of promotional activity. Budget is also further divided to different promotional activities [2].

New drug entity takes about 12 years in average to come from research lab to market. After a new drug discovery, pharmaceutical company gets patent rights of their medicines. Only 5 in 5000 drugs are approved for preliminary clinical trials. For many drugs, the research and development cost is quite high and companies may struggle to make enough money for further development of drugs. Technical innovations in clinical trials can be helpful to reduce research and development costs. For example, using wearable devices and new sensors can automatically gather and analyze the data this can reduce the cost and speed of trails. Moreover, emerging technology such as organ-on-a-chip (OOC) has a huge potential to reduce the overall cost of testing drugs on a subject [3].

Medical representatives are focused to promote drugs from marketing point of view, so they can tell about their beneficial effects more and tell less about possible side effects. Pharmaceutical companies should spend a good amount of money to improve their skills and competences rather than just to be focusing on marketing.

There is a need to understand what products medical representatives are going to present, and there should be clear goals and strategy placed beforehand. Some physicians have a specific list of prescribing medication therefore It would be waste of resources to send them constant reminders. Physicians will prescribe these mostly in case when patient's exact situation is unknown [4].

In above mentioned model patients are mostly ignored in approaching. The methods utilized are not as direct to patients or common public. People in future will become more aware what to get. Sometimes treatment totally depends on patient's behavior, for example if a patient is already positive for a particular medication then he or she will most likely subscribe it. Free samples are usually given to physicians with a hope that they will prescribe these samples or medication, but this happens mostly in opposite, physician switch to other free samples and takes the benefit rather giving pharmaceutical companies the ultimate benefit.

3 Smart Pharma: A Futuristic Approach

People are becoming more and more aware of drugs due to the use of various technological tools. The increasing public awareness would make pharmaceutical industries difficult to hide facts and figures as well as data related to drugs. This change from thinking to infrastructure and behavior should be improvised. Otherwise, the pharmaceutical current approach would be hard to realize in the coming years.

Smart pharma is an approach, which is going to strengthen the relation among physician, patients, and pharmaceutical industries. The following are the proposed behavioral changes needed to change the existing approach with the smart pharma concept.

Patient Empowerment: Patient empowerment is one of the biggest challenges. Continuous innovation is making people aware of products they are consuming and giving suggestions on beneficial or negative effects on their physical health [5]. Pharmaceuticals should contribute in making software to handle the privacy content of the patients actually taking their medication. They must also introduce online portals, help or suggestive therapy, devices, applications about a particular use of medication and its handling. This application will also guide what kind of hospitals and physician are available to treat a particular indication with multiple attractive offers. Pharma will help in paying charges and other life diet modification.

Patient Record as Family Member: Patients should be treated as family rather than medicinal testbeds. Empowered people will define success of smart pharma [6]. Smart pharma will have a record of patients that are actually benefited with their medication. They will also get timely reviews from their patients. This will help in innovations, needed in previous medication with more aesthetically good and compliance approach. To achieve this goal, we need to create new scientific methods and frameworks. Smart pharma will have an updated record of their customers as family members.

Customized Medication: Customized medication and compounding pharmacies should work for individual consumer rather on individual medicinal product for all society. Human machinery has different pharmacokinetics and pharmacodynamics, which means how drug will react to human body and in opposite how body will react to medication [7]. This can be achieved by launching small compounding pharmacies with company label. These successful small units will be converted to big units. These small units will have patients record, small manufacturing machinery, patient life history, habits and behavior towards disease. Telemedicine practices will require professional approach [8].

Continuous Engagement: Continuous engagement especially for chronic diseases is needed as medications are prescribed for lifetime. Smart pharma will have their data relating to diseases and genetics of consumers. Continuous reminder will be delivered to set patient compliance with therapy and post therapy. These reminders will include chronic diseases alarms for making them more consistent with the medications. They can organize different diseases related programs and awareness campaigns. These programs include different medical tests, behavioral and life modification tutorials, defining different chronic diseases, medication product description and motivational lessons, etc.

Careful Utilization of Incentives: Careful utilization of incentives by knowing the actual users of products should have more focus. In case of chronic diseases and permanent disabilities, gifts and incentives will be shared between patient and physician for encouragement. Continuous reliance with therapy, following the behavioral modification with application services provided by the particular Smart pharma will help in listing constant reviews to keep product alive in market.

Careful Utilization of Budget: Pharmaceutical industries are spending huge resources for marketing. The old system of product promotion that is generally based on physician will become less effective. Pharmaceutical industries will have to shift their budget for marketing on more ground level. Where pharmaceutical and patients can understand each other and less budget will be utilized to the areas which have less benefit. Proactive and strategized plans are required.

4   Proposed Framework for Efficient Healthcare Ecosystem

The proposed model above in Fig. 1 has the ability to cope with future challenges. This will make a healthier connection between patient and Smart pharma. There is a direct approach proposed for patient engagement and overall revenue. The placebo unit, shown in Fig. 1, will act as extension of pharma and suggest direct approaches in order to make direct contact with the consumers. The proposed strategies of placebo unit are:

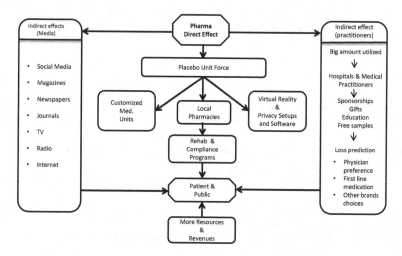

Fig. 1. Proposed framework for efficient healthcare ecosystem.

- It will help in patient customized units, providing application for privacy setups and software to patients for their medications.
- It will also help in preparing marketing budget of Smart pharma to be more focused on patients rather than physician.
- It will also make connections with available pharmacies for collection of patients' data regarding medication and will have a control on their provided inventory.
- For chronic diseases, it will make a permanent symbiotic relationship between pharma and patients.
- It will also provide best facilities to patients who are using the medication and in opposite will get the ultimate benefits and economy.

Indirect approach shown in Fig. 1 is mostly governed by legislative authorities. Legislation on indirect methods are becoming strict because many things we cannot directly indicate to patients on media. Drugs can cause dependency and the ones who have short therapeutic window can seriously harm large population, so understanding between patients and pharma is required because old model will be less effective in future.

5   Conclusions

In this paper, we have proposed a generic framework for efficient healthcare ecosystem which has a number of objectives to close the gap between traditional system and futuristic approach, especially to make a strong connection between Smart pharma and patients. We have discussed that the patient empowerment may bring a big change in the whole healthcare system when consumers will become more aware of what actually they are utilizing. There is a need of many behavioral changes as we proposed in our paper. The ultimate goal is to focus on actual utilizer of product. Further research is required for the detail study of our proposed model.

References

1. Norman, J., Madurawe, R.D., Moore, C.M., Khan, M.A., Khairuzzaman, A.: A new chapter in pharmaceutical manufacturing: 3D-printed drug products. Adv. Drug Deliv. Rev. **108**, 39–50 (2017)
2. Findlay, S.D.: Direct-to-consumer promotion of prescription drugs. Pharmacogenomics **19**(2), 109–119 (2001)
3. Zhang, B., Radisic, M.: Organ-on-a-chip devices advance to market. Lab Chip **17**(14), 2395–2420 (2017)
4. Lexchin, J.: Interactions between physicians and the pharmaceutical industry: what does the literature say? CMAJ: Can. Med. Assoc. J. **149**(10), 1401 (1993)
5. Williams, S.J., Martin, P., Gabe, J.: The pharmaceuticalisation of society? A framework for analysis. Sociol. Health Illn. **33**(5), 710–725 (2011)
6. Gellad, Z.F., Lyles, K.W.: Direct-to-consumer advertising of pharmaceuticals. Am. J. Med. **120**(6), 475–480 (2007)
7. Harris, R.Z., Benet, L.Z., Schwartz, J.B.: Gender effects in pharmacokinetics and pharmacodynamics. Drugs **50**(2), 222–239 (1995)
8. Olivier, C., Williams-Jones, B., Godard, B., Mikalson, B., Ozdemir, V.: Personalized medicine, bioethics and social responsibilities: re-thinking the pharmaceutical industry to remedy inequities in patient care and international health. Curr. Pharmacogenomics Pers. Med. (Former. Curr. Pharmacogenomics) **6**(2), 108–120 (2008)

Sign Language Translator System

Alin Florian Stoicescu, Razvan Craciunescu[(✉)], and Octavian Fratu

University Politechnica of Bucharest, Bucharest, Romania
razvan.craciunescu@upb.ro

Abstract. This paper presents a low-cost wireless sign language translator for interpreting and having a conversation between deft and non-deft persons. The system is a glove-like one with sensors embedded in every finger of the glove as to fusion the information from multiple sources and accurately providing an output of the sign language. The paper presents the hardware modules and the software workflows that were used to implement the system and it shows a first prototype of the system. The achieved accuracy, in terms of sign detection, is around 85%.

Keywords: Sign language · Wireless systems · Sensors · IoT

1 Introduction

All around world we can find women and men unable to speak through their mouth or which are deaf or even worse, both, ever since they were born and due to something that happened during their life. They do not represent a majority, indeed, and some people might never have this type of person amongst their friends or in their entourage or they might not even meet one in their life, but they do exist and they do need our help.

There are research attempts to close de gap between the deft group and others. In [1] the authors presented a a sign language apparatus built using a glove with movement sensors on fingers, used to produce time series of data. The editing apparatus, as it was called, was using a sign language word dictionary for storing the processed data, a sentence data editing divider for reading out the time series data and adding predetermined additional information to produce time series data and an animation synthesizer to create an animation movement for the present sign. Also, in [2] the authors design a case with a touch screen display located on its face, a microprocessor for word, letters and number translation into videos with a real person performing the translation. The device consisted into a memory for words database and the complementary video. The purpose of the project was to translate a user input data selected from the screen and to display the corresponding returned video output.

The purpose and motivation of this paper is to try to fill the gap of communication between the deft and others, giving them a way in which they could have a normal conversation. This gap should be filled using a low-cost and robust solution. Hence, the paper presents a sign language translator, sign language being a dialect where the communication is possible without the means of acoustic sounds. All the letters are based on sign patterns, movements and orientations of the hand, so that the device is presented in the form of a glove.

O. Fratu et al. (Eds.): FABULOUS 2017, LNICST 241, pp. 83–88, 2018.
https://doi.org/10.1007/978-3-319-92213-3_13

This paper is organized as follows. Section 2 describes the implemented system, Sect. 3 presents the results and Sect. 4 concludes this paper.

2 The Implemented System

2.1 The Hardware Modules

The hardware modules connections are based on the microcontroller which is the heart of the project, meaning it connects and gives life to everything. The Flex sensors are used on every finger of the hand to measure how bend a finger is and by fusioning the data with the accelerometer and the Contact sensor to determine what is the letter that the user is showing at a given time. Then, the microcontroller, gathers data from all flex sensors, from contact sensors and from accelerometer, processes data and passes it further, remotely, to another microcontroller which communicates with a LCD (Fig. 1).

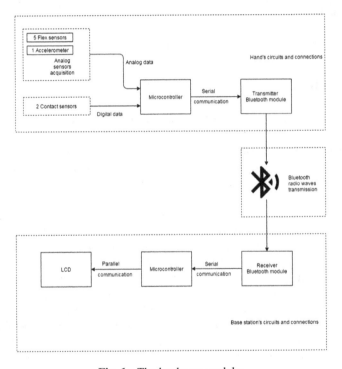

Fig. 1. The hardware modules

2.2 The Software Applications

Based on the modules shown in Fig. 1 it can be easily understood that we have 2 main blocks. The hand block and the base station block. Both these blocks have separate workflows that should follow and that are programmed in the microcontroller. The hand software application is divided into two main areas, one for initializations and the other one for ongoing processes.

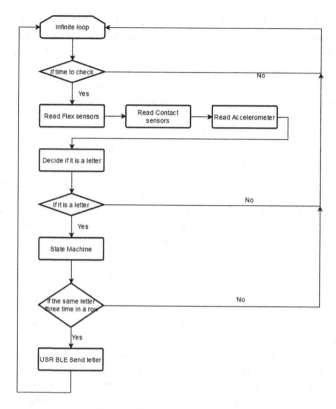

Fig. 2. The glove application

For the initialization part, we should initialize the used PIN's state, the oscillator clock, the ADC, the Interrupts, Enhanced Universal Asynchronous Receiver Transceiver (EUSART), the Bluetooth low energy modules and a Timer. All these initializations are necessary before the main application start and are describing the initial state of the system.

The main application, the one that does the sign translation is presented in Fig. 2. The presented workflow should continuously run, creating a never-ending program with its functionality described below: The code is contained into an infinite loop of a while instruction with the condition to run if the initial condition is true. The time, to check condition, is represented by a flag change by a timer interrupt at each 150 ms. The reading sensors sequence is divided into analog data readings and digital data for contact sensors: Digital data readings are simple, they can be either high value (logic 1) or low value (logic 0), with the actual value of the pin being hold into a register called PORT. To read analog data, several changes are required, beside configuring the module as it was indicated above and placing it in the startup zone: Enable the ADC module; Select the channel corresponding to the PIN where the device is connected; Give time to the module to start and to select a channel by introducing a few microseconds delay; Start the conversion; Wait for the conversion to finish; Disable the

ADC module; Get the result from the ADRESH and ADRESL registers The sign language translator is based on American Sign Language Alphabet (ASL) [3], each letter having its own sign. The differences between the marks being given by the degree of bending of the fingers, the positioning of the hand, the movement or the contact between certain fingers. Based on the data read from the flex sensors, a decision is taken on how much each finger is bent and a certain value is assigned. Based on the data read from accelerometer, the hand's position is determined and a value is also assigned. All the assigned values will be concatenated into a single string and compared with a predefined and previously calculated string for each of the characters. The decision is taken only based on the flex sensors and accelerometer in order to diminish the number of processes, since based on the data received from these sensors, the application is able to distinguish about 85% of the characters. For the rest of the characters, the application is using contact sensors and the same accelerometer, this time used in another approach: Contact sensors are used to decide between "r", "u" and "v", the only difference being the contact between the index finger and the middle finger, while the finger's bend and hand's position is the same; This time, the accelerometer is used to determine the movement which is the only difference between "i" and "j" and between "d" and "z.

Once decided if it is or not an alphabet letter, the letter is either passed to a state machine or the application will wait for the next timer interrupt. The **state machine** is used to check the credibility of the letter, since it could happen for the hand to be in a certain position corresponding to a certain letter in the exact moment of the reading procedure, but in fact it could have just passing by, resulting in erroneous data transmission. The principle of operation is simple, checking the current letter with the previous one and if they are the same, it can move to the next state. The previous letter refers to the decision made based on the sensors readings at the previously timer interrupt, thus the state machine advances to a new state or goes to the first state at each timer interrupt. Once the state machine reaches state 3, meaning that the same letter was found 3 times in a row, the equivalent of 450 ms, it can be decided that a letter has been made and will be sent, using EUSART, towards the Bluetooth module which will further send using radio waves to the base station's Bluetooth module. In the initializing process, the EUSART peripheral was used in a Full-Duplex communication so it can configure the Bluetooth module, sending commands and receiving the confirmation. In the runtime process, a Full-Duplex communication is no longer required, the glove sending data to the base station when a certain letter has been detected, the data exchanging becoming simplex and the Bluetooth device acting as a transmitter.

After a letter has been sent, a flag is activated as a safety measure, in order to avoid character's spamming (to transmit the same character forever). From now on, when a timer interrupt occurs, it will be checked whether the new letter is the same as the last one sent: If they are the same and the flag is still active, the program will no longer enter into the state machine; If the characters are different and the flag is still active, the flag will be disabled, the program will reach the state machine's first state and from now on it can follow its normal path shown in Fig. 2.

The base station's application is way simpler, given the fact that it has no sensors, resulting in no need to create a timer and wait for its interrupt or to configure an ADC module. The only thing it does is to process nothing during its run-time until an

EUSART receive interrupt occurs, meaning a letter was transmitted. When a letter was received, his job is to manage the LCD, printing the target slave's MAC address on the first line and checking if there is enough space on the second line for character printing. If it has received a character and there is no empty slot to display it, it will clear the display, reprint the MAC address on the first line, set the cursor on the second line and display the received character. After the initialization process, the EUSART interface is kept in a Simplex transmission with the current Bluetooth device acting as a receiver.

3 Results

From the point of view of flex sensors, these were few important variables which changed the original readings, from a free mode, into something hard to predict and with certain calibrations required. The most important factor was the difference between finger's lengths and their capability to bend and this time not between people, but the same person's fingers. Thus, each finger required its own configuration based on its range of values. The range of values was decided by reading the voltage level given while the hand was acting and making all the sign contained in the American Sign Language.

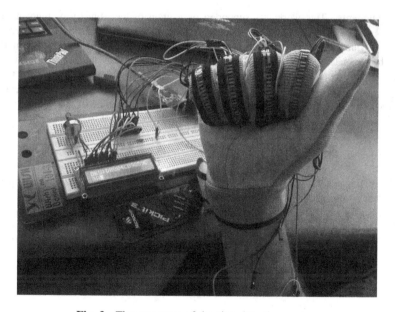

Fig. 3. The prototype of the sign detection system

For all the signaling problems we've could identify the cause using a Logic Analyzer which can measure both digital and analog signals. The device has a computer compatible application that can create a history of the measured signals. The user can also select if he uses a certain protocol and the application will translate the level of voltage into the respective code.

After the calibration process of the accelerometer and the flex sensor's data for the user specifications, the application could distinguish most of the letters, the only problems seem to be to determine the signs that involve movement. In the current configuration, the same accelerometer is used for position and movement detection, sometimes making the decision difficult. The module was used to determine the position of the hand based on the acceleration on each axis and the movement, using the gyroscope as a direction indicator and thus, using some decisional blocks, we can identify the existence of the movement. In Fig. 3 can be seen the glove doing the A letter and the base station printing the slave's device MAC address on the first row and the character on the second, in front of an arrow.

4   Conclusions and Future Work

In this paper, we presented the results of a sign detector system that can be used in understand a basic conversation with a deft person. We plan to extend our work to add other signs that represents a whole world to understand also a fast pace conversation. Also, given the Bluetooth capabilities of the system, the base station module could be implemented inside a smartphone application for easier and more practical usage.

Acknowledgments. This work was supported by a grant of the Ministry of Innovation and Research, UEFISCDI, project number 5 Sol/2017 within PNCDI III, by the Sectoral Operational Programme Human Resources Development 2007–2013 of the Ministry of European Funds through the Financial Agreement POSDRU/159/1.5/S/132397 and by the ERDF funded project "Research Ecosystems for development and innovation of IT&C services and products for a society connected to IoT – NETIO". The authors thank to SES, the world-leading operator of ASTRA satellites, for their kind support in presentation and publishing of this paper.

References

1. Ikeda, H., Sagawa, H., Sakiyama, T., Ohki, M., Kaneko, Y.: Sign language editing apparatus. US patent number US 5990878 A (1999)
2. Ander, B., Anderm, S.: Sign language translator. US patent number S 8566077 B2 (2013)
3. Baker, A., van den Bogaerde, B., Pfau, R., Schermer, T. (eds.): The Linguistics of Sign Languages: An Introduction. John Benjamins Publishing Company, Amsterdam (2016)

Analysis of Relay Selection Game in a Cooperative Communication Scenario

Razvan Craciunescu[1(✉)], Simona Halunga[1], and Albena Mihovska[2]

[1] University Politechnica of Bucharest, Bucharest, Romania
razvan.craciunescu@upb.ro
[2] Aarhus University, Aarhus, Denmark

Abstract. This paper analyzes the performances of a proposed set of functions that model the relay selection process in a cooperative communication scenario. The proposed behavior and influence functions create a mechanism for selecting the best relays to be used to send certain types of data. The mechanism is based on a Nash Equilibrium (NE) algorithm and on a marriage equation, that predicts the degree of satisfaction between married couples. We consider an opportunistic cooperative communication settings in which multiple nodes are competing for a poll of relay nodes. The performances are evaluated in terms of comparison between the bit error rate of the proposed mechanism and the direct communication, using Matlab.

Keywords: Relay selection · Nash Equilibrium · Marriage equation
Behavior function · Cooperative communication · Resource allocation

1 Introduction

When we are talking about cooperative communication we are talking about a field that was and is on the hot investigated areas. Even more, in the context of 5G rising there will be a need of transferring the information to relevant receivers as is the case of a poll of sensors that want to forward their information to a destination node that is several hops away. For this poll of sensors there should be a poll of relays to forward that information and the best relay for each sensor should be selected. Moreover, the poll of sensors of the poll of relays is not stable (i.e. a relay can be on or off conserving energy). Hence a mechanism that can be flexible and independent of the number of relays or the number of transmitters is required.

Current research papers presented the performances of cooperative communication (CC) in comparison with direct communication (DC). In [1] Lee et al. proposed a max-min-max cooperative relay selection based on the signal intensity. Thus, a higher diversity gain and a higher system throughput was achieved in comparison with DC. In [2] Guo and Carrasco proposed a MAC protocol for improving the transmission rate by using high rate station as an assistant for low rate ones. Moreover, relay networks are also used in mobility scenarios to dynamically select a relay for improving the delay and capacity of the transmitter. In [3] the authors proposed a routing algorithm for efficient resource allocation in MANET and in [4] a group two-hop CC algorithm is proposed for delay improvement.

© ICST Institute for Computer Sciences, Social Informatics and Telecommunications Engineering 2018
O. Fratu et al. (Eds.): FABULOUS 2017, LNICST 241, pp. 89–94, 2018.
https://doi.org/10.1007/978-3-319-92213-3_14

Another extensively used mechanisms for CC is the game theory in the context of relay selection. The research is concentrated on rate improvement by selecting the best relay from a poll of relays [5]. This problem is different formulated from the Chinese restaurant game (i.e. choose the best table such that the satisfaction is maximized) [6] or using the auction theory (i.e. efficient matching buyers with sellers) [7].

In this paper, we used the mechanism proposed by the authors in [9], and evaluated the improvements in BER against SNR for different scenarios in a cooperative communication model.

This paper is organized as follows. Section 2 describes the proposed mechanism algorithm and the mathematics behind it; Sect. 3 shows simulated results and Sect. 4 concludes this paper.

2   Relay Selection Mechanism

2.1   The Behavior Function

The following mechanism translate the behavior function, that models the relation between the partners of a married couple, to a selection relay behavior function.

The node that initiates the communication will be denoted as SN (source node). The node that is used to relay the communication is denoted as RN (relay node) The relationship between these two nodes is defined in (1) and (2) [9]:

$$B_{RN(n+1)} = I_{SN \to RN}(B_{SN^n}) + r_{n_1}B_{RN^n} + a \tag{1}$$

$$B_{SN(n+1)} = I_{RN \to SN}(B_{RN^n}) + r_{n_2}B_{SN^n} + b \tag{2}$$

In (1) we have the following notations: $B_{RN(n+1)}$ is the notation of the RN behavior at $n + 1$, and it is a score determined by the following values; $ISN \to RN$ is the value of the Influence of the source node on relay node; the function is described in Sect. 2.2; r_{n_1} is a parameter, which considers the free resources of node RN at time n. It has values between [0; 0.9], where 0 means that 100% of the resources are occupied and 0.9 means that 100% of the resources are free; B_{RN^n} is the behavior function score at the previous moment of time; a/b is a constant defining the Device Class. The parameter takes its values as integer ones in the range [4; 20] [9]; n represents the current moment in time/number of iterations.

(2) is the mirrored imagine of (1) with the addition that RN is replaced by SN. This equation scores the behavior of the SN with regards of the RN.

As demonstrated in [9] "Theorem 1. The behavior function is convergent" is true, thus, concluding that the stability is achieved faster as the free resources are lower.

2.2   The Influence Function

The *Influence* (from (1) and (2)) is a function of the *Influenced Behavior*. It describes the influence that one node (RN or SN) has on the connected node (SN or RN) and its main usage is to evaluate the connection by rewarding beneficial partners and penalizes the non-beneficial ones.

The influence score is calculated based on (3). The different parameters values will be chosen by the CC system administrator. The values to choose from are defined in [9].

$$I = \alpha I_L + \beta I_{CA} + \gamma I_{PE} + \delta I_S + \varepsilon I_T + \eta I_{CH} + \lambda I_{EP} + \mu I_{CP} \tag{3}$$

All the parameters from (3) are described in [9]. When searching for the best neighbors a node is sending its expectation and the weights of the above parameters can be relevant or 0, thus sending just the interest parameters in each context.

2.3 The Relay Selection Game

The relay selection game, described in [9] has the outcome of selecting the best relay such that the overall performance of the CC system is optimal.

The system has a M source nodes, denoted as {SN1, ... SNM) each of them with selfish requirements (i.e. they want to choose the relay so that they maximize their requirements). Each of the sources will select one of the N relay nodes, denoted as {RN1 ... RNN}, N >= M. Each source can have only one relay that relays its data and the relay can be assigned to only one source node. The optimal strategy (denoted as (*)) is the solution of a *Maximum Weighted Bipartite Matching* (MWBM) problem applied to a graph [10]. The game is described in [9].

The utility function is defined as in (4) and takes into consideration how much the current SN node selection deviates from the optimal strategy.

$$U(s_i, s_{-i}) = -\left| B_{RN_i^{n+1}} - B_{RN_i^{n+1}}^* \right| + \frac{\sum_{k \neq i} \left| B_{RN_k^{n+1}} - B_{RN_k^{n+1}}^* \right|}{M - 1} \tag{4}$$

The game has a Strictly Dominant Strategy Equilibrium and, thus, a unique NE strategy as demonstrated in [9].

2.4 The Relay Selection Algorithm

As described in [9] the results of Sects. 2.1, 2.2 and 2.3 are converted into the algorithm described by the diagram in Fig. 1. This algorithm is used for the relay selection results described in Sect. 3.

3 Results

For the simulations Matlab was used. Using the selection algorithm described in Sect. 3 we compared the performances, in terms of bit error rate (BER) of the overall CC system (with 50 relays and 40 source nodes) with a direct communication between a SN and a RN. Also, we compared the performances of the best and worst communication pair of nodes (SN-RN) from the CC system and a DC between random selected

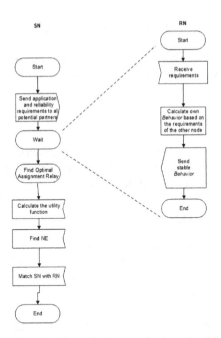

Fig. 1. The relay selection mechanism algorithm

nodes from the SN and RN poll. The communication is done using OFDM with 64 carriers and a CP length of 4 samples from the number of samples in the OFDM symbol, 64QAM for the modulation and 10^8 transmitted bits. The channel fading model adopted is Rayleigh. The source and relay nodes are situated on a 50 km x 50 km area. The sources are equally distributed on one edge of the area and the

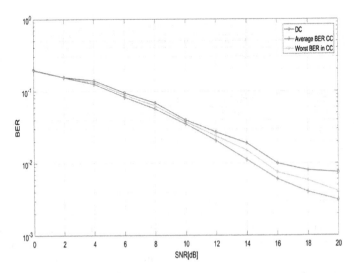

Fig. 2. BER curves for a direct communication (blue), average BER of the CC (red) and the worst BER of the CC pairs (yellow) (Color figure online)

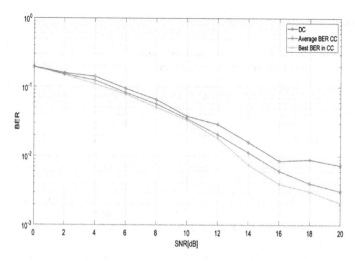

Fig. 3. BER curves for a direct communication (blue), average BER of the CC (red) and the best BER of the CC pairs (yellow) (Color figure online)

relays are scattered on the area. The closes relay is at 25 km away from the edge where the source nodes are positioned.

For Figs. 2 and 3 we can conclude that if we choose a random node pair (SN, RN) (the blue line) the performances are worst if we are going to compare them with the worst, average or best BER in the CC system. As the Signal to Noise (SNR) increases the difference between the CC and DC performances also increases. Hence, only in the case of a poor communication the systems behave the same. Even more, the usage of behavioral functions in corroboration with game theory improves even more the relay selection and the overall performances of a communication system [9].

4 Conclusions

In this paper, we presented the results of a game theory selection algorithm for relay selection. The authors presented a novel utility function based on a behavior and influence function and, demonstrated that using this utility function the game achieves a Strictly Dominant Strategy Equilibrium. The paper also demonstrated the results of 50 relays, 40 source nodes in comparison with a direct communication between random selected pairs of relay-source nodes from the poll. The paper demonstrated that using the same pairs of source-relay nodes in a CC system is better, in terms of bit error rated, to a stand-alone direct communication between a random pair from the same poll of nodes.

Acknowledgments. This work was supported by a grant of the Ministry of Innovation and Research, UEFISCDI, project number 5 Sol/2017 within PNCDI III and by Ministry of European Funds through the Financial Agreement POSDRU/159/1.5/S/132397. The authors thank to SES, the world-leading operator of ASTRA satellites, for their kind support in presentation and publishing of this paper.

References

1. Lee, H., Hwang, H., Kim, S., Roh, B., Park, G.: Cooperative RS selection schemes for IEEE 802.16 j networks. In: Military Communications Conference, MILCOM 2013, pp. 1290–1295. IEEE, San Diego (2013)
2. Guo, T., Carrasco, R.: CRBAR: cooperative relay-based autorate MAC for multirate wireless networks. IEEE Trans. Wirel. Commun. **8**, 5938–5947 (2009)
3. Liu, J.J., Gao, J.T., Jiang, X.H., Nishiyama, H., Kato, N.: Capacity and delay of probing-based two-hop relay in MANETs. IEEE Trans. Wirel. Commun. **11**(11), 4172–4183 (2012)
4. Liu, J.J., Jiang, X.H., Nishiyama, H., Kato, N.: Generalized two-hop relay for flexible delay control in MANETs. IEEE/ACM Trans. Netw. **20**(6), 1950–1963 (2012)
5. Baidas, M.W., Bahbahani, M.S.: Game-theoretic modeling and analysis of relay selection in cooperative wireless networks. Wirel. Commun. Mob. Comput. **16**(5), 500–518 (2016)
6. Wang, C.Y., Chen, Y., Liu, K.J.R.: Sequential Chinese restaurant game. IEEE Trans. Signal Process. **61**(3), 571–584 (2013)
7. Li, Y., Liao, C., Wang, Y., Wang, C.: Energy-efficient optimal relay selection in cooperative cellular networks based on double auction. IEEE Trans. Wirel. Commun. **14**(8), 4093–4104 (2015)
8. Gottman, J., Murray, J., Swanson, C., Tyson, R., Swanson, K.R.: The Mathematics of Marriage Dynamic Nonlinear Models. A Bradford Book, Cambridge (2005)
9. Craciunescu, R., Mihovska, A., Prasad, R., Halunga, S.: Use of behavior and influence functions for relay selection in cooperative communications. In: 2015 IEEE Globecom Workshops (GC Wkshps), pp. 1–6, San Diego (2015)
10. West, D.B.: Introduction to Graph Theory, 2nd edn. Prentice Hall, Upper Saddle River (2001)

Estimation Algorithm for Large MIMO System

Carmen Voicu[(⊠)], Mădălina Berceanu, and Simona V. Halunga

Telecommunications Department, Electronics,
Telecommunications and Information Technology Faculty,
University "Politehnica" of Bucharest, Bucharest, Romania
carmen.voicu@radio.pub.ro

Abstract. In multiuser Large MIMO communication systems, signal recovery is a relevant factor for ensuring a safe and reliable communication, especially when the users are intercorrelated. Solutions for interference minimization include analysis regarding source coding/decoding techniques, channel coding/decoding methods and multiuser detection algorithms. This paper illustrates the performance improvement brought by convex optimization technique in Large MIMO systems when the channel is affected by AWGN and Rice fading. The performance is evaluated for different sets of spreading sequences (Walsh-Hadamard and PN) and based on the simulation results several conclusions are highlighted and further improvement will be proposed for fading effects reduction and interference minimization.

Keywords: Large MIMO · Convex optimization · POCS algorithm
Multiuser MIMO · Rice fading

1 Introduction

In the last decades many studies have been made regarding the Multiple-Input Multiple-Output (MIMO) technology because of its advantages including superior data rates, range and reliability without requiring additional bandwidth or transmit power. If initially the research has been focused on point-to-point MIMO links [1], recently the multi-user MIMO system brings more benefits due to spatial multiplexing. Thus, MU-MIMO is used in modern wireless standards, including in IEEE 802.11n, 3GPP LTE/LTE Advanced, and mobile WiMAX systems [2].

In order to be able to achieve better performance in terms of throughput and energy efficiency, Massive MIMO system, also known as Large-Scale Antenna System or Large MIMO, has been proposed [3]. The transmitter/receiver is equipped with a very large number of service antennas (e.g. hundreds) which are working fully coherent and adaptive. This approach considerably eliminates the effects of noise fading and other interferences, allowing thus to improve the spectral efficiency and robustness of the system [4].

Although Massive MIMO system has many advantages, there are still many challenges to be studied. In [1] it is presented the importance of user scheduling, which in conventional MIMO implementation can be avoided using more complex signal

© ICST Institute for Computer Sciences, Social Informatics and Telecommunications Engineering 2018
O. Fratu et al. (Eds.): FABULOUS 2017, LNICST 241, pp. 95–100, 2018.
https://doi.org/10.1007/978-3-319-92213-3_15

processing to separate spatially correlated users. Other issue represents the channel state information (CSI), which has to be known by the multi-user Massive MIMO system in order to advance the capacity gain offered by it [4, 5]. Thus [6] shows that the use of TDD (time-division duplexing) allows the system to "learn" the channel, for both uplink and downlink. However, as the number of antennas increases this becomes a difficult task. Other challenge caused by the high number of antennas is the implementation of coders and detectors with reasonable complexity.

The scope of this paper is to analyse the effects of the correlated users on the performance of an uplink Large MIMO system, when Rice fading occurs on the communication channel. At the base station an algorithm based on projection onto convex sets is proposed to eliminate the interference between the users.

The remainder of this article is organized as follows. The benefits of using convex optimization are discussed in Sect. 2. Section 3 presents the proposed algorithm and the results obtained. Finally, conclusions are drawn in Sect. 4.

2 Convex Optimization

The optimization methods are very useful in addressing challenges in many domains. Numerous communication issues can be cast as or can be transposed into convex optimization problems, which facilitate their analytic and numerical solutions [7]. The convex optimization has been successfully applied in several domains in wireless communications and signal processing. The success of this class of optimization techniques is due to their features. During the years, a lot of efficient and fast algorithms for resolving convex optimization problems have been developed and implemented, and a part of them have a significant impact in area of MIMO, OFDM and 3G/4G wireless systems, which makes convex optimization a good candidate for wireless communications [8].

The convex optimization is used in Massive MIMO as well. In [9] the authors propose signal detection schemes for massive overloaded MIMO. The signal detection is formulated as a convex optimization problem, which can be solved via a fast algorithm based on Douglas-Rachford splitting. In [10], an energy efficient antenna selection algorithm based on convex optimization for Massive MIMO system has been proposed.

In mathematics, convex optimization refers to the minimization of a convex objective function subject to convex constraints. In this paper, we are interested in projections onto convex sets (POCS), which is a method to find a point in the intersection of two closed convex sets or to find the minimum distance between these sets.

3 System Model and Parameters

In the following an uplink transmission of a Massive MIMO system is considered. First the system is considered an ideal one, in which the users are totally uncorrelated one another, and then the real situation is analysed, in which, because of fading or other impairments, the users are getting correlated one another. A general block diagram of the system is presented in Fig. 1.

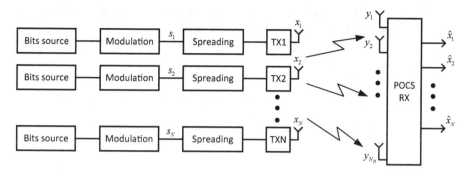

Fig. 1. System model

The base station (BS), represented in our scheme by the POCS RX block, is equipped with N_R receive antennas and N_T transmission antennas, one for each user. It was assumed perfect CSI at the transmitter and at the BS. In the case of multiuser MIMO system, the signal from a user, after dispreading and demodulation, may be considered as interference for the others, so the number of users is limited by multiuser interference, noise and fading. The $N_R \times 1$ received signal vector at BS can be written as the combination of all signals transmitted from all users:

$$\mathbf{y} = \sqrt{p}\sum_{k=1}^{N} \mathbf{h}_k\mathbf{x}_k + \mathbf{n} = \sqrt{p}\mathbf{H}\mathbf{x} + \mathbf{n}, \tag{1}$$

where p is the average signal to noise ratio, $\mathbf{n} \in \mathbb{C}^{N_R \times 1}$ is white Gaussian noise vector with mean equal to zero and variance one, $\mathbf{x} = [x_1, x_2, \ldots, x_N]^T$ is the matrix of the transmitted signal from all users and $\mathbf{H} \in \mathbb{C}^{N_t \times N}$ is the channel matrix between the N users and the BS, where $\mathbf{h}_k$ is a $N_R \times 1$ vector which represents the channel vector between the kth user and the BS.

The scope of the following proposed algorithm is to detect signals transmitted by the users from the received BS signal. In the uplink, multiuser detection can be used. The problem can be formulated as:

$$\hat{\mathbf{x}} = \arg \min_{x \in S^N} \left\| \mathbf{y} - \sqrt{p}\mathbf{H}\mathbf{x} \right\|^2, \tag{2}$$

where S is the finite alphabet of x_k, $k = 1, 2, \ldots, N$. The problem (2) is a least square problem with a finite-alphabet constraint. It is well known that linear least squares problems are convex optimization problems, thus the POCS algorithm can be applied.

A $N_R \times N$ linear detection matrix which contains the correlation coefficients between the users, r_k, denoted by $\mathbf{R}$, it is introduced in (1) as follows:

$$\mathbf{y} = \sqrt{p}\mathbf{R}\mathbf{H}\mathbf{x} + \mathbf{n}. \tag{3}$$

In this way, the information sent by the users is decoded independently. From (3), the kth stream of $\mathbf{y}$ which is used to decode x_k is given by:

$$\mathbf{y}_k = \underbrace{\sqrt{p}\mathbf{r}_k\mathbf{h}_k x_k}_{desired\ signal} + \underbrace{\sqrt{p}\sum_{\substack{p \neq k}}^{N}\mathbf{r}_k\mathbf{h}_p x_p}_{interuser\ interference} + \underbrace{\mathbf{n}}_{noise}. \tag{4}$$

Considering the initial estimate of the problem (2), the least square solution:

$$\hat{\mathbf{x}}_{LS} = \left(\mathbf{R}^H\mathbf{R}\right)^{-1}\mathbf{R}^H\hat{\mathbf{x}}_{MF}, \tag{5}$$

where $\hat{\mathbf{x}}_{MF}$ is the output of the matched filter. Further, at stage $k + 1$ the POCS estimation can be written as:

$$\hat{\mathbf{x}}_{POCS}^{(k+1)} = \hat{\mathbf{x}}_{POCS}^{(k)} + \left(\sigma^2\mathbf{I} + \mathbf{R}^H\mathbf{R}\right)^{-1}\mathbf{R}^H\left(\hat{\mathbf{x}}_{MF} - R\hat{\mathbf{x}}_{POCS}^{(k)}\right), \tag{6}$$

where σ^2 is the noise estimated variance and $\mathbf{I}$ is the identity matrix.

For the evaluation of our algorithm we consider that four baseband users are sending binary data streams towards the same BS. We analysed the performance when data is transmitted using different modulation schemes and the users are separated by Walsh-Hadamard and PN signature sequences. The communication channel is affected by AWGN and Rice fading, we study the situation of a rural area when the users have line of sight with the BS.

First, we would like to study the differences between our algorithm and the MMSE one, which is already used on Massive MIMO for the same purpose. If perfectly orthogonal Walsh codes of length 32 are used to separate the users, there is no difference between the performance obtained. However, if PN codes of length 31 are used as signature sequences, there is a small correlation between the user that cannot be eliminated and the POCS algorithm reduce its effects, as can be shown in Figs. 2 and 3. For this case 5 antennas at the BS and QPSK modulation have been used.

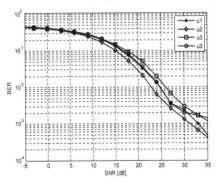

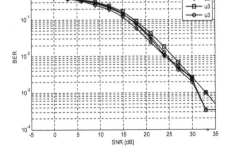

Fig. 2. MMSE algorithm, PN codes, 1×5 MIMO

Fig. 3. POCS algorithm, PN codes, 1×5 MIMO

Figure 2 presents the results obtained by MMSE algorithm when PN codes of length 31 are used, and it can be easily observed that, because of inter-correlation between the users the performance is limited to a BER = 10^{-3} for SNR = 35 dB. When the POCS algorithm is used, Fig. 3, the performance archived by each user is slightly improved, but this improvement is very small.

Further are presented the results obtained in the same scenario and with the optimization algorithm for different types of modulation. Figure 4 shows the performance achieved when the BS is equipped with 2 receive antennas and PN codes are used. It can be noted that, even for the lowest order modulation, the signal cannot be recovered even at high SNR, since the BER is very high. Increasing the number of antennas might bring an improvement of the results as has been previously shown.

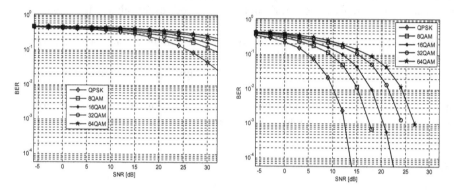

Fig. 4. POCS algorithm, PN codes, 1×2 MIMO

Fig. 5. POCS algorithm, Walsh codes, 1×10 MIMO

Thus, we increase the numbers of antennas at the BS from 5 to 10 to see how much the performance of the system is increased. In Fig. 5 are presented the results for Walsh and it is obvious that the performance is significantly improved even for high order modulation, reaching a BER around 10^{-3} for a signal to noise ratio less than 27 dB.

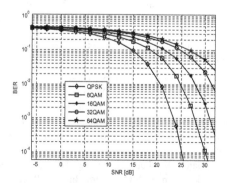

Fig. 6. POCS algorithm, PN codes, 1×10 MIMO

When the Walsh codes are replaced with PN codes the results get worse (see Fig. 6) in comparison with those from Fig. 5, but better from those from Fig. 4 when BS has only 2 antennas. Also, if we compare the results for the QPSK modulation, we can see that increasing the BS' antennas from 5 (Fig. 3) to 10 (Fig. 6) we have a gain of almost 9 dB for a bit error rate of 10^{-3}.

4   Conclusion and Future Work

The present paper illustrates the behaviour of an estimation algorithm, based on convex optimization, for Large MIMO systems. The presented algorithm can reduce the undesired effects of non-orthogonality of spreading sequences and fading. Furthermore, when Walsh codes are used the algorithm achieves good results, also as the number of BS' antennas increase.

Future work implies to change the random data sent on the communication channel to one that contains visual information (images or video streaming). The quality of the recovered data can be analysed using different quality metrics and the effect of the algorithm in data estimation will also be analysed (Video Quality Metric, Structural Similarity Index etc.). Also different types of channel coding, like Turbo and LDPC, which are suitable for 5G technologies, will be tested together with the algorithm.

References

1. Lu, L., Li, G.Y., Swindlehurst, A.L., Ashikhmin, A., Zhang, R.: An overview of massive MIMO: benefits and challenges. IEEE J. Sel. Top. Sign. Process. **8**(5), 742–758 (2014)
2. Li, Q., Li, G., Lee, W., Lee, M.I., Mazzarese, D., Clerckx, B., Li, Z.: MIMO techniques in WiMAX and LTE: a feature overview. IEEE Commun. Mag. **48**(5), 86–92 (2010)
3. Björnson, E., Sanguinetti, L., Hoydis, J., Debbah, M.: Optimal design of energy-efficient multi-user MIMO systems: is massive MIMO the answer? IEEE Trans. Wirel. Commun. **14**(6), 3059–3075 (2015)
4. Wang, C.-X., Wu, S., Bai, L., You, X., Wang, J., Lang, C.-L.: Recent advances and future challenges for massive MIMO channel measurements and models. Sci. China Inf. Sci. **59**(2), 1–16 (2016)
5. Papadopoulos, H., Wang, C., Bursalioglu, O., Hou, X., Kishiyama, Y.: Massive MIMO technologies and challenges towards 5G. IEICE Trans. Commun. **E99-B**(3), 602–621 (2015)
6. Marzetta, T.L.: Noncooperative cellular wireless with unlimited numbers of base station antennas. IEEE Trans. Wirel. Commun. **9**(11), 3590–3600 (2010)
7. Luo, Z.Q., Yu, W.: An introduction to convex optimization for communications and signal processing. IEEE J. Sel. Areas Commun. **24**(8), 1426–1438 (2006)
8. Vorobyov, S.A., Cui, S., Eldar, Y.C., KinMa, W., Utschick, W.: Optimization techniques in wireless communications. EURASIP J. Wirel. Commun. Netw. **1**, 1–2 (2009)
9. Hayakawa, R., Hayashi, K., Sasahara, H., Nagahara, M.: Massive overloaded MIMO signal detection via convex optimization with proximal splitting. In: EUSIPCO, Budapest, pp. 1383–1387 (2016)
10. Bibo, H., Yuanan, L., Gang, X., Fang, L., Feng, N.: Antenna selection for downlink transmission in large scale green MIMO system. In: 4th IEEE International Conference Network Infrastructure and Digital Content (IC-NIDC), pp. 312–316 (2014)

Quantitative Theory of Signal Inversion in RFID

Dan Tudor Vuza[1], Reinhold Frosch[2], Helmut Koeberl[2],
Idlir Rusi Shkupi[2], and Marian Vlădescu[3(✉)]

[1] Institute of Mathematics of the Romanian Academy, Bucharest, Romania
danvuza@hotmail.com
[2] Freaquent Froschelectronics GmbH, Graz, Austria
{reinhold.frosch,helmut.koeberl,
idlir.rusi}@freaquent.com
[3] Optoelectronics Research Center, "Politehnica" University,
Bucharest, Romania
marian.vladescu@gmail.com

Abstract. Inversion is a phenomenon that affects the signal received by an RFID reader from a transponder in an unwanted way, as it creates zones of non-communication on the reader antenna. In a previous work we have shown how to locate and evaluate inversion with the aid of 2D maps produced with an automated scanner. The present paper supplements that work with a theory that clarifies the dependence of inversion on the parameters of the transponder circuit and on the magnetic coupling between antenna and transponder.

Keywords: RFID · Reader · Transponder · Signal inversion
Automated scanner

1 Introduction

A measure of the performance of Radio-Frequency Identification (RFID) systems is the quality of the signal received by the reader from the transponder (called tag in what follows). Clearly it depends on the position of the tag on the reader antenna and as such it should be tested at all positions to be expected in the targeted application. The main parameter varying with position is the magnetic coupling between reader antenna and tag coil. For a tuned tag the amplitude of the baseband signal demodulated by the reader varies monotonically with the absolute value of the coupling. However with detuned tags and with readers that do demodulation with an envelope detector a more intricate phenomenon may occur. There may be areas on the antenna for which the signal from a detuned tag placed there is the mirror image of the one normally expected; such a signal is called inverted. The areas with inverted and with normal signals are separated by zones of pure phase modulation where the output of an envelope detector has zero magnitude and no communication is possible. For this reason it is important for the developer to be able to locate those zones. The developers have been warned against this phenomenon in an NXP application note [1], where a graphical example is presented in the form of a 2D diagram that displays inversion in function of reader antenna and tag

© ICST Institute for Computer Sciences, Social Informatics and Telecommunications Engineering 2018
O. Fratu et al. (Eds.): FABULOUS 2017, LNICST 241, pp. 101–106, 2018.
https://doi.org/10.1007/978-3-319-92213-3_16

coil detuning, the position of the tag being fixed. The authors of the present paper have been interested in how and where inversion may occur when the tag is displaced over the reader antenna. In our previous work [3] we have described an automated scanner with the aid of which one can obtain 2D maps of inversion. It is the purpose of the present paper to supplement that work with a quantitative theory of inversion, under the assumption that the reader antenna is tuned but the tag coil may be detuned to various degrees. In Sect. 2 we recall some basic facts, namely the model of the RFID system used in the subsequent discussion and the definition of a numerical measure V_{12}, already discussed in [2, 3], whose sign is determinant for the occurrence of inversion. The computation of V_{12} in [2, 3] has been based on a first order Taylor development and did not realistically reflect the inversion second order dependence on the coupling. The theory of Sect. 3 starts from an algebraic approach that gives the exact sign of V_{12} and hence allows for a precise discussion of inversion in terms of the coupling and of the circuit parameters of the tag. Finally Sect. 4 presents some experimental illustrations of the theory obtained with the 2D scanner.

2   Models and Definitions

Figure 1 presents the model of a typical RFID system in which the reader is of current-driven type and employs an envelope detector as demodulator. The reader feeds the antenna with a current of constant amplitude I_A and frequency ω. Because of the mutual inductance M_{TA} between the tag coil and the reader antenna a voltage is induced in the tag coil, the rectified version of which being used by the tag for powering its internal circuits. The tag transmits data to the reader via the procedure of load modulation: switching between the two resistors R_1 ($=R_T$ in Fig. 1) and R_2 ($=R_T \parallel R_{MOD}$) internal to the tag determines, because of the mutual inductance, a change in the effective impedance Z_A of the antenna circuit and hence a change in the antenna voltage sensed by the reader. When no tag is present on the antenna, Z_A is resistive and equals R_A as the antenna circuit is tuned to ω. When a tag is present with the switch positioned for R_i ($i = 1, 2$), the antenna impedance becomes $R_A + \Delta Z_i$.

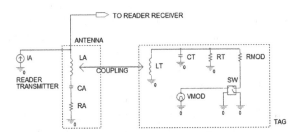

Fig. 1. Model of an RFID system.

The concept of ideal magnitude of the baseband signal extracted by the reader as defined in [2, 3] is fundamental for evaluating the quality of the received signal. Let V_1 be the amplitude of the antenna voltage when the tag switch is open and let V_2 be the amplitude of that voltage when the tag switch is closed. The ideal signal magnitude V_{12} is defined as the difference $V_1 - V_2$; it is ideal in the sense that its absolute value would be the amplitude of the baseband signal output by the envelope detector provided that the transients were short enough with respect to the duration of the bit interval. V_{12} is a signed quantity given by

$$V_{12} = I_A R_A \left(\left| 1 + \frac{\Delta Z_1}{R_A} \right| - \left| 1 + \frac{\Delta Z_2}{R_A} \right| \right). \tag{1}$$

Performance evaluation tests may use V_{12} as a measure of quality of the received signal, since the higher is the absolute value $|V_{12}|$ of V_{12} the lesser is the probability of bit decoding error. In general, the larger is the coupling $|M_{TA}|$, the higher is V_{12}; this is especially true for tuned tags, for which the resonant circuit composed of L_T and C_T in Fig. 1 is tuned to ω. For detuned tags the situation is complicated by the phenomenon of signal inversion: there may be areas on the reader antenna where $V_{12} > 0$ and areas of inversion where $V_{12} < 0$ separated by zones where V_{12} is nearly zero. In the zones where V_{12} is nearly zero the demodulated signal is mainly composed of transients, with the consequence that the bit decoding would most certainly fail.

3   Theory of Inversion

In [2] the following approximate expression for V_{12} has been given under the assumption that $\Delta Z_i / R_A$ are small quantities,

$$V_{12} \approx k^2 I_A R_A Q_A \frac{(Q_1 - Q_2)(1 - Q_1 Q_2 \Delta_T^2)}{(Q_1^2 \Delta_T^2 + 1)(Q_2^2 \Delta_T^2 + 1)}, \tag{2}$$

where $k^2 = M_{TA}^2 / L_T L_A$ denotes the square of the magnetic coupling between the reader antenna and the tag coil, Δ_T represents the detuning $1 - L_T C_T \omega^2$, $Q_A = L_T \omega / R_A$ is the quality factor of the reader antenna and $Q_i = R_i / L_T \omega$ are the quality factors of the tag corresponding to the open ($i = 1$) and closed ($i = 2$) positions of the switch. The approximation consisted in using in (1) the Taylor development up to first order

$$|1 + Z| = 1 + \text{Re} Z + \dots \tag{3}$$

for a small complex number Z. Since k^2 is the only quantity in (2) that varies with the position of the tag on the reader antenna and it is always positive, the approach based on (2) may leave the impression that the occurrence of inversion is dependent only on the detuning Δ_T and is independent of the tag position. However such dependence exists as a second order effect. For analyzing it we start from the identity

$$|1 + Z_1| - |1 + Z_2| = \frac{|1 + Z_1|^2 - |1 + Z_2|^2}{|1 + Z_1| + |1 + Z_2|}. \tag{4}$$

Further, the numerator of (4) may be computed by using

$$|1 + Z|^2 = 1 + 2\mathrm{Re}Z + |Z|^2 \tag{5}$$

which finally gives the new approximative formula that we shall use, obtained by neglecting the small complex numbers Z_1 and Z_2 in the denominator of (4):

$$|1 + Z_1| - |1 + Z_2| \approx_S \mathrm{Re}Z_1 - \mathrm{Re}Z_2 + \frac{|Z_1|^2 - |Z_2|^2}{2}. \tag{6}$$

In (6) the sign $\approx_S$ means that the right term is an approximation of the left term with the additional quality that the signs of the two terms coincide, without any approximation. When using (6) in (1) we find the approximation of V_{12}:

$$V_{12} \approx_S I_A \left(\mathrm{Re}\Delta Z_1 - \mathrm{Re}\Delta Z_2 + \frac{|\Delta Z_1|^2 - |\Delta Z_2|^2}{2R_A} \right). \tag{7}$$

In terms of our model of Fig. 1 we have

$$\Delta Z_i = k^2 L_A L_T \omega^2 \frac{1 + jR_iC_T\omega}{R_i\Delta_T + jL_T\omega}. \tag{8}$$

By substituting (8) in (7) and performing the algebra we arrive at the approximate formula for the analysis of inversion, exact as far as sign is concerned:

$$V_{12} \approx_S k^2 I_A R_A Q_A \frac{(Q_1 - Q_2)\left(1 - Q_1 Q_2 \Delta_T^2 + k^2 Q_A (Q_1 + Q_2)(\frac{1}{2} - \Delta_T)\right)}{(Q_1^2 \Delta_T^2 + 1)(Q_2^2 \Delta_T^2 + 1)}. \tag{9}$$

Since we always have $Q_1 > Q_2$ and the denominator in (9) is positive we finally obtain the formula for the sign of V_{12} to be used in the analysis of inversion, in which $\mathrm{sgn}(x)$ stands for the sign of x:

$$\mathrm{sgn}(V_{12}) = \mathrm{sgn}\left(1 - Q_1 Q_2 \Delta_T^2 + k^2 Q_A (Q_1 + Q_2)(\frac{1}{2} - \Delta_T)\right). \tag{10}$$

The discussion of inversion comprises several cases.

(A) $\Delta_T < 1/2$ and $Q_1 Q_2 \Delta_T^2 \leq 1$. The right term in (10) is positive and inversion does not occur. In particular this covers the case $\Delta_T = 0$ of tuned tags.

(B) $\Delta_T < 1/2$ and $Q_1 Q_2 \Delta_T^2 > 1$. Inversion occurs as soon as k verifies

$$k^2 < \frac{Q_1 Q_2 \Delta_T^2 - 1}{Q_A (Q_1 + Q_2)(\frac{1}{2} - \Delta_T)}. \tag{11}$$

Since the coupling may be made as small as wished by placing the tag farther from the antenna, it follows that inversion can occur in principle for the considered case. Of course in reality the communication might stop before reaching the needed distance.

(C) $\Delta_T = 1/2$ and $Q_1 Q_2 \leq 4$. Inversion does not occur.
(D) $\Delta_T = 1/2$ and $Q_1 Q_2 > 4$. Inversion occurs irrespective of the magnitude of k.
(E) $\Delta_T > 1/2$ and $Q_1 Q_2 \Delta_T^2 \geq 1$. Inversion occurs irrespective of the magnitude of k.
(F) $\Delta_T > 1/2$ and $Q_1 Q_2 \Delta_T^2 < 1$. Inversion occurs as soon as k verifies

$$k^2 > \frac{1 - Q_1 Q_2 \Delta_T^2}{Q_A (Q_1 + Q_2)(\Delta_T - \frac{1}{2})}. \tag{12}$$

However, being a magnetic coupling, k must also verify $k^2 \leq 1$. Therefore inversion may occur only if

$$\frac{1 - Q_1 Q_2 \Delta_T^2}{Q_A (Q_1 + Q_2)(\Delta_T - \frac{1}{2})} < 1. \tag{13}$$

4 Experimental Results

The automated scanner described in [3] works by displacing the tag over the reader antenna through a systematic 2D movement while the system computes V_{12} for each tag position. Figure 2 shows the changes in the demodulated signal as the tag passes successively over the non-inverted area, the boundary zone and the inverted area. The signal in Fig. 2B consists mainly of transients and cannot be decoded; the arrows point at those parts of the signal where one clearly observes that V_{12} vanishes.

The colors used in the 2D maps of V_{12} obtained with the scanner are red for non-inverted areas and blue for inverted areas; for the reader not disposing of the color figures graphs of the middle vertical sections through the maps have been included. The black and white maps show in black the positions at which the decoding of some data bit failed; the arrows on those maps point at the no-communication zones that separate the inverted and the non-inverted areas. Figure 3A shows the case of a tuned tag for which inversion does not occur. Figure 3B illustrates case B of the discussion in Sect. 3; one observes that indeed inversion occurs in the areas of lower coupling near the edges of the antenna. Figure 3F illustrates case F which is the most tricky to achieve since besides condition (12) on the coupling it needs condition (13) on the circuit parameters which might not be true for the tags available to the developer. For

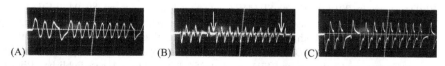

Fig. 2. (A) Not inverted signal; (B) signal at the boundary between non-inverted and inverted areas; (C) inverted signal.

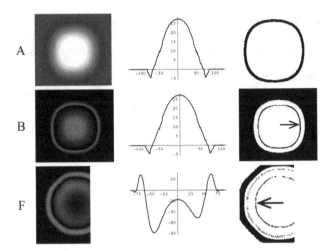

Fig. 3. Color map of V_{12}, graph of section and map of incorrect bit decoding for no inversion (A), inversion case B and inversion case F. (Color figure online)

this reason the map for this example has been obtained with a tag simulator with components carefully adjusted to satisfy (13); details about tag simulators are given in [4]. As predicted by (12) inversion occurs in the central area where coupling is higher.

5   Conclusions

We have exposed an exact theory, as far as the sign is concerned, of the dependence of inversion on the parameters of the tag circuit and on the magnetic coupling between reader antenna and tag. We have shown that inversion is associated with lower coupling in case of slightly detuned tags and possibly with higher coupling in case of heavily detuned tags, the latter case occurring only if the parameters of the tag circuit allow it. Each of the main cases of inversion has been illustrated with a map obtained with the 2D scanner. Together, the theory and the scanner provide useful insights into a phenomenon the RFID system developer should be aware of.

References

1. NXP Semiconductors N.V.: Read/write devices based on the HITAG read/write IC HTRC110 (2010). www.nxp.com/docs/en/application-note/AN98080.pdf
2. Vuza, D.T., Frosch, R., Gugganig, M., Vlădescu, M.: Test and measurement procedures for RFID systems. In: 2014 IEEE 20th SIITME Conference Proceedings, pp. 89–94. IEEE (2014)
3. Vuza, D.T., Vlădescu, M., Pascu, L.: Automated platform for characterization of RFID reader antennas. In: 2014 IEEE 20th SIITME Conference Proceedings, pp. 131–134. IEEE (2014)
4. Vuza, D.T., Frosch, R.: RFID readers for the HDX protocol - a designer's perspective. In: Current Trends and Challenges in RFID, pp. 229–254. InTech Open Access Publisher, Rijeka (2011)

Architecture of a Wireless Transport Network Emulator for SDN Applications Development

Alexandru Stancu$^{(\boxtimes)}$, Alexandru Vulpe, Simona Halunga, and Octavian Fratu

University Politehnica of Bucharest, 060042 Bucharest, Romania
{alex.stancu, alex.vulpe}@radio.pub.ro,
{shalunga, ofratu}@elcom.pub.ro

Abstract. Software-Defined Networking is no longer just a paradigm, but a novel architecture that is gaining momentum in the industry, covering all aspects of a network, from campus networks and data-centers, to optical transport and microwave networks. In Wireless Transport networks, the emergence of the Microwave Information Model, ONF TR-532, in late December 2016, is an important milestone in integrating SDN into such networks. Having the right tools for evaluating the model and for developing SDN applications based on it, is very important. This paper proposes an architecture of a Wireless Transport Network Emulator (WTE), based on TR-532, which enables SDN application developers to implement and test such software programs, based on the microwave model, without the need of owning expensive wireless transport devices in the process.

Keywords: Software-Defined Networking · Network Emulator
Wireless transport networks

1 Introduction

With the advancement of technology in aspects such as processing power or increased storage and with the increased multimedia content and streaming on the Internet, traditional networks began to show their limitations. Software-Defined Networking (SDN) is a novel architecture that proposes to mitigate those limitations and thus to advance the networking industry as well, making networks more agile and vendor independent [1].

SDN decouples the networks' data and control planes, moving the control logic inside an external entity, called the SDN Controller, making the network elements simple forwarding devices, which would just move the packets according to what instructions they get from the control plane. This makes the networks programmable through software applications that run on top of the SDN Controller, increasing their agility. In this respect, SDN becomes a key enabler for technologies like Cloud Computing, Internet of Things (IoT), or, more recently, 5G communication networks.

SDN is emerging in all aspects of a network, from campus and data centers to optical transport, wireless transport networks and even Internet exchange points. This momentum is maintained by organizations like the Open Networking Foundation

© ICST Institute for Computer Sciences, Social Informatics and Telecommunications Engineering 2018
O. Fratu et al. (Eds.): FABULOUS 2017, LNICST 241, pp. 107–112, 2018.
https://doi.org/10.1007/978-3-319-92213-3_17

(ONF), which militates for the adoption of SDN through the development of open standards and opensource software ecosystems. The Wireless Transport (WT) Project is part of the Open Transport Working Group inside ONF and has been focusing on the development of the Microwave Information Model, a data model that describes in an abstract, vendor independent manner, wireless transport devices. Three Proofs of Concept (PoCs) [2–4]) were successfully conducted inside this project, resulting in the formal release of the Microwave Information Model, as ONF TR-532 [5]. This data model, which refers also another model developed by ONF, the Core Information Model, TR-512, should be implemented by equipment vendors in their devices and can be used by SDN application developers for creating software programs that could ease the management of wireless transport networks. Such applications could be, as demonstrated also in the PoCs: detection of aberrances in the network configuration (comparison between the values configured on the devices and the values from the planning database), performance monitoring, rerouting applications etc.

Since the information model was only recently released, in December 2016, it is not yet available embedded in the wireless transport devices' software. Having the right tools for emulating entire wireless transport networks, that expose this data model, without the need of owning such expensive equipment, is an important advantage for SDN application developers, because they do not need to wait for the model being available in the devices for implementing and testing their software.

The main contribution of this paper is proposing an architecture for a Wireless Transport Network Emulator. Several options are analyzed. The Emulator should have the ability to simulate Network Elements exposing the aforementioned information models, and links between different interface layers of those elements.

The remainder of the paper is organized as follows: Sect. 2 presents similar work that was done in the field of emulators for SDN, Sect. 3 illustrates the proposed architecture of the Wireless Transport Network Emulator, while Sect. 4 concludes the paper.

2 Related Work

Several methods for development and testing of network applications or protocols exist, from experimental testbeds, which are expensive but have the advantage of utilizing the real hardware that the network uses, to simulations or emulation of networks. Simulations are fast and easy to deploy, usually requiring only a laptop or a personal computer, but have an important disadvantage: under the same conditions, the simulation results are not always replicable and consistent. Emulations, on the other hand, are executed in real-time and have replicable results.

Since SDN is not a mature technology yet, only a few options for simulating or emulating software-defined networks exist. The most notorious solution, used on a large scale is Mininet [6, 7]. It is an emulation framework, written in Python, that can create hosts, switches, routers and links between them using a single Linux kernel. Everything is done in software, and because of its flexibility it is easily extendable. The focus of Mininet is on the OpenFlow protocol, which is used between the forwarding devices and the SDN Controller. It is considered an important tool in the context of

SDN, having purposes from testing the OpenFlow protocol to teaching SDN principles to students, as described in [8]. Other tools that can be used in the context of SDN are ns-3 [9], or EstiNet [10]. The former provides support only for the OpenFlow protocol, but it is not developed anymore and it is not compatible with the latest versions, while the latter, although it has an ability to provide performance results for SDN applications in a consistent, replicable and correct manner, it only supports one southbound protocol, the same OpenFlow.

Software tools that provide NETCONF as a southbound protocol do not exist yet, probably because YANG models that describe network devices in an abstract, vendor independent manner, have just started to emerge. The Wireless Transport Emulator, whose architecture is proposed in this paper, is intended to fill in this gap in the research community and provide a simple to use emulator for SDN applications developers, which exposes the recently emerged information models.

3 Architecture of WTE

The architecture proposed for the Wireless Transport Emulator is somewhat similar to Mininet. It was chosen not to extend the existing solution, but to create a new one, for two main reasons: (i) Mininet is based on OpenFlow, and the WTE will be based on the NETCONF protocol, exposing YANG models as defined by TR-532 and TR-512, (ii) Mininet uses a Python API that the user can use for implementing its own network topology, so one would need to know basic Python for creating a custom network; the WTE approach is different, providing a topology configuration file, in JSON format, that describes the Network Elements, different layers of interfaces described by the Core Information Model and links between those interfaces. This provides the ability for the user to create a custom network without the need of having any programming skills, just by describing the topology in a specific format.

The WTE should be able to simulate Network Elements that run a NETCONF server, exposing the aforementioned YANG models through a *management* interface, which should be used by an SDN controller to connect to the simulated device. Also, the emulator should support links between interfaces at different layers, both inside the NE and between different NEs. The hosts emulation is different that Mininet, meaning that they are not separate processes accessible through *ssh*.

The architecture of the WTE is based on two main pillars: a NETCONF server implementation and a Python framework that glues everything together. Each Network Element should be simulated as a docker container, isolated from the rest of the applications of the host that runs the emulator. The docker container should run a Linux image and the NETCONF server inside. With this approach, the NETCONF servers will be separated, not interfering with one another. This offers flexibility and extensibility to the emulator. One can implement its own docker container that runs a NETCONF server of choice, as long as it can be run on Linux. An example of NETCONF server based on TR532 is described in [11]. It is a C implementation that could easily be modified to run inside a docker container, providing the NETCONF functionality that the WTE proposes to offer.

The Python framework should represent the core of the WTE. It should be responsible for interpreting the JSON file that describes the topology of the emulated network, reading any other configuration that the WTE might have and then generating the topology. This generation implies several steps: after the topology JSON file is parsed, the framework is responsible for creating and starting the docker containers associated with the NEs (this implies starting also the NETCONF server inside the container), creating the interfaces described by the user, along with the necessary connections between them, and creating the links between the devices. After everything is set in place, the framework should expose a Command Line Interface (CLI), which is topology aware and provides the user the ability of interacting with both the network and the framework. Also, a cleanup ability is needed in the framework so that everything can be stopped when the emulation has ended, so that the environment can be ready for the next run.

A high-level overview of the WTE components when emulating a simple linear topology containing three devices is illustrated in Fig. 1. The idea behind the emulator is that all traffic that can be passed between the simulated NEs is only Layer 2 traffic (Ethernet), so we should achieve network isolation between the NEs at higher layers. This can be done through docker networks. Each simulated NE, in order to have its own management interface, isolated from the other devices, can have its own docker network. A more detailed overview of a single NE can be seen in Fig. 2.

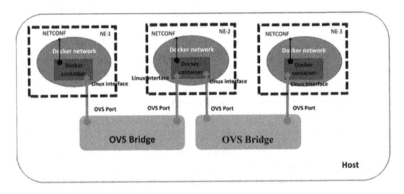

Fig. 1. High-level overview of the WTE components.

There are two proposed solutions for emulating links between two network elements. The first solution implies using a software switch, Open vSwitch (OVS).

Each physical interface defined for a wireless transport device is emulated as a Linux network interface inside its corresponding docker container. For connecting two interfaces from different containers, an OVS bridge can be created and used for connecting the two interfaces, as seen in Fig. 1. Modeling link characteristics, such as bandwidth or latency, can be done using the QoS features provided by OVS. Emulating a single connection between two interfaces implies creating an OVS bridge for each link. If multiple Linux interfaces were to be connected in the same bridge, they would have connectivity between one another and this is not the intention of the emulator.

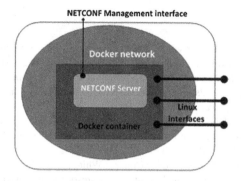

Fig. 2. Overview of the components of a simulated device.

The second proposed solution is more feasible and easier to implement. It consists of replacing the OVS bridge with a *veth* (virtual Ethernet) pair. This feature, which is present in Linux, creates a virtual pipe between the two ends, transferring data between them. The first advantage over the previous proposal is that if an interface will malfunction or set to administratively *down* by the user, the other end will notice that and will go *down*. In the case of an OVS bridge, if one interface connected to the bridge is *down*, the other interface is not affected. The second advantage would be using Linux tool *tc* for emulating the link characteristics, which is easier than using the QoS in OVS.

4   Conclusion

SDN is beginning to have an increased presence in all aspects of the networks nowadays, and through the work done in research communities and in organizations like the ONF, that promotes its adoption through the development of open standards and open-source software ecosystems, it will keep its momentum and will eventually mature as a solution.

Having the right tools that can help both the standardization process and the SDN ecosystem, by aiding software programmers to develop SDN applications from a very early stage, is of vital importance. This paper aims of doing exactly that, by proposing an architecture and the main components of a Wireless Transport Emulator that should aid interested users in simulating wireless transport networks, containing devices that expose the Microwave and Core Information Models.

Acknowledgements. This work was supported by a grant of the Ministry of Innovation and Research, UEFISCDI, project number 5 Sol/2017 within PNCDI III and partially funded by UEFISCDI Romania under grant no. 60BG/2016 Intelligent communications system based on integrated infrastructure, with dynamic display and alerting - SICIAD and by University Politehnica of Bucharest, through the Excellence Research Grants Program, UPB GEX, Identifier: UP - BEXCELENTA2016, project Platform for Studying Security in IoT, contract number 96/2016 (PaSS-IoT).

References

1. Kreutz, D., Ramos, F.M., Verissimo, P.E., Rothenberg, C.E., Azodolmolky, S., Uhlig, S.: Software-defined networking: a comprehensive survey. Proc. IEEE **103**(1), 14–76 (2015)
2. Wireless Transport SDN Proof of Concept White Paper, September 2015. https://www.opennetworking.org/images/stories/downloads/sdn-resources/white-papers/ONF_Microwave_SDN_PoC_White_Paper%20v1.0.pdf
3. Wireless Transport SDN Proof of Concept 2 Detailed Report, June 2016. https://www.opennetworking.org/images/stories/downloads/sdn-resources/technical-reports/Wireless_Transport_SDN_PoC_White_Paper.pdf
4. Third Wireless Transport SDN Proof of Concept White Paper, December 2016. https://www.opennetworking.org/images/stories/downloads/sdn-resources/technical-reports/Third-Wireless-Transport-SDN-Proof-of-Concept-White-Paper.pdf
5. ONF TR-532 – "Microwave Information Model", Version 1.0. https://www.opennetworking.org/images/stories/downloads/sdn-resources/technical-reports/TR-532-Microwave-Information-Model-V1.pdf
6. Heller, B.: Reproducible network research with high-fidelity emulation. Ph.D. thesis. Stanford University (2013)
7. Lantz, B., O'Connor, B.: A mininet-based virtual testbed for distributed SDN development. ACM SIGCOMM Comput. Commun. Rev. **45**(5), 365–366 (2015)
8. Lisa, Y., McKeown, N.: Learning networking by reproducing research results. ACM SIGCOMM Comput. Commun. Rev. **47**(2), 19–26 (2017)
9. Riley, G.F., Henderson, T.R.: The *ns-3* network simulator. In: Wehrle, K., Güneş, M., Gross, J. (eds.) Modeling and Tools for Network Simulation, pp. 15–34. Springer, Heidelberg (2010). https://doi.org/10.1007/978-3-642-12331-3_2
10. Wang, S.-Y., Chou, C.-L., Yang, C.-M.: EstiNet OpenFlow network simulator and emulator. IEEE Commun. Mag. **51**(9), 110–117 (2013)
11. Stancu, A., Vulpe, A., Fratu, O., Halunga, S.: Default values mediator used for a wireless transport SDN Proof of Concept. In: 2016 IEEE Conference on Standards for Communications and Networking (CSCN), Berlin, pp. 1–6 (2016). https://doi.org/10.1109/cscn.2016.7784889

Neural Network Based Architecture for Fatigue Detection Based on the Facial Action Coding System

Mihai Gavrilescu$^{(\boxtimes)}$ and Nicolae Vizireanu

Department of Telecommunications, University "Politehnica" of Bucharest,
1-3 Iuliu Maniu Blvd, 06107 Bucharest 6, Romania
mike.gavrilescu@gmail.com, warticol@gmail.com

Abstract. We present a novel non-invasive neural network based three layered system for detecting fatigue by analyzing facial expressions evaluated using the Facial Action Coding System. We analyze 16 Action Units pertaining to eye and mouth regions of the face. We define an Action Units map containing Action Unit intensity levels for each frame in the video sequence and we analyze this map in a pattern recognition task via a feed-forward neural network. We show that emotion-induced frontal face recordings offer more information in the training stage, while for testing stage the random dataset can be used with no major impact on accuracy, specificity and sensitivity. We obtain over 88% accuracy in intra-subject tests and over 83% for inter-subject tests and we show that our system surpasses the state-of-the-art in terms of accuracy, specificity, sensitivity and response time.

Keywords: Neural networks · e-health · Bioengineering
Facial expression recognition · Image processing

1 Introduction

Most research conducted in the area of facial expression recognition is focused on face recognition or emotion detection. The current paper takes another challenge, proposing a novel non-invasive neural-network based system for fatigue detection using the Facial Action Coding System (FACS). Although this task has been researched in other papers, the current research novelty is in how the architecture is designed as well as the use of feed forward neural networks for this task. Such a system would prove useful in a variety of tasks as monitoring the physical fatigue of a subject reveals the health condition of the person, but also can be used for real-time driver fatigue detection, fatigue being one of the main reasons for car accidents around the globe.

In the following chapter we will present the state-of-the-art in the area of fatigue detection based on facial features.

© ICST Institute for Computer Sciences, Social Informatics and Telecommunications Engineering 2018
O. Fratu et al. (Eds.): FABULOUS 2017, LNICST 241, pp. 113–123, 2018.
https://doi.org/10.1007/978-3-319-92213-3_18

2   Related Work

Although the vast majority of research papers in the area of facial expression recognition are focused on face recognition or emotion detection, there are several research papers where facial features were used for fatigue detection.

Researchers in [1] use Facial Action Coding System (FACS) evaluated using Gabor filters with different frequencies and orientations and classified by means of a cascaded AdaBoost with the purpose of determining driver's fatigue. The proposed method is tested on a database based on ground truth information and it shows promising results in the context of a driver monitoring system. Similarly [2] presents a novel method for detecting daily fatigue using color consistent area correction in the preprocessing phase to reduce the environment illumination. Two kinds of color spaces are determined in the grey level co-occurrence matrix and a backward propagation algorithm is used for detection. The accuracy of the system reaches up to 92.3% with a self-built image database.

Kawamura et al. [3] study the changes of luminance in facial images to determine fatigue. Because these changes are usually influenced by vital signs such as heart rate and blood pressure, the level of fatigue is considered predictable with high accuracy by combining these features with the changes of luminance in the facial area. 13 facial parts are used to estimate subject's fatigue using feature values based on luminance changes for each facial part. The results show accuracy of up to 92%. In [4], facial videos acquired in a realistic environment, with natural lighting, where subjects are allowed to voluntarily move their head were used in order to determine physical fatigue. Facial feature point tracking method was used by combining a "good feature to track" and "supervised descent method". The experimental results show the proposed system outperforms video-based existing systems for physical fatigue detection. Similarly, in [5] a fatigue monitoring system is presented which analyzes eye blinking, head nod and yawning. The method employed to extract facial characteristics in time and frequency domain is mean-variance, for eye blink a Haar-like cascade classifier is used, while for yawning the Canny Active Contour method is employed. The testing of this system shows promising results.

Optical imaging through digital cameras installed on car dashboard is another method used for detecting driver fatigue [6]. The camera detects and tracks the driver face and a non-contact photoplethysmography (PPG) method is applied to get multiple physiological signals (brainwave, cardiac and respiratory pulses) which are used for measuring fatigue levels. These are assessed by studying the alteration of facial feature such as eye, mouth, and head. In order to extract information from the facial features, supervised descent method (SDM) with scale-invariant feature transform (SIFT) is used, while, for classifying the fatigue levels, support vector machine (SVM) methods are employed. [7] presents another research that aims detecting driver fatigue levels by evaluating facial features based on statistical local features, Local Binary Patterns (LBP) being used for person-independent fatigue facial expression recognition. The research shows that LBP features perform stably and robustly over a broad range of fatigue-affected face images. AdaBoost is employed to learn the most discriminative fatigue facial LBP features from a pool of LBP features. These Boost-LBP features show better performance than state-of-the-art.

Given the above described state-of-the-art, we are proposing a novel neural-network based system for determining fatigue levels based on facial features analyzed by means of the Facial Action Coding System. Details on the proposed architecture are presented in the next chapter.

3 Proposed Architecture

As previously mentioned, the current paper proposes a novel neural network-based system for detecting fatigue based on facial features collected via Facial Action Coding System (FACS).

The Facial Action Coding System (FACS) [8] is a framework developed by Eckman and Freisen which divides the face into a set of Action Units (AUs) that are correlated with the activity of different facial muscles. The AUs can be additive (meaning that if a specific AU is triggered it will determine the trigger of another AU) or non-additive (meaning that the triggering of a specific AU is independent from the triggering of other AUs). FACS has showed very good results in determining hidden emotions and we are using it in a fatigue detection task as it offers more reliability compared to other methods of analyzing the face.

In order to achieve the task of detecting fatigue based on FACS, we design an architecture on three layers and we will present each layer in the following paragraphs. The architecture is also depicted in Fig. 1.

The base layer has the main purpose of acquiring facial features from each region of the face and determine if a specific AU is present or not, and, if present, at which intensity. For this the video frame containing the frontal face is normalized and the face is detected by means of Viola-Jones face detection algorithm, then the same algorithm is used for detecting the face components. We analyze only 16 out of the 46 FACS AUs, choosing only the ones known to convey important information for detecting fatigue (mostly linked to eyes and mouth) in order to avoid overcomplicating the architecture as well as overfitting the neural network, therefore in the base layer three components are being detected: Eye, Brow, and Mouth. For each of these components we use specific classifiers to determine the presence/absence and intensity of the AUs pertaining to that specific region such as:

- *Eye component:* Gabor jets-based features have been successfully used for ana-lyzing the eye features providing classification rates of over 90% as well as fast convergence, surpassing other state-of-the-art methods [9]. Because of these strong points, we use them in our work as well, alongside with Support Vector Machines (SVMs) for the AU classification task. The AUs classified in this component are: *AU5* (Upper Lid Raiser), *AU7* (Lid Tightener), *AU43* (Eyes Closed), *AU45* (Blink).
- *Brow component:* We use again the same Gabor Jets with Support Vector Machines (SVMs) method as the one used for the Eye component. The AUs classified in this component are: *AU1* (Inner Brow Raiser), *AU2* (Outer Brow Raiser), *AU4* (Brow Lowerer).

– *Mouth component:* We use active contour classifiers [10] to classify the AUs pertaining to this component. The AUs classified are: *AU8* (Lips toward each Other), *AU10* (Upper Lip Raiser), *AU12* (Lip Corner Puller), *AU15* (Lip Corner Depressor), *AU16* (Lower Lip Depressor), *AU20* (Lip Strecher), *AU23* (Lip Tightener), *AU25* (Lips Part), *AU28* (Lip Suck).

Each of the AU classifiers are previously trained so that they offer over 90% accuracy in cross database tests on Cohn-Kanade [11] and MMI [12] databases.

The three components presented above will fetch to an *intermediary layer* the presence/absence of a specific AU as well as their intensity levels, as follows: *A – Trace* (classification score between 15 and 30), *B – Slight* (classification score between 30 and 50), *C – Marked and Pronounced* (classification score between 50 and 75), *D – Severe or Extreme* (classification score between 75 and 85), *E – Maximum* (classification score over 85), *O – AU is not present* (under 15 classification score). All these scores will be used to compute an *AU activity map* which will have the following structure: (A1A, A2C, A4A, etc.) where A1A means that the Action Unit AU1 was classified with level A of intensity. This *AU activity map* computed in the intermediary layer will contain a row for each frame from the video sequence, each row describing the intensity scores for the analyzed action units. The map is fetched to the top layer which will take the final decision regarding whether the analyzed subjects shows signs of fatigue or not.

In *the top layer* we use a neural network which analyzes the map built in the intermediary layer, in a pattern recognition task, and based on that it determines if the subject is affected by fatigue or not. Because it's a pattern recognition task in a bottom-up layered architecture without feedback loops, the neural network used is a feed-forward neural network as it is efficient for pattern recognition tasks. The neural network has one input layer, one hidden layer, and an output layer. The input layer contains 30 consecutive rows from the AU activity map, hence it has 450 input nodes which are normalized in the [0, 1] interval, such that level A = 0.2, level B = 0.4, level C = 0.6, level D = 0.8, level E = 0.9, 0 – if AU not present. We choose 30 consecutive rows because we are considering a framerate of 30 frames/second, hence 30 consecutive rows pertain to 1 s of the video sequence which is high enough to catch microexpressions and low enough to avoid overfitting the neural network. The output layer has only one node with a binary result, 0 meaning that the subject doesn't show signs of fatigue while 1 means that signs of fatigue are detected. As backpropagation shows the best performance and fast convergence in pattern recognition tasks [13] we employ it as a method for training the neural network. The neural network activation function is determined to be the log sigmoid after trial-and- error. Also through trial and error, trying to minimize the Average Absolute Relative.

Error (AARE), the optimal number of hidden nodes is determined to be 780. Gradient descent algorithm is used for learning the weights and biases of the neural networks until AARE is as low as 0.005. The optimal learning rate is 0.5 and the optimal momentum is 0.02. 50000 training epochs are needed to train the system and it took an average of 3 h to complete on an Intel i7 testbed. Nguyen-Widrow weights initialization is used to evenly distribute the initial weights for each neuron in the input layer.

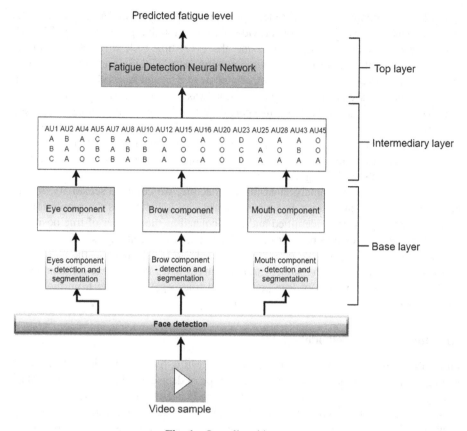

Fig. 1. Overall architecture.

The platform used for implementing the architecture is Scala (as programming language) using Spark MLib library. We used a Java Virtual Machine (JVM) and Eclipse as Integrated Development Environment (IDE). The application has a complexity of around 40.000 code lines and it took an average of 1.5 h to train the feed-forward neural network. The JVM is running on a system with Intel i7 processor, 8 GB of RAM memory, and using Linux Solaris 11.3 as an operating system.

4 Experimental Results

In order to thoroughly test the proposed architecture, we built our own database containing recordings of frontal facial expressions from 64 subjects when watching videos inducing the 6 basic emotions (Sadness, Fear, Happiness, Anger, Surprise, Disgust) from the LIRIS-ACCEDE database [14] as well as in random scenarios. Because the videos existing in the LIRIS-ACCEDE database typically have between 8 and 12 s, we combined more videos for the same emotion in a one minute video-sequence as we needed longer videos for both training and testing. The 64 subjects were recorded six times in three months, every time collecting one frontal face video recording of their reactions when watching each of the six emotion inducing videos (referred to as controlled dataset), as well as five frontal face video recordings in complete random scenarios (when no emotion was induced; referred to as random dataset). They were also asked to self-report their fatigue levels in each session when their face was recorded. Subjects were 32 males and 32 females with ages between 18 and 35, participating in accordance with the Helsinki Ethical Declaration. We have tested the system in both intra-subject and inter-subject methodologies and the results are presented in the following subchapters.

In order to assess the precision of the architecture, we compute sensitivity, specificity and accuracy for all tests conducted. Sensitivity is defined as the proportion of positives that are correctly identified and is calculated as the number of true positives divided by the sum of true positives and false negatives. Specificity is defined as the proportion of negatives that are correctly identified and is calculated as the number of true negatives divided by the sum of true negatives and false positives. Accuracy is calculated as the proportion of true positive and true negative results from the entire number of results.

4.1   Intra-subject Methodology

Intra-subject methodology refers to training and testing the system with samples pertaining to the same subject, but alternating the type of dataset used in training as well as testing stages (controlled, random, or controlled and random). The tests are repeated for all subjects and until all combinations of samples are exhausted. Averaged results are detailed in Table 1. As it can be observed, the higher accuracy is obtained when the controlled dataset is used for both training and testing, specifically when 24 samples are used for training and 12 for testing. In this case the accuracy reached 88.5%, while specificity is 94.5% and sensitivity is 97.2%. We notice that if we change the testing dataset from controlled to random the accuracy of the system shows a decrease of only 2% compared to when random dataset is used for training purposes when the accuracy dropped with 7%. This shows that the controlled dataset offers a lot more important information in the training stage, while for testing any random recordings of the subject can be used, offering similar accuracy, specificity and sensitivity. This is important as it offers the possibility for real-time monitoring of a subject, who will only need to watch emotion inducing videos when he/she first uses the application and further it can be monitored in random situations with over 88% accuracy. In terms of processing time, the time needed to detect fatigue when controlled dataset is used in training and random dataset for testing is no more than six seconds, making the system fast enough to be used for real-time monitoring.

We also conducted a further test for determining which of the six emotions ads the most value to the testing stage in order to detect fatigue with high accuracy. Results are detailed in Table 2.

Table 1. Fatigue detection accuracy, specificity and sensitivity in intra-subject tests.

Type of training samples	Type of test samples	Number of training samples/number of test samples	Accuracy (%)	Specificity (%)	Sensitivity (%)	Average time to converge to a result (s)
Controlled	Controlled	12/24	86.6	93.4	96	6
Controlled	Controlled	18/18	87.4	94	97.2	6
Controlled	Controlled	24/12	88.5	94.5	97.5	5
Random	Random	12/18	78.3	78	76.5	11
Random	Random	18/12	80.5	83	82	11
Random	Random	24/6	81.2	85	84.5	10
Controlled	Random	36/30	88.2	93	96.2	6
Random	Controlled	30/36	81.4	85	84.4	13
Controlled + Random	Controlled + Random	44/22	87.7	92.2	95.8	7

Table 2. Fatigue detection accuracy, sensitivity and specificity for intra-subject tests and for different emotions induced in the training dataset.

Emotion	Accuracy (%)	Sensitivity (%)	Specificity (%)
Happiness	**95.4**	**97.8**	**97.5**
Anger	79.4	80.3	84.2
Fear	**92.3**	**90.2**	94.3
Disgust	**95.4**	**95.2**	**94.1**
Surprise	70	70.1	75.4
Sadness	**95.2**	**98.5**	**98.2**

It can be observed that videos inducing emotions such as Happiness, Disgust and Sadness can be used to detect fatigue with over 95% accuracy, sensitivity, and specificity, while for other emotions results are lower.

4.2 Inter-subject Methodology

For inter-subject methodology we trained the system on multiple subjects and we tested it on a brand new subject, alternating both the number of subjects involved in training and testing as well as the type of datasets used (controlled or random). The tests were repeated using a leave-one-out approach until all combinations of subjects were exhausted. Averaged results are detailed in Table 3.

As it can be observed, results are similar with the ones obtained in intra-subject tests, in the sense that the highest accuracy is obtained when controlled dataset is used in both training and testing stages, specifically when 63 subjects were used in training and the system was tested on the remaining one, case when we obtained over 84% accuracy, and over 88% sensitivity and specificity. We make the same observation as in intra-subject tests that changing the test dataset to the random one only reduces the accuracy with 1%, as opposed to changing the training dataset to random when the accuracy is reduced with 8%. This shows again that the controlled dataset ads more value in the training stage, which is important if we consider building this application

Table 3. Fatigue detection accuracy, sensitivity and specificity in inter-subject tests.

Type of training samples	Type of test samples	Number of subjects involved in training/number of test subjects	Accuracy (%)	Sensitivity (%)	Specificity (%)	Average time to converge to a result (s)
Controlled	Controlled	32/32	81.2	86	86.2	9
Controlled	Controlled	48/16	83.3	87	87.2	8
Controlled	Controlled	63/1	84.3	88.5	88.4	8
Random	Random	32/32	73.3	76.1	75.4	18
Random	Random	48/16	75.2	78	77.4	16
Random	Random	63/1	76.2	79.2	78.8	15
Controlled	Random	63/1	83.2	87.4	86.8	9
Random	Controlled	63/1	76.4	80	80.2	15
Controlled + Random	Controlled + Random	63/1	82.5	85.5	84.5	10

for real-time monitoring, as the emotions need to be induced only when the application is first used, while it can be further assessed in totally random scenarios, completely ad-hoc.

The highest time needed to converge to a result is nine seconds when controlled dataset is used for training and random dataset for testing, which makes the approach fast and attractive for fatigue detection in real-time monitoring systems.

We have conducted a similar test as in intra-subject methodology to determine which emotion ca better be used to detect fatigue, and we reach similar results as in intra-subject tests, reaching over 89% accuracy, and over 90% specificity and sensitivity for Happiness, Disgust and Sadness, while for other emotions the accuracy is lower. These results are detailed in Table 4.

Table 4. Fatigue detection accuracy, sensitivity and specificity in inter-subject tests and for different emotions induced in the training dataset.

Emotion	Accuracy (%)	Sensitivity (%)	Specificity (%)
Happiness	**89.3**	**97.8**	**97.5**
Anger	77.2	75	78
Fear	**88.5**	**86.7**	89.2
Disgust	**91.2**	**90.2**	**90.5**
Surprise	68.4	63	64.2
Sadness	**89.4**	**93.4**	**93**

4.3   Comparison with State-of-the-Art

We have tested the other methods used in [2, 3, 7] on our dataset and our approach offered higher accuracy, sensitivity and specificity than the state-of-the-art as well as faster convergence. Results are detailed in Table 5.

Table 5. Comparison with state-of-the-art.

Work	Year	Method used	Accuracy (%)	Time to compute results (seconds)
[2]	2017	Color consistent area correction	85.3	15
[3]	2017	Luminance changes	86.2	16
[7]	2015	SVM with Boost- LBP features	83	25
Current work	2017	Feed-Forward Neural Network	*Intra-subject: 88% Intra-subject (emotion controlled testing): 95%* (Happiness, Sadness, Disgust) *Inter-subject: 83% Inter-subject (emotion controlled testing): 89%* (Happiness, Sadness, Disgust)	6–15

As it can be observed, our approach using a feed-forward neural network for determining the fatigue levels surpasses in terms of accuracy with 3% the results obtained when using color consistent area correction [2] and with 2% the results obtained when luminance changes [3] are used. Our approach also offers up to 5% more accuracy compared to the methods where SVM with Boost-LBP features [7] were used. In terms of execution time, our approach is faster than all other methods in state of the art, the time to compute results being lower than 15 s.

5 Conclusions

We presented a non-invasive neural network based system for fatigue detection by analyzing facial expressions acquired by means of the Facial Action Coding System. We only analyze 16 Action Units which are considered to be linked to fatigue and we propose a three layered architecture such that the base layer determines the facial action unit presence and intensity level, the intermediary layer builds a map containing AU details for each frame in the video sequence, and the top layer contains a feed-forward neural network trained to detect fatigue by analyzing the map built in the intermediary layer in a pattern recognition task.

We describe the database constructed by recording 64 subjects in both controlled (emotion is induced) and random (no emotion is induced) scenarios as well as self-reports of their fatigue level for each recording session. We have tested the system in both intra-subject and inter-subject methodologies and we have shown that emotion-induced frontal face recordings offer more information in the training stage, while for testing stage the random dataset can be used without impacting the accuracy, specificity and sensitivity of the system too much. This is an important observation, as users will only have to watch emotion inducing videos when they first use this application, while further real-time monitoring can be done ad-hoc, in random scenarios. We obtain over 88% accuracy, over 93% specificity and over 96% sensitivity in intra-subject tests and over 83% accuracy, over 87% sensitivity and over 86% specificity for inter-subject tests when controlled dataset is used for training and random dataset for the testing stage. Results are computed in no more than 9 s, making such system fast and attractive for real-time monitoring applications. We have tested other methods from the state-of-the-art on our own database and have shown that our method surpasses them in terms of accuracy, sensitivity, specificity as well as response time. We have also analyzed which emotion used in the testing stage can offer the highest accuracies for fatigue detection and we concluded that these are Happiness, Disgust and Sadness, offering over 95% accuracy for intra-subject tests and over 89% accuracy for inter-subject tests. This information can be used to further tune the system by focusing on these three emotions for achieving higher accuracy which will be the direction of our future work.

References

1. Koon, L.Y., Suandi, S.A.: AU measurements from cascaded adaboost for driver drowsiness detection. In: 2013 8th IEEE Conference on Industrial Electronics and Applications (ICIEA), June 2013
2. Chen, J., et al.: Fatigue detection based on facial images processed difference algorithm. In: 2017 13th IASTED International Conference on Biomedical Engineering (BioMed), February 2017
3. Kawamura, R., Takemura, N., Sato, K.: Mental fatigue estimation based on luminance changes in facial images. In: IEEE International Symposium on Systems Integration (SI), February 2017
4. Haque, M.A., Irani, R., Nasrollahi, K., Moeslund, T.B.: Facial video-based detection of physical fatigue for maximal muscle activity. IET Comput. Vis. **10**(4), 323–329 (2016)
5. Giao, Y., Zeng, K., Xu, L., Yin, X.: A smartphone-based driver fatigue detection using fusion of multiple real-time facial features. In: 2016 13th IEEE Annual Consumer Communications and Networking Conference (CCNC), March 2016
6. Tayibnapis, I.R., Koo, D.Y., Choi, M.K., Kwon, S.: A novel driver fatigue monitoring using optical imaging of face on safe driving system. In: 2016 International Conference on Control, Electronics, Renewable Energy and Communications (ICCEREC), January 2017
7. Zhang, Y., Hua, C.: Driver fatigue recognition based on facial expression analysis using local binary patterns. Optik – Int. J. Light Electron Opt. **126**(23), 4501–4505 (2015)
8. Ekman, P., Friesen, W.V.: Facial Action Coding System: Investigator's Guide. Consulting Psychologists Press, Palo Alto (1978)
9. Mikhail, M., Kaliouby, R.E.: Detection of asymmetric eye action units in spontaneous videos. In: 2009 16th IEEE International Conference on Image Processing (ICIP), Cairo, pp. 3557–3560 (2009)
10. Liu, X., Cheung, Y.M., Li, M., Liu, H.: A lip contour extraction method using localized active contour model with automatic parameter selection. In: 20th International Conference on Pattern Recognition (ICPR), pp. 4332–4335, August 2010

11. Tian, Y., Kanade, T., Cohn, J.F.: Recognizing action units for facial expression analysis. IEEE Trans. Pattern Anal. Mach. Intell. **23**(2), 97–115 (2001)
12. Pantic, M., Valstar, M.F., Rademaker, R.: Web-based database for facial expression analysis. In: Maat, L. (ed.) Proceedings of IEEE International Conference on Multimedia and Expo (ICME 2005), pp. 317–321, July 2005
13. Xiaoyuang, L., Bin, Q., Lu, W.: A new improved BP neural network algorithm. In: 2nd International Conference on Intelligent Computation Technology and Automation, pp. 19–22, October 2009
14. Baveye, Y., Dellandrea, E., Chamaret, C., Chen, L.: LIRIS-ACCEDE: a video database for affective content analysis. IEEE Trans. Affect. Comput. **6**(1), 43–55 (2015)

Using Off-Line Handwriting to Predict Blood Pressure Level: A Neural-Network-Based Approach

Mihai Gavrilescu[(⊠)] and Nicolae Vizireanu

Department of Telecommunications, University "Politehnica" of Bucharest,
1-3 Iuliu Maniu Blvd, 061071 Bucharest 6, Romania
mike.gavrilescu@gmail.com, warticol@gmail.com

Abstract. We propose a novel, non-invasive, neural-network based, three-layered architecture for determining blood pressure levels of individuals solely based on their handwriting. We employ four handwriting features (baseline, lowercase letter "f", connecting strokes, writing pressure) and the result is computed as low, normal or high blood pressure. We create our own database to correlate handwriting with blood pressure levels and we show that it is important to use a predefined text for the handwritten sample used for training the system in order to have high prediction accuracy, while for further tests any random text can be used, keeping the accuracy at similar levels. We obtained over 84% accuracy in intra-subject tests and over 78% accuracy in inter-subject tests. We also show there is a link between several handwriting features and blood pressure level prediction with high accuracy which can be further exploited to improve the accuracy of the proposed approach.

Keywords: Neural networks · E-health · Bioengineering · Image processing

1 Introduction

Although used as a means of communication for millennia, only recently handwriting has been studied in relationship with psychological and medical conditions of the writer, in a rather new research area called graphology. Typically graphology is used to identify, analyze and interpret different behavior aspects of the writer as well as medical conditions he/she might have, analyzing handwriting features such as: the trajectory of the writing [1], the way letters are written (letter "t" and letter "y" [2]) or the weight of strokes. Several of these features are employed in the current work in a neural-network based approach for predicting blood pressure levels based on handwriting. Such an approach will provide a non-invasive and less costly alternative to other more invasive ways of determining blood pressure levels which are typically assessed by means of costly equipment. The proposed approach can also provide a baseline for predicting other medical or behavioral conditions (such as lying, which is often linked to an increase in blood pressure). The approach is also original as it involves building a novel three-layered architecture based on a feed-forward neural network, but also because it treats the task of predicting blood pressure from handwriting as a pattern recognition task.

© ICST Institute for Computer Sciences, Social Informatics and Telecommunications Engineering 2018
O. Fratu et al. (Eds.): FABULOUS 2017, LNICST 241, pp. 124–133, 2018.
https://doi.org/10.1007/978-3-319-92213-3_19

In the following chapters we will present the state-of-the-art in the area of hand-writing recognition, focusing our attention on systems that use handwriting to predict different medical conditions of the writer.

2 Related Work

As mentioned before, our system aims predicting blood pressure based on off-line handwriting hence we will present the state-of-the-art in terms of predicting medical conditions by analyzing handwritten samples of an individual.

Grace et al. [3] propose a way of investigating the relationship between the grip and pinch strength in handwriting and the Autism Spectrum Disorder (ASD). They have analyzed 51 children which were divided into two groups (children with no ASD and children in the autism spectrum), each child being asked to take a test which would assess its pinch and grip strength, as well as the pencil control and writing activity independence. Their research showed that grip strength was correlated with pencil control in both analyzed groups, but with legibility only in the children without ASD which shows that grip and pinch are important features for children development tasks.

Another medical condition which was analyzed by means of handwriting is Parkinson's disease (PD), knowing the fact that PD is typically associated with micrographia. Micrographia refers to the decrease in letter size as well as increase in the movement time and decrease and frequent changes in the speed and acceleration of writing. Drotar et al. [4] propose a template to collect handwriting during different tasks which are specifically designed to determine as many aspects of micrographia as possible. Their proposed approach, tested on 75 subjects, showed an accuracy of 80% in classifying subjects suffering from PD. Similarly, in [5] several metrics are developed in order to describe micrographia, such as size-reduction, ink utilization, and pixel density. These are used to compute scores for signatures of 12 subjects in order to predict if they are suffering from PD or not. The results show significant differences in terms of pixel density between subjects suffering from PD and non-PD suffering subjects and showed promising results for developing such a system that could be used as an alternative to other dynamic sampling methods for PD diagnosis which involve specialized and costly equipment.

Bhaskoro and Supangkat [6] present a research where handwriting is analyzed with the purpose of discriminating between subjects suffering from diabetics' disease and healthy subjects. They used a term frequency – inversed document frequency method to analyze the levels of resemblance of the handwriting features in the vector space model and, tested on 56 subjects, the method offered an accuracy of 81.8%.

Neuromuscular disorders are also analyzed in [7] with the aid of handwriting movement analysis which segments the handwriting strokes in order to evaluate the motor control abilities of neuromuscular disorders and those of people who do not suffer from them. The results are promising and show that such an approach can be used to assist the diagnosis of such disorders.

With all the above-mentioned research, our paper proposes building a non-invasive feed-forward neural network-based system able to determine the blood pressure level of the writer solely by analyzing his/her handwriting. This could offer a non-invasive and less costly alternative to current approaches which are more invasive and need more expensive equipment to determine the blood pressure level of a patient.

3 Proposed Architecture

3.1 Graphology Analysis and Blood Pressure Types

As mentioned previously, the area of research which studies handwriting for determining psychological, behavioral or medical conditions of the writer is called graphology. There are tens of handwriting features which can be used to analyze writing [8], but in this paper we will only use the following: baseline, lowercase letter "t", connecting strokes, and writing pressure. We will describe each of them in the following paragraphs.

Baseline refers to the direction on which the writing flows. An *ascending baseline* is typically associated with easy going, happy people, *descending baseline* is associated with pessimistic people, while *leveled baseline* is associated with people with high reasoning abilities. All these psychological features can have an impact on the blood pressure hence the reason why we have chosen this handwriting feature (e.g. happiness is know to lower blood pressure).

Lowercase letter "f" refers to how the letter "f" is written. We use it because it provides clues about the precision of the writing which can convey information about blood presure as well: *cross-like lower case letter "f"* is related to increase levels of concentration, *angular loop* refers to strong reaction to obstacles, *narrow upper loop* refers to narrow minded people, *angular point* refers to persons who can get easily revolted, *balanced lowercase letter "f"* is typically associated with leadership abilities.

Connecting strokes refer to how letters are connected one with another to form a word. *Strongly connected* letters are an indicator of people who can easily adapt to change, *medium connected* letters refer to persons who like changing environments often, and *not connected* means the person has difficulties adapting to change.

Writing pressure refers to the amount of pressure that is applied by the writer on the paper and this is the most commonly used handwriting feature to assess the blood pressure level of the writer. *A medium writer* is a person who is moderately affected by traumas (and is typically associated with normal blood pressure), *light writer* is a person who easily gets over traumas (typically associated with low blood pressure), and *heavy writer* refers to persons who are deeply affected by traumas (and is typically associated with high blood pressure).

Analyzing these handwriting features we aim building a non-invasive system able to predict blood pressure levels. We divide the subjects analyzed into three categories, based on their blood pressure:

- Subjects with low blood pressure (Systolic: 70–90, Diastolic: 40–60)
- Subjects with normal (ideal) blood pressure (Systolic: 90–130, Diastolic: 60–85)
- Subjects with high blood pressure (Systolic: over 130, Diastolic: over 85)

In the following subchapter we will present the architecture of the proposed system and will describe in detail each of the three component layers.

3.2   Overall Architecture

As previously mentioned, we design a feed-forward neural-network based system on three layers: base layer (where the handwriting is normalized and letters are split), a middle layer (where a matrix is computed for each letter in the handwritten sample), and a top layer (where the decision regarding the blood pressure of the subject is taken). The architecture is depicted in Fig. 1.

The *base layer* has the main purpose of taking the handwritten sample in the form of a scanned image and converting it to a set of handwriting features. The contrast of the image is first increased in order to better distinguish the letters and features such as connecting strokes or writing pressure, then the area of the handwritten sample where the handwritten text is present is cropped and converted into greyscale.

Letters are then split and cropped from the image using a junction-based segmentation algorithm as used in [9] which has showed good results at segmenting characters closely linked together. The cropped character is then provided as input to a feature extraction block.

The feature extraction block implements a set of algorithms for each handwriting feature analyzed. For *baseline,* a polygonization method is used [10], a technique where a polygon is delimited around the handwritten text and its relation with the overall structure of the page is studied. For *lowercase letter "f"* the algorithm used is template matching where the letter is compared to 50 templates for letter "f" and based on the matching score the handwriting feature is determined for each letter "f" in the text. For *connecting strokes,* we analyze them using the same junction based segmentation algorithm [9] by scoring the connections between two consecutive letters in the handwritten sample. *Writing pressure* makes use of a grey level thresholding algorithm [11], which studies the thickness of the writing and determines if it is light, medium or heavy.

Each of these features collected for each letter in the handwritten sample are sent to the middle layer where each result is binary coded. Hence, for *baseline* we will have the following possible values: 100 – Ascending, 010 – Descending, 001 – Leveled, for *lowercase letter "f"* we will have as possible values: 10000 – Cross-like, 01000 – Angular Loop, 00100 – Balanced, 00010 – Angular Point, 00001 – Narrow Upper Loop, 00000 – not a lowercase letter f, for *connecting strokes* we have 100 – Not Connected, 010 – Medium connectivity, 001 – Strongly connected, and for *writing pressure* the binary codes will be: 100 – Light Writer, 010 – Medium Writer, 001 – Heavy Writer. Hence, for each letter in the handwritten sample, we will have a row in the Letters matrix; for example a row like [100][10000][010][100] will mean ascending baseline – 100, cross-like letter "f" – 10000, medium connectivity – 010, light writer – 100. This matrix is fetched to the top layer which will analyze it in a pattern recognition task using a neural network in order to determine the blood pressure level of the writer (low, normal or high).

In the top layer we will have a neural network that is trained in order to determine the blood pressure level of the writer by only analyzing the previously mentioned features. Being a pattern recognition task in a bottom-up architecture with no feedback

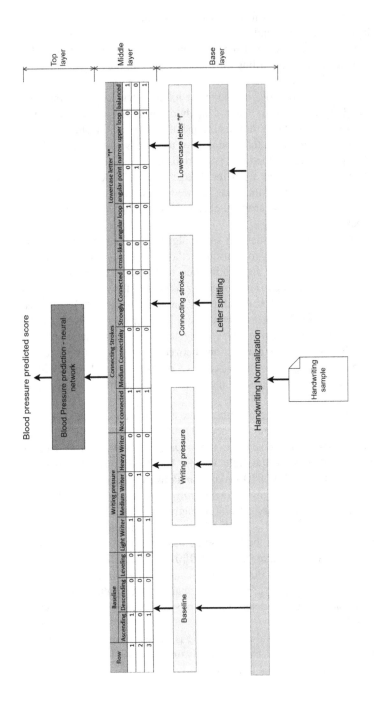

Fig. 1. Overall architecture.

loops, the neural network employed is feed-forward and the training method used is backpropagation which is known to offer good results and fast convergence in such tasks. The neural network has three layers: an input layer, one hidden layer, and the output layer. The Letters matrix formed in the middle layer is provided as input to the neural network every 70 letters in order to avoid overfitting the neural network (we are also considering we don't have more than 70 letters on a row; if more than 70 letters are present on a row, only the first 70 letters will be taken into account). As for each letter we will have 14 binary numbers, the input layer will therefore have 980 nodes. The output layer will have only one node which will provide a score on a scale from 1 to 3 (1 – Low Blood Pressure, 2 – Normal Blood Pressure, 3 – High Blood Pressure). In the training phase the Average Absolute Relative Error (AARE) is computed as the difference between what is expected and what is determined and the neural network's weights are tuned to accommodate better results. Through trial and error it was determined that the optimal number of hidden nodes is 1120 with an AARE of 0.005. For learning the weights and biases of the neural network, gradient descent algorithm is employed while for the initialization of weights in the input node Nguyen-Widrow weights initialization method was used. The optimal learning rate is 0.01, the optimal momentum 0.03 and the number of training epochs needed 50000.

In the following chapter we will present the experimental results obtained when testing the previously described system.

4 Experimental Results

In order to test the proposed architecture, due to lack of any publicly available database to use, we have created our own datasets by asking 18 subjects (9 males and 9 females with ages between 18 and 45, participating in accordance with Helsinki Ethical Declaration) to provide each three handwritten samples at three different times as well as acquired their blood pressure each time they provided these samples. Out of the three handwriting samples, one of them contained a pre-defined text from *The London Letter* (a standard request exemplar used by graphologists in handwriting analysis [8] because the text is designed in such manner as to provide relevant information for all the handwriting features we analyze), while the other two handwriting samples contained texts which were freely chosen by subjects, but needed to contain at least 200 words. We have used this database for both testing and training the system proposed. We therefore divided the two handwritings into two different datasets which we tested in both intra-subject and inter-subject methodologies: controlled dataset (pre-defined text is used – *The London Letter*), random dataset (text freely chosen by the writer containing minimum 200 words).

4.1 Intra-subject Methodology

For intra-subject methodology we trained and tested the system on handwriting samples attributed to the same subject, by alternating the type of the dataset used (controlled, random or controlled and random). Results can be found in Table 1.

Table 1. Blood pressure prediction accuracy and average number of rows in intra-subject tests.

Type of training samples	Type of test samples	Number of training samples/number of test samples	Accuracy (%)	Specificity (%)	Sensitivity (%)	Avg. no. of handwritten rows analysed
Controlled	Controlled	2/1	86.4	82.2	87.4	4
Controlled	Random	3/6	84.4	78.2	85.2	5
Random	Controlled	3/3	74	70.2	79.5	10
Random	Controlled	3/6	74.5	71.3	79.2	10
Controlled + Random	Random	8/1	80.4	77.5	84	7

As it can be observed, the highest prediction accuracy as well as results in terms of specificity and sensitivity are obtained when the controlled dataset is used for both training and testing the system, reaching over 86% accuracy. However, the results are kept considerably high when the controlled dataset is used in training while the system is tested on random dataset, the decrease being of only 2% in terms of accuracy. This shows that the most important thing is to have a well-chosen pre-defined text used for training purposes, while for testing purposes any text can be used and the accuracy is still high. This is important as in a real application the subject will only have to write a pre-defined text when he first uses the application, while for all other subsequent measures he can freely write any text he wants. This is also sustained by the fact that when random dataset was used for training, the results were 10% lower than when using the controlled dataset.

The average time taken to compute the results in the case where the controlled dataset is used for training purposes is 15 s (the average number of rows to analyze is 5 and analyzing a row takes on average 3 s) which makes such an application suitable for real time implementation as it is very fast.

4.2   Inter-subject Methodology

The same tests were conducted in an inter-subject methodology, which means that we trained the proposed system on handwriting samples coming from a set of writers and we tested it on handwriting samples coming from a different writer not involved in training. The results are similar, the highest accuracy, specificity and sensitivity being obtained when the controlled dataset is used for training, up to 7% higher accuracy than when random dataset is used in the training stage. This shows consistency for the proposed system, the accuracy provided in this methodology being 78.3%. The remaining 21.7% typically refers to blood pressure levels which were mistaken with their neighbor values (such that low blood pressure is mistaken with normal blood pressure, normal blood pressure with high blood pressure and vice versa) for which better algorithms for level discrimination should be proposed. Results can be observed in Table 2.

Table 2. Blood pressure prediction accuracies and average number of rows in inter-subject tests.

Type of training samples	Type of test samples	Number of subjects involved in training/number of test subjects	Accuracy (%)	Specificity (%)	Sensitivity (%)	Avg. no. of handwritten rows analysed
Controlled	Controlled	9/9	76.2	73	76.2	10
Controlled	Controlled	12/6	78	75.2	79.3	8
Controlled	Controlled	17/1	78.9	76	82.2	7
Random	Random	9/9	71	67.4	73.2	13
Random	Random	12/6	72.1	68	74	14
Random	Random	17/1	72.5	69.2	74.2	16
Controlled	Random	17/1	78.3	75.4	81	7
Random	Controlled	17/1	70.4	68.4	73.2	15
Controlled + Random	Controlled + Random	17/1	77.8	74.3	80.2	9

The average time needed to converge to a result when the controlled dataset is used in training stage is 30 s, which also shows that such an application is fast and can be an attractive alternative to other more expensive ways and equipment used for assessing the blood pressure of an individual.

4.3   Links Between Handwriting Features and the Blood Pressure Levels

In order to determine the links between the handwriting features we are studying and the blood pressure levels, we have created a residual application which counts the number of appearances for each handwriting feature when a specific level is detected with over 90% accuracy. Table 3 depicts these relationships which can be further used to tune the system and increase its accuracy even more.

Table 3. Correlation between handwriting features and the blood pressure levels.

Blood pressure levels	Most present handwriting features in the letters matrix
Low blood pressure	Writing pressure – light writer
	Ascending baseline
Normal blood pressure	Writing pressure – medium writer
	Connecting strokes – strongly connected
	Lowercase letter "f" – cross like
High blood pressure	Writing pressure – heavy writer
	Descending baseline
	Connecting strokes – not connected
	Lowercase letter "f" – angular point

5 Conclusions

We propose a novel, non-invasive, neural-network based system with an architecture on three layers with the purpose of determining the blood pressure of a subject solely based on his/her handwriting. The architecture contains a base layer where the scanned handwriting is normalized, the handwritten text is split into letters and for each letter four handwriting features are determined (baseline, writing pressure, lowercase letter "f", and connecting strokes), a middle layer where a binary matrix is computed containing rows for each line in the handwriting sample and depicting the handwriting features for each letter using a combination of binary codes, and a top layer containing a feed-forward neural network trained via backpropagation to determine the blood pressure level by studying the patterns in the binary matrix computed in the middle layer.

We have created our own database containing handwriting samples collected from 18 subjects as well as their corresponding blood pressure. The database is divided into controlled dataset (the written text is pre-defined) and random dataset (the written text is freely chosen by the writer). We have shown that in both intra-subject and inter-subject methodologies, the controlled dataset ads more value in the training stage, offering up to 10% better accuracy for intra-subject tests and 7% for inter-subject tests compared to when the random dataset is used for training. This is an important observation as for such an application the subject will only have to write a pre-defined text at the beginning in order to train the system, and after that he can write any text, hence it will involve less effort from their side, while the accuracy is kept at similar levels. We obtained over 84% accuracy, over 78% specificity and over 85% sensitivity for intra-subject tests and over 78% accuracy, over 75% specificity and over 81% sensitivity for inter-subject tests. The time needed to converge to a result was no more than 30 s, making such approach more attractive comparted to other more expensive ways of assessing the blood pressure.

We have also showed there is a link between several handwriting features and prediction with high accuracies of each of the three blood pressure levels which can be further exploited to tune the system and reach better accuracies. Also the fact that the non-accurate results are typically mistaken with neighbor levels (low blood pressure is typically mistaken with normal blood pressure, normal blood pressure is typically mistaken with high blood pressure and vice-versa) shows the need for other algorithms to be integrated in this approach to better discriminate between blood pressure levels which will be the direction of our future research.

References

1. Naghibolhosseini, M., Bahrami, F.: A behavioral model of writing. In: International Conference on Electrical and Computer Engineering (ICECE), pp. 970–973, December 2008
2. Champa, H.N., Anandakumar, K.R.: Automated human behavior prediction through handwriting analysis. In: 2010 First International Conference on Integrated Intelligent Computing (ICIIC), September 2010

3. Grace, N., Enticott, P.G., Johnson, B.P., Rinehart, N.J.: Do handwriting difficulties correlated with core symptomology, motor proficiency and attentional behaviors. J. Autism Dev. Disord. 1–12 (2017)
4. Drotar, P., Mekyska, J., Smekal, Z., Rektorova, I.: Predicition potential of different handwriting tasks for diagnosis of Parkinson's. In: 2013 E-Health and Bioengieering Conference, pp. 1–4, November 2013
5. Zhi, N., Jaeger, B.K., Gouldstone, A., Sipahi, R., Frank, S.: Toward monitoring Parkinson's through analysis of static handwriting samples: a quantitative analytical framework. IEEE J. Biomed. Health Inf. **21**, 488–495 (2017)
6. Bhaskoro, S.B., Supangkat, S.H.: An extraction of medical information based on human handwritings. In: 2014 International Conference on Information Technology Systems and Innovation (ICITSI), pp. 253–258, November 2014
7. Liu, M., Wang, G.: Handwriting analysis for assistant diagnosis of neuromuscular disorders. In: 2013 6th International Conference on Biomedical Engineering and Informatics (BMEI), February 2014
8. Morris, R.N.: Forensic Handwriting Identification: Fundamental Concepts and Principles. Academic Press, Cambridge (2000)
9. Jayarathna, U.K.S., Bandara, G.E.M.D.C.: A junction based segmentation algorithm for offline handwritten connected character segmentation. In: Computational Intelligence for Modelling, Control and Automation, 2006 and International Conference on Intelligent Agents, Web Technologies and Internet Commerce, p. 147, 28 Nov 2006–1 Dec 2006
10. Djamal, E.C., Ramdlan, S.N., Saputra, J.: Recognition of handwriting based on signature and digit of character using multiple of artificial neural networks in personality identification. In: Information Systems International Conference (ISICO), 2–4 December 2013
11. Coll, R., Fornes, A., Llados, J.: Graphological analysis of handwritten text documents for human resources recruitment. In: 12th International Conference on Document Analysis and Recognition, pp. 1081–1085, July 2009

SDWN for End-to-End QoS Path Selection in a Wireless Network Ecosystem

Eugeniu Semenciuc, Andra Pastrav, Tudor Palade,
and Emanuel Puschita[(⊠)]

Communication Department, Technical University of Cluj-Napoca,
G. Baritiu 26-28, 400027 Cluj-Napoca, Romania
{eugeniu.semenciuc,andra.pastrav,tudor.palade,
emanuel.puschita}@com.utcluj.ro

Abstract. In recent years, a significant increase of mobile data traffic has been observed, resulting in more complex and diverse network services. Thus, it becomes more difficult to fulfill the requirements of QoS-sensitive applications. The emergence of new technologies such as Cloud Computing, Software Defined Networking and Network Function Virtualization provides an excellent ecosystem for QoS routing solutions to support real-time applications requirements in wireless networks. The scope of this paper is to propose a Software Defined Wireless Network controller implementation to determine the appropriate end-to-end QoS path in a wireless network ecosystem. The proposed solution is based on Bayesian reasoning and Fuzzy logic algorithms.

Keywords: QoS routing · End-to-end QoS path · Wireless network ecosystem
Bayesian reasoning · Fuzzy logic

1 Introduction

The development of Internet and telecommunication technologies in the last couple of years established a well-connected and communicative information society. New applications and services like social networking, multimedia, Voice over IP (VoIP), virtual reality, mobile applications and Internet of Things (IoT), generate a big amount of data and require a scalable, high performance, energy efficient and reliable networking infrastructure to provide strict Quality of Service (QoS). Meeting these requirements is getting more challenging each day with existing network architecture and devices due to their limited capabilities. Thereby the Software Defined Network (SDN) paradigm has emerged [1].

SDN is a network architecture that consists of three layers: applications, control plane and data plane plus a set of interfaces [2]. SDN architecture separates the control plane (that makes decisions about where traffic is sent), and the data plane (which contains the devices responsible for traffic forwarding) [2]. The applications use specific Northbound interfaces (NBIs) to enforce their policies in the data plane, while the SDN controller uses Southbound interfaces (SBIs) to communicate with the network equipment [2]. Due to programmability of SDN controllers and network devices, the introduction of new protocols and improvements requires only modifications of

© ICST Institute for Computer Sciences, Social Informatics and Telecommunications Engineering 2018
O. Fratu et al. (Eds.): FABULOUS 2017, LNICST 241, pp. 134–140, 2018.
https://doi.org/10.1007/978-3-319-92213-3_20

software programs, creating a more flexible, extensible and open framework for network design and upgrade. Such attractive features of SDN provoke the implementation of the SDN architecture into wireless networks, resulting in the emergence of Software Defined Wireless Networks (SDWN) [3].

Wireless network ecosystems consist of different technologies, services and network nodes that create a complex hybrid access network with specific requirements like mobility management, dynamic channel configuration and rapid client re-association. With the increase of the diversity of network services, fulfilling the QoS requirements becomes more and more challenging. Since the SDN approach was proved to be successful on legacy wired networks, it becomes intensely adopted by other networks such as wireless, mobile and sensor networks. Therefore, the scope of this paper is to propose a solution that determines a feasible end-to-end QoS path in a wireless network ecosystem based on SDWN concept. The originality of the proposed solution consists in (1) the use of selective probing to estimate the network state, (2) the estimation of new application performances using Bayesian reasoning, and (3) the classification of available routes based on multiple metrics (delay, jitter, packet loss) integrated in a Fuzzy logic algorithm.

The remainder of the paper is organized as follows. In Sect. 2 the most notable open-source SDN controller are compared. Section 3 introduces some attempts to enhance QoS support using SDWN. Section 4 describes the proposed Fuzzy logic QoS solution in a SDWN architecture. Finally, Sect. 5 concludes the paper.

2 SDN Controllers

The SDN architecture is managed by a central controller that enables on-demand resource allocation, self-service provisioning and virtual networks. The controller is a fundamental part of the SDN architecture. A set of programming languages, architectures, APIs, and protocols have been adopted by controllers [4, 5]. Various SDN controller features are compared in Table 1.

Table 1. Feature-based comparison of the most popular open source SDN controllers.

	Language	Architecture	SBI APIs	NBI APIs	Storage
ONOS	Java	Flat distributed	OpenFlow1.5 OVSDB, BGP, SNMP, PCEP NETCONF, P4, IS-IS, OSPF	REST API	RAFT LOG
Open Daylight	Java	Flat distributed	OpenFlow1.4, NETCONF, OVSDB, CEP, BGP, LTSP, SNMP	REST API RESTCONF	In memory datastore
NOX	C++	Centralized	OpenFlow 1.0	REST	WheelFS
IRIS	Java	Centralized	OpenFlow 1.0, 1.3, OVSDB	REST API	Mongo

OpenFlow [6] is the first communication interface defined between control and data layers of an SDN architecture, and permits switches to update their flow table entries to take corresponding actions per the incoming flows and defined rules.

Considering specific application constraints, we have selected OpenDaylight and ONOS as the best choices, thanks to their distributed architecture, wider applications, topology discovery and stability. In [7] ONOS and OpenDaylight performances are compared using Cbench and Mininet. The results show that ONOS has good performance on clusters, link-up, switch-up and throughput.

3   SDWN and QoS Support

Open Roads [8] was one of the first efforts in the development of a wireless SDN architecture, based on OpenFlow, NOX controller and FlowVisor. This solution was deployed on Cambridge University Campus Network. In this framework, OpenFlow separates control of the forwarding plane, SNMP protocol allows for device configuration and FlowVisor creates the network slices and ensure isolation between them. Therefore, multiple scenarios can be run on the same physical infrastructure and researchers can easily adopt SDN paradigms in cellular networks.

OpenRadio [9] proposes a novel architecture that provides modular and declarative programming capability for the entire wireless stack. Because multiple blocks at the PHY and MAC layers are reused across multiple wireless protocols (3G, 4G, WLAN) OpenRadio decouples wireless protocol definition from the hardware, offering the possibility of defining and customizing protocols programmatically. The processing plane includes actions, signal processing operations. The decision plane, includes rules, responsible for choosing which actions must be performed.

CloudMAC [10] presents a new management distributed architecture for WLAN systems by moving the MAC layer processing to virtual machines connected by an OpenFlow network. CloudMAC architecture consists of Virtual APs (VAPs), Wireless Termination Points (WTPs), an OpenFlow switch and an OpenFlow controller. This architecture enables several new applications, such as dynamic spectrum use, on-demand AP and downlink scheduling. The performance evaluation has shown that CloudMAC achieves good performance and seamlessly interworks with standard IEEE 802.11 stations.

In [11] Xu et al. proposes a SDWN multipath-transmission (MP-SDWN) solution. Using an extension of Floodlight OpenFlow, the MP-SDWN provides network slicing to support multiple virtual WLANs running on the same physical infrastructure. Also, it introduces the multi-connection virtual access point (MVAPs) concept, which forms the same virtual access point over different physical APs. Based on MVAP, all the traffic from a user can be transmitted over multiple APs simultaneously, thus increasing the throughput considerably. The experiment results show that compared to WiFi, MP-SDWN achieves notable throughput improvement.

In [12] the load imbalance problem is examined by proposing a centralized Software Defined LTE RAN (SD-LTE-RAN) framework and a new QoS Aware Balance (QALB) algorithm. The solution provides QoS satisfaction using Priority Set Scheduler (PSS). PSS tries to allocate more resources for higher priority UEs according to their configured GBRs (Guaranteed Bit Rate). The study results are based on simulations realized using NS-3 simulator and they show that QALB obtains better QoS data rates and decreases the total network overload by 15% compared to existing algorithms. As shown in [11, 12] SDN permits QoS decisions based on network state, but to the best of our knowledge, none of the existing mechanisms estimates the future performances using Bayesian Networks and Fuzzy Logic.

4 Fuzzy QoS Support in SDWN

Although the SDWN concept is quite new and not standardized, it offers support for a stable and mature development ecosystem. Nearly all proposed QoS solutions use SDWN and NFV (network function virtualization) to manage in a better way available resources, offer load balancing and provide different queuing techniques. However, there are a few solutions that approach QoS routing in wireless access networks, and even fewer that consider composite metrics.

This section proposes a solution to determine the appropriate end-to-end QoS path in a wireless network ecosystem using the SDWN paradigm. The proposed implementation represents a transition of the QoS support mechanism presented in [13] to SDWN architecture to obtain a more flexible, robust and scalable solution.

In [13] the proposed algorithm was integrated with QualNet simulator and the simulations results showed estimation accuracy and good learning capabilities.

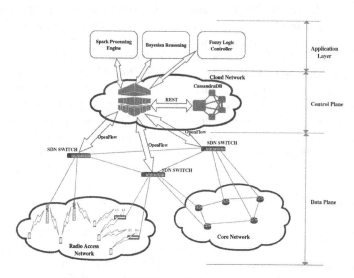

Fig. 1. SDWN based QoS support model.

As shown in Fig. 1, the selected architecture is based on ONOS controller that manages the core wired network and the radio access network and uses OpenFlow to communicate with data plane. The pseudocode of the algorithm is presented above:

```
Step1. Gathering Intelligence
foreach (node){
 if (packet) {
      computeDelay();computeJitter();getBandwidth();
      sendPacketToONOS();savePacketInDB();}}
Step2. Estimate QoS performances of a new Application:
sendsAppRequirementsToONOS();estimateQoS();
makesFuzzyDecisions();sendsPathToSource();
estimateQoS () {
 getHistoryDBData(source,destination,appData);
 List<QoSData> learningData;groupBy(AppID);
 foreach (route){
  assign(delay, jitter, bandwidth)
          to QoS{POOR,MODERATE,GOOD,EXCELLENT}}
 P(metric= QoSValue|DBData) = (1 + #(QoSValue))/(3+N);}
```

A NoSQL database cluster is considered for network state parameters storage. Thereby ONOS controller will have the global view of the network based on applications performance logging. Additionally, to maintain a more accurate and current network state, a probing mechanism is proposed considering applications characteristics [13]. The probes are sent in a hop-by-hop manner, from the source to the destination node. Each intermediate node analyzes the performance in terms of the QoS parameters and updates the database with new results. Central controller will use this information to perform Bayesian reasoning to estimate the performance of each path for applications. To classify these routes, a Fuzzy algorithm, named Fuzzy Logic Controller (FLC) is being used. FLC is described by the following steps: 1 - using defined membership functions, applied for metrics, such as delay, jitter, bandwidth, the affiliation degree to each fuzzy set is determined; 2 - fuzzy linguistic rules for inputs obtained in the previous step are evaluated and 3 - a percentage, characterizing the performance of the route, is issued by applying defuzzification [14].

The data processing and estimation tasks will be implemented as an ONOS application using Apache Spark, cluster-computing framework. Apache Spark contains the MLlib (Machine Learning Library), which due to its distributed memory-based architecture performs nine times faster than the disk-based implementations.

With increasingly sophisticated ways of probing and recording network activities, the network data analysis becomes a Big Data problem. Different algorithms can be applied on these data, to predict and estimate future network behavior, and to create an central controller which learns to manage the network on its own. To experimentally evaluate the proposed SWDN concept, we will use Mininet-WiFi [15].

5 Conclusions

This paper proposes a QoS support based on SDWN concept to estimates the future network performance based on previous network states and selects an end-to-end path that fulfills the application requirements. The particularities of this solution are: probing to save network states in a distributed NoSQL database, centralized data processing and decision taken by ONOS controller using Bayesian reasoning and Fuzzy logic algorithms. Conducted studies confirm that SDWN and Machine Learning represent a promising QoS solutions for wireless network ecosystems.

Acknowledgement. This paper was partially supported by a grant of the Ministry of Innovation and Research, UEFISCDI, project number 6 Sol/2017 within PNCDI III and by a grant of the Ministry of National Education and Scientific Research, RDI Programme for Space Technology and Advanced Research - STAR, project number 116/2016.

References

1. Kreutz, D., Ramos, F., Esteves Verissimo, P., Esteve Rothenberg, C., Azodolmolky, S., Uhlig, S.: Software-defined networking: a comprehensive survey. Proc. IEEE **103**, 14–76 (2015)
2. Masoudi, R., Ghaffari, A.: Software defined networks: a survey. J. Netw. Comput. Appl. **67**, 1–25 (2016)
3. Akyildiz, I., Lin, S., Wang, P.: Wireless software-defined networks (W-SDNs) and network function virtualization (NFV) for 5G cellular systems: an overview and qualitative evaluation. Comput. Netw. **93**, 66–79 (2015)
4. The OpenDaylight Platform—OpenDaylight. https://www.opendaylight.org/
5. Open Network Operating System. http://onosproject.org/
6. McKeown, N., Anderson, T., Balakrishnan, H., Parulkar, G., Peterson, L., Rexford, J., Shenker, S., Turner, J.: OpenFlow. ACM SIGCOMM Comput. Commun. Rev. **38**, 69 (2008)
7. Yamei, F., Qing, L., Qi, H.: Research and comparative analysis of performance test on SDN controller. In: 2016 First IEEE International Conference on Computer Communication and the Internet (ICCCI) (2016)
8. Yap, K., Kobayashi, M., Sherwood, R., Huang, T., Chan, M., Handigol, N., McKeown, N.: OpenRoads. ACM SIGCOMM Comput. Commun. Rev. **40**, 125 (2010)
9. Bansal, M., Mehlman, J., Katti, S., Levis, P.: OpenRadio. In: Proceedings of the First Workshop on Hot Topics in Software Defined Networks - HotSDN 2012 (2012)
10. Dely, P., Vestin, J., Kassler, A., Bayer, N., Einsiedler, H., Peylo, C.: CloudMAC - an OpenFlow based architecture for 802.11 MAC layer processing in the cloud. In: 2012 IEEE Globecom Workshops (2012)
11. Xu, C., Jin, W., Zhao, G., Tianfield, H., Yu, S., Qu, Y.: A novel multipath-transmission supported software defined wireless network architecture. IEEE Access. **5**, 2111–2125 (2017)
12. Farshin, A., Sharifian, S.: A chaotic grey wolf controller allocator for Software Defined Mobile Network (SDMN) for 5th generation of cloud-based cellular systems (5G). Comput. Commun. **108**, 94–109 (2017)

13. Semenciuc, E., Pastrav, A., Palade, T., Puschita, E.: Performance evaluation of a Cloud-based QoS support mechanism. In: 2016 International Conference on Communications (COMM) (2016)
14. Zadeh, L.: Theory of fuzzy sets. Electronics Research Laboratory, College of Engineering, University of California, Berkeley, Berkeley, CA (1977)
15. Fontes, R., Afzal, S., Brito, S., Santos, M., Rothenberg, C.: Mininet-WiFi: emulating software-defined wireless networks. In: 2015 11th International Conference on Network and Service Management (CNSM) (2015)

Intelligent Low-Power Displaying and Alerting Infrastructure for Secure Institutional Networks

Alexandru Vulpe[✉], Marius Vochin, Laurentiu Boicescu, and George Suciu

Telecommunications Department, University Politehnica of Bucharest,
Bucharest, Romania
{alex.vulpe,george.suciu}@radio.pub.ro, marius.vochin@upb.ro,
lboicescu@elcom.pub.ro

Abstract. This paper proposes an intelligent displaying and alerting system, based on a scalable low-power communication infrastructure. The system is designed to offer dynamic display capabilities using the ePaper technology, as well as to enable indoor location-based services such as visitor guidance and alerting capabilities using iBeacon-compatible mobile devices. The system is designed primarily for educational and research institutions, allowing remote authentication through eduroam-type technology performed by the user's distant institution of affiliation. As such, secure access based on locally-defined policies is to be implemented, as well as multiple levels of access, from guests to system administrators. An analysis concerning the dependency of system power consumption on the value of the advertising interval of the iBeacon frames is performed. Based on this, recommendations are made to the institution regarding the optimization of system configuration.

Keywords: ePaper · iBeacon · Alerting system · Indoor positioning
Low power display

1 Introduction

With the ever-increasing use of technology in all life aspects, a sustainable and easily managed system for digital and up-to-date room signage for offices, meeting rooms, and conferences has become the next challenge for modern office buildings. The emergence of Internet of Things (IoT) and digital interactions using electronic paper (ePaper) technology has marked a new phase of development in this direction. The new technology relies on ambient light reflection instead of a backlight, as well as a screen that only consumes a significant amount of energy during the update phase. Such digital displays offer good visibility of information in all light conditions, with the benefit of a low power consumption. The same can be said about iBeacon, which relies on the Bluetooth Low Energy (BLE) standard to create stationary constellations of low-power beacons to determine the indoor position of mobile terminals [1].

© ICST Institute for Computer Sciences, Social Informatics and Telecommunications Engineering 2018
O. Fratu et al. (Eds.): FABULOUS 2017, LNICST 241, pp. 141–150, 2018.
https://doi.org/10.1007/978-3-319-92213-3_21

However, because these technologies are still relatively new, their use requires extensive computer programming skills to access and manage displayed information. The current level of technology relies on the user either micro-managing individual displays, or writing complex scripts for the dissemination of multiple information flows and dynamic update of these displays.

There are several companies that offer display and notification solutions based on wireless ePaper. All these solutions are, generally, based on three elements:

- Display, which can be either ePaper or LCD (Liquid Crystal Display);
- Communication infrastructure, which can be based on Wi-Fi, 3G or Bluetooth/ZigBee;
- Content management and publishing application.

Most solutions are focused on static content display and less on dynamic content. There are also digital signage applications which focus on complex content, both static and dynamic, but in this case, a more complex infrastructure is required, and a low power consumption or flexible infrastructure is no longer the target [2].

The paper proposes an intelligent displaying and alerting system (SICIAD) that relies on wireless ePaper and iBeacon technologies to create custom displays for both static and dynamic information, as well as to ease the indoor orientation of guests. The system is currently undergoing testing and preliminary results from real-world deployment are available in [3].

Although the system is primarily designed for public institutions like universities or government buildings, some of its applications may include public transport, exposition and commercial centers, museums and both indoor or outdoor amusement parks. Any organization may benefit from an indoor positioning and orientation system, as well as a centrally-managed display and alerting system.

The paper is organized as follows. Section 2 presents the envisioned architecture, while Sect. 3 details use cases of the SICIAD project. Some preliminary results are given in Sect. 4, while Sect. 5 draws the conclusions.

2 SICIAD Architecture

The SICIAD project was proposed in order to capitalize on existing advanced technology available at a company's premises, as described in Sect. 2. It targets the development of an intelligent system that can dynamically display information and provide notification on certain events. For this, it proposes the development of an integrated management application for the infrastructure and wireless ePaper displays, along with an interface for connecting to internet calendar, several access levels and e-mail message programming. The proposed high-level architecture is depicted in Fig. 1.

The implemented management console will enable the dynamic display of information, either on ePaper devices connected to the infrastructure and without wired power supplies, or on the users' cell phones, using beacons based on the iBeacon technology. An internet calendar interface with email entry will be created, allowing the display of event schedule, as well as an electronic notice board for announcements, commercials, etc.

An application for the operation and monitoring of the system's state parameters is to be implemented, offering the ability to send generated alerts through technologies like e-mail, GSM SMS, ePaper displays in areas of interest, or iBeacon messages.

The intelligent system will analyze data from IoT sensors (temperature, CO_2, smoke, gas) to identify threats, send alerts through its available means, or even automatically initiate emergency evacuation and facilitate the avoidance of problem areas and to provide guidance towards safe exits (including aid for the hearing impaired).

The infrastructure will be designed and implemented using the economic operator's LANCOM ePaper and iBeacon existing technologies, as well as generic open-source technologies available to the university.

The economic operator will be able to implement the system in domains like: universities, schools, conference halls, hospitals, etc.

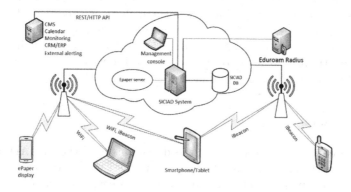

Fig. 1. High-level SICIAD architecture

The Lancom ePaper Server comes integrated with features for displaying user-provided images, as well as generating (rendering) ePaper images based on the user's specifications. All operations, including ePaper display management, display tasks, image upload and image generation, are performed through the system's XML API (Application Programming Interface).

Pre-rendered images can also be directly uploaded to the ePaper Server, also through XML API calls. For the system to function properly, the images must be encoded in BASE64 format and then sent using the API.

Finally, the API can also be used to manage the ePaper displays, remotely gain information regarding their status, or even access the system's logs: including uploaded images and performance data.

As such, the first step in the design and development of SICIAD has been to create a system capable of interacting with the API to send images and tasks for each available display. First and foremost, performance data for the ePaper Server, as well as the displays, is necessary to decide how to proceed further. Moreover, it must be determined if the low-power displays used can work within the system's constraints (specifically as an emergency alerting system).

Since the server is written in Java, for consistency purposes, it has been chosen that SICIAD will also be based on the same programming language, making it a platform-independent software as well. To simplify access to the test system, it has been implemented as a web application.

The system's initial components include:

- An HTTP client, capable of sending all API calls and capturing (and identifying) responded data, offering access to full HTTP information for analysis;
- An XML parser, used to process performance data and convert it to CSV format, for further analysis;
- An integrated database, to store complete test data;
- And a basic web interface, for sending manually-generated XML requests to the ePaper Server API.

The current version of SICIAD focuses solely on centrally managing the information displayed on the ePaper devices, leaving all management functions to the already implemented Lancom tools. In its current design phase, the system uses iBeacon devices integrated in the Lancom Access Points to provide indoor location services. However, the use of stand-alone BLE devices is also considered, to enable a more accurate location of users.

3   Use Cases

Several use cases are envisioned for the development of the SICIAD architecture, based on the project's objectives. Here, wireless ePaper devices are used to display static or dynamic information, while the iBeacon technology can enable smartphone apps to provide guidance, custom advertisements or even location-based alerts. Several use cases are proposed:

1. **Dynamic or static announcements and notifications in public transport stations.** In this scenario, the ePaper will display the schedule of public transport associated with a stop, along with a short map of the surrounding areas and the transport network, and other useful information. There will also be dynamic information such as the remaining time until a public transport vehicle arrives or temporary changes of the schedule.
2. **Dynamic display of information in educational and research institutes and visitor guidance.** Wireless ePaper displays can be used to replace traditional notice boards. As such, a hierarchical architecture could allow each room's administrator to present information regarding schedule, special events, contests and projects. Furthermore, additional information could be managed by the upper hierarchy of the institute. For large organizations, visitors could be guided using an iBeacon-based in-door positioning system.

3. **Dynamic display of alerts and emergency evacuation.** An intelligent monitoring system can determine safety threats and automatically enact pre-defined evacuation plans. Here, ePaper displays can be used to show the best route for evacuation, while iBeacons can be used to broadcast alerts or guide visitors towards exits through smartphone applications.

4. **Guidance for customers in large shopping areas/malls.** Here, ePaper is used along with beacons. ePaper can ensure the display of price tags, and can also dynamically modify them. For instance, based on information from beacons, it can enlarge the font if there is a senior person or with eyesight problems. Also, a loyal customer may get a lower price and notifications regarding the existence of such price.

5. **Guidance and notifications for museum visitors.** In this scenario ePaper is used for tagging exposition halls and exhibition pieces, as well as marking the visitation route. Also, beacons will enable, via a smartphone app, an interactive electronic guide of the exhibition.

6. **Tourist information and guidance in national and adventure parks.** Here, beacons are used, via a smartphone app, for providing information on tourist landmarks in the area, as well as for providing interactive audio guide.

Based on the above use cases, as well as the details presented in Sect. 2, it can be concluded that ePaper displays controlled over a wireless network can be used to fulfil SICIAD's main objectives. More important, the use of wireless technology simplifies the deployment of the system, since additional wiring or power sources will not be necessary. However, several special cases result from the use-case analysis.

First off, the ePaper displays (including the Lancom ePaper displays proposed for use in the system's architecture) are designed to work at a low level of power consumption. This means a slow refresh rate of the displayed information, when changes occur. For static information, this is not an issue: all the displays can be updated in the off hours, when no one is using them. However, an issue may arise when trying to display urgent dynamic notifications, like the emergency evacuation alert from the sixth use case. For such cases, further study is needed regarding the wireless ePaper response time.

The specifications of Lancom ePaper displays indicate a battery life time between 5 and 7 years, if the displayed information is changed four times a day [4]. For more interactive applications (like the first use case), or improving response times for emergency situations, additional power sources may be needed, which may come in the form of solar panels in outdoor deployments (when battery replacement may become an issue).

Secondly, the Lancom WiFi Access Points integrate iBeacon technology. This offers a simple means of determining whether a mobile smart device is in close range of the access point, but a larger iBeacon network is necessary for determining exact indoor position. As such, further work may relate to the integration of stand-alone iBeacon devices in the SICIAD architecture.

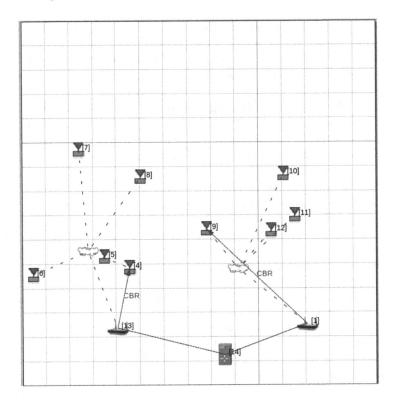

Fig. 2. Scenario topology simulated in EXata

The above use cases highlight three general use cases for the SICIAD system:

1. **Dynamic display system** - which updates the ePaper devices based on a set predefined rules, either automatically or at the user's request;
2. **Visitor guidance system** - relying on BLE iBeacon emitters to pin-point the users' locations and provide indoor navigation assistance and location based services;
3. **Dynamic alerting system** - relying on components from the previous use cases and superseding their displayed/broadcasted information. In case of an alert, the system will store the previous normal running state, proceed to alerting (or even evacuating all visitors) and, once the alert has passed, restore it.

4   Evaluation

In order to determine the battery behavior of standalone iBeacons in the SICIAD architecture, we devised a topology that resembles as closely as possible the network in the BEIA company building that would be used to implement iBeacons in the SICIAD architecture. The battery behavior is important as it will serve as a metric for deciding the advertising interval of iBeacon. A very small interval (100 ms as recommended by Apple) will likely lead to a fast discharge of the beacon battery. Whereas a high interval (larger than 1000 ms) might lead to a drop in the positioning accuracy for applications like indoor positioning.

We used EXata Network Simulator [5] in order to send iBeacon frames to receiving devices. The transmission is modeled as a Constant Bit Rate (CBR) application, as BLE (iBeacon) frames have a constant size and a constant transmission interval. Figure 2 shows the scenario topology.

The battery models available in EXata were used to capture the characteristics of real-life batteries and to enable the analysis of the discharge behavior under different system loads without resorting to time consuming and expensive prototyping.

The analysis was conducted using two battery models:

1. **Service Life Battery Model.** This model estimates the total service life of the battery and uses a model developed by Sarma and Rakhmatov [6] as an abstraction of the real battery. It can be used for different particular batteries, provided that one has the rated capacity vs. discharge current.
2. **Residual Life Battery Model.** This model estimates the remaining service life of the battery and, similar to the service life battery model above, will need a battery efficiency plot to estimate the discharge rate.

Table 1. Simulation parameters

Parameter	Value
Packet size	30 bytes
Packet transmission interval	100; 200; 350; 700; 1000 ms
Simulation length	24 s
Battery model	Service life; Residual life
Battery type	Duracell-AAA
Initial battery charge	1200 mAhr

The two battery models where used, together with varying rates of advertising interval, to see the effect of the value of the interval on the battery life. Table 1 shows the main parameters used.

Results are shown in Figs. 3, 4 and 5. From Fig. 3 we can notice that the consumed energy does not decrease linearly. We see that the rate of decrease is higher at lower transmission intervals (which was of course to be expected) but we see that going from 700 towards 1000 ms, the rate of energy consumption has a very small value. If we look at Fig. 4, we can make the same observation. The residual battery capacity tends to increase as the transmission interval decreases. This means that the battery of the beacon will last longer when having a higher

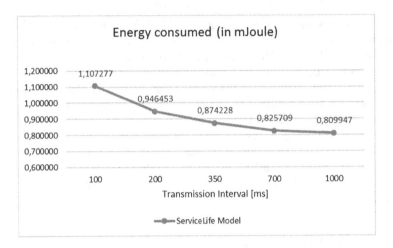

Fig. 3. Energy consumed

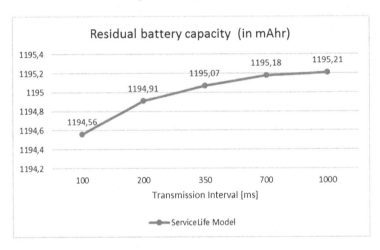

Fig. 4. Residual battery capacity [Service Life model]

transmission interval (which only makes sense, as one needs to transmit once every second, and not 10 times per second).

We analysed the same parameter using the Residual Life Model (Fig. 5). Although the curve is similar, we can see that the values predicted are more optimistic than the Service Life model. We also notice that, in terms of absolute values, the Service Life model estimates a higher discharge rate for the beacon battery. Several conclusions now can be drawn by putting the results together. It is plain to see that by using the recommended transmission interval (100 ms) the battery would deplete in a very short time. However, increasing the transmission interval ten-fold (to 1000 ms) does not lead to a 10-fold drop in the discharge rate. The battery life will last between 13 and 30% longer (depending on the battery model that was used). Taking into account the residual battery capacity together with the consumed energy curve, the recommendation for the company would be to choose and advertising interval between **350** and **600** ms as that accommodates both a good indoor positioning accuracy as well as a good battery discharge rate.

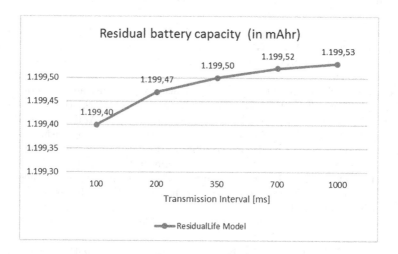

Fig. 5. Residual battery capacity [Residual Life model]

5 Conclusions

The paper presents a displaying and alerting system, based on an integrated communication infrastructure. The system offers dynamic display capabilities using the ePaper technology, as well as enables in-door location-based services such as visitor guidance and alerting using iBeacon-compatible mobile devices. While the iBeacon emitters integrated in the used Wireless access points can enable location-based services, accurately determining each users' location may require additional, battery-powered BLE beacons. Such a network (or constellation) of beacons could provide a more elegant indoor guidance system, due to its effectiveness at a range of several meters (compared to several centimeters for NFC tags). Moreover, although the investment in Beacon devices may be significant, the already widespread use of compatible smart devices may reduce the necessity of other hand-held devices. Future work with the project will include the development of the system's management console, along with the further investigation of ePaper response times and iBeacon functional range, as well as the proposed architecture's scalability, performance and security.

Acknowledgement. This work has been funded by UEFISCDI Romania under grant no. 60BG/2016 "Intelligent communications system based on integrated infrastructure, with dynamic display and alerting - SICIAD" and partially funded University

Politehnica of Bucharest, through the "Excellence Research Grants" Program, UPB - GEX. Identifier: UPB - EXCELENTA - 2016 project Research projects "Intelligent Navigation Assistance System", contract number 101/2016 (SIAN) and "Platform for Studying Security in IoT", contract number 96/2016 (PaSS-IoT).

References

1. Ahn, S., Song, S., Yang, J., Oh, H., Choi, J.K.: Web-based multi-screen digital signage. In: 2014 IEEE 3rd Global Conference on Consumer Electronics (GCCE), pp. 244–245, Tokyo (2014). https://doi.org/10.1109/GCCE.2014.7031154
2. Vochin, M., Vulpe, A., Suciu, G., Boicescu, L.: Intelligent displaying and alerting system based on an integrated communications infrastructure and low-power technology. In: WorldCist 2017 - 5th World Conference on Information Systems and Technologies, Porto Santo Island, Madeira, Portugal, 11–13 April 2017 (2017)
3. Sykes, E.R., Pentland, S., Nardi, S.: Context-aware mobile apps using iBeacons: towards smarter interaction. In: Proceedings of the 25th Annual International Conference on Computer Science and Software Engineering, pp. 120–129 (2015)
4. Lancom Wireless ePaper Displays Specification sheet. https://www.lancomsystems. com/fileadmin/produkte/lc_wireless_epaper_displays/LANCOM-Wireless-ePaperDisplays-EN.pdf
5. EXata - Network Emulation. http://web.scalable-networks.com/exata-network-emulation-software
6. Rakhmatov, D.N., Vrudhula, S.B.K.: An analytical high-level battery model for use in energy management of portable electronic systems. In: Proceedings of the 2001 IEEE/ACM International Conference on Computer-Aided Design (ICCAD 2001), pp. 488–493. IEEE Press, Piscataway (2001)

On the Regularization of the Memory-Improved Proportionate Affine Projection Algorithm

Roxana Mihăescu, Cristian Stanciu, and Constantin Paleologu[✉]

University Politehnica of Bucharest, Bucharest, Romania
{cristian,pale}@comm.pub.ro

Abstract. In order to improve the performance of the conventional algorithms used for network and acoustic echo cancellation, we can exploit the sparseness character of the echo paths (i.e., a small percentage of the impulse response components have a significant magnitude while the rest are zero or small). In this paper, we consider the memory-improved proportionate affine projection algorithm (MIPAPA), which represents an appealing choice for echo cancellation. In this context, we focus on the regularization of this algorithm, relating the regularization parameter to the signal-to-noise ratio. In this way, the algorithm can operate properly in different noisy conditions. Simulation results indicate the good performance of the proposed solution.

Keywords: Adaptive filters · Echo cancellation
Memory-improved affine projection algorithm (MIPAPA)
Regularization

1 Introduction

The main goal in echo cancellation is to model an unknown system, i.e., the echo path [1,2], similar to a system identification problem. Nevertheless, the echo paths (for both network and acoustic echo cancellation scenarios) are sparse in nature, i.e., a small percentage of the impulse response components have a significant magnitude while the rest are zero or small. The sparseness character of the echo paths inspired the idea to "proportionate" the algorithm behavior, i.e., to update each coefficient of the filter independently of the others, by adjusting the adaptation step size in proportion to the magnitude of the estimated filter coefficient [3]. Following this idea, many proportionate-type algorithms were developed for echo cancellation, e.g., see [4] and the references therein.

In this work, we focus on the memory-improved proportionate affine projection algorithm (MIPAPA) [5]. As compared to most of its counterparts, the MIPAPA takes into account the "history" of the proportionate factors. Moreover, this also helps to reduce the computational complexity.

© ICST Institute for Computer Sciences, Social Informatics and Telecommunications Engineering 2018
O. Fratu et al. (Eds.): FABULOUS 2017, LNICST 241, pp. 151–157, 2018.
https://doi.org/10.1007/978-3-319-92213-3_22

The MIPAPA requires a matrix inversion within its update. Due to the nature of the input signal (which is mainly speech), this matrix can be very ill-conditioned. Consequently, it needs to be regularized before inversion by adding a positive constant to the elements of its main diagonal. In practice, it was found that the value of this regularization term is highly influenced by the level of the system noise [6].

In this paper, we present a solution for choosing the constant regularization parameter of the MIPAPA, aiming to attenuate the effects of the noise in the adaptive filter estimate. Simulations performed in the context of both network and acoustic echo cancellation indicate the robustness of the algorithm in different noisy conditions.

2   Memory-Improved Proportionate Affine Projection Algorithm

The improved proportionate affine projection algorithm (IPAPA) [7] is one of the most popular algorithms used for echo cancellation. It results as a straightforward combination of the affine projection algorithm (APA) [8] and the improved proportionate normalized least-mean-square (IPNLMS) algorithm [9]. The IPAPA is defined by the following equations:

$$\mathbf{e}(n) = \mathbf{d}(n) - \mathbf{X}^T(n)\widehat{\mathbf{h}}(n-1), \tag{1}$$

$$\widehat{\mathbf{h}}(n) = \widehat{\mathbf{h}}(n-1) + \alpha\mathbf{G}(n-1)\mathbf{X}(n)\left[\delta\mathbf{I}_P + \mathbf{X}^T(n)\mathbf{G}(n-1)\mathbf{X}(n)\right]^{-1}\mathbf{e}(n), \tag{2}$$

where $\mathbf{e}(n)$ is the error signal vector of length P (with P denoting the projection order), $\mathbf{d}(n) = \left[d(n)\ d(n-1)\ \cdots\ d(n-P+1)\right]^T$ is a vector containing the most recent P samples of the desired signal, superscript ^{T} denotes the transpose operator, $\mathbf{X}(n) = \left[\mathbf{x}(n)\ \mathbf{x}(n-1)\ \cdots\ \mathbf{x}(n-P+1)\right]$ is the input data matrix, where $\mathbf{x}(n) = \left[x(n)\ x(n-1)\ \cdots\ x(n-L+1)\right]^T$ is a vector containing the most recent L samples of the input signal $x(n)$,

$$\mathbf{G}(n-1) = \text{diag}\left[g_0(n-1)\ g_1(n-1)\ \cdots\ g_{L-1}(n-1)\right] \tag{3}$$

is a diagonal matrix containing the proportionate (or gain) factors, α represents the step-size of the algorithm, δ is the regularization parameter, and $\mathbf{I}_P$ is the $P \times P$ identity matrix. The proportionate factors are evaluated as [9]

$$g_l(n-1) = \frac{1-\kappa}{2L} + (1+\kappa)\frac{\left|\widehat{h}_l(n-1)\right|}{2\sum_{l=0}^{L-1}|\widehat{h}_l(n-1)|}, \quad 0 \le l \le L-1, \tag{4}$$

where κ $(-1 \le \kappa < 1)$ is a parameter that controls the amount of proportionality. Looking of the equations that define the IPAPA, i.e., (1) and (2), it can be noticed that the classical APA [8] is obtained for $\mathbf{G}(n-1) = \mathbf{I}_L$ (where $\mathbf{I}_L$ is the $L \times L$ identity matrix), while the IPNLMS algorithm [9] results when $P = 1$.

In practice, it would be very computationally expensive (and also inefficient) to compute the matrix product $\mathbf{G}(n-1)\mathbf{X}(n)$ in the classical way (i.e., matrices multiplication). Hence, taking into account the diagonal character of the matrix $\mathbf{G}(n-1)$, we can evaluate

$$
\begin{aligned}
\mathbf{P}(n) &= \mathbf{G}(n-1)\mathbf{X}(n) \\
&= \left[\mathbf{g}(n-1)\odot\mathbf{x}(n)\; \mathbf{g}(n-1)\odot\mathbf{x}(n-1)\cdots\mathbf{g}(n-1)\odot\mathbf{x}(n-P+1)\right],
\end{aligned} \tag{5}
$$

where $\mathbf{g}(n-1) = \left[g_0(n-1)\; g_1(n-1)\cdots g_{L-1}(n-1)\right]^T$ is a vector containing the diagonal elements of $\mathbf{G}(n-1)$ and the operator $\odot$ denotes the Hadamard product. Using (5), the IPAPA update (2) can be rewritten as

$$
\widehat{\mathbf{h}}(n) = \widehat{\mathbf{h}}(n-1) + \alpha\mathbf{P}(n)\left[\delta\mathbf{I}_P + \mathbf{X}^T(n)\mathbf{P}(n)\right]^{-1}\mathbf{e}(n). \tag{6}
$$

However, the IPAPA does not take into account the "proportionate history" of each coefficient $\widehat{h}_l(n-1)$, with $l = 0,1,\ldots,L-1$, but only its proportionate factor from the current time sample, i.e., $g_l(n-1)$. Therefore, let us consider a modified approach in order to take advantage of the "proportionate memory" of the algorithm, by choosing the matrix [5]

$$
\mathbf{G}_l(n-1) = \mathrm{diag}\left[g_l(n-1)\; g_l(n-2)\cdots g_l(n-P)\right]. \tag{7}
$$

In this manner, we take into account the "proportionate history" of the coefficient $\widehat{h}_l(n-1)$, in terms of its proportionate factors from the last P time samples. Thus, the matrix from (5) becomes

$$
\begin{aligned}
&\mathbf{P}'(n) \\
&= \left[\mathbf{g}(n-1)\odot\mathbf{x}(n)\; \mathbf{g}(n-2)\odot\mathbf{x}(n-1)\cdots\mathbf{g}(n-P)\odot\mathbf{x}(n-P+1)\right]
\end{aligned} \tag{8}
$$

and consequently, the update (6) is

$$
\widehat{\mathbf{h}}(n) = \widehat{\mathbf{h}}(n-1) + \alpha\mathbf{P}'(n)\left[\delta\mathbf{I}_P + \mathbf{X}^T(n)\mathbf{P}'(n)\right]^{-1}\mathbf{e}(n). \tag{9}
$$

We refer to this algorithm as the "memory" IPAPA (MIPAPA) [5].

The advantage of this modification is twofold. First, the MIPAPA takes into account the "history" of the proportionate factors from the last P steps. Second, the computational complexity is lower as compared to the IPAPA. This is (8) can be recursively evaluated as

$$
\mathbf{P}'(n) = \left[\mathbf{g}(n-1)\odot\mathbf{x}(n)\; \mathbf{P}'_{-1}(n-1)\right], \tag{10}
$$

where the matrix $\mathbf{P}'_{-1}(n-1)$ contains the first $P-1$ columns of $\mathbf{P}'(n-1)$. Thus, the columns from 1 to $P-1$ of the matrix $\mathbf{P}'(n-1)$ can be used directly for computing the matrix $\mathbf{P}'(n)$ [i.e., they become the columns from 2 to P of $\mathbf{P}'(n)$].

Besides, let us examine the matrix to be inverted in the classical IPAPA, as compared to the case of the MIPAPA. In the first case, this matrix is $\mathbf{M}(n) = \delta\mathbf{I}_P + \mathbf{X}^T(n)\mathbf{P}(n)$, which is symmetric but does not have a time-shift character.

On the other hand, the matrix to be inverted in the MIPAPA is not symmetric, but has a time-shift property, which allows us to evaluate

$$\mathbf{M}'(n) = \begin{bmatrix} \delta + \mathbf{x}^T(n)\left[\mathbf{g}(n-1) \odot \mathbf{x}(n)\right] & \mathbf{x}^T(n)\mathbf{P}'_{-1}(n-1) \\ \mathbf{X}^T_{-1}(n-1)\left[\mathbf{g}(n-1) \odot \mathbf{x}(n)\right] & \mathbf{M}'_{P-1}(n-1) \end{bmatrix}, \quad (11)$$

where the matrix $\mathbf{M}'_{P-1}(n-1)$ contains the first $P-1$ columns and $P-1$ rows of the matrix $\mathbf{M}'(n-1)$ [i.e., the top-left $(P-1) \times (P-1)$ submatrix of $\mathbf{M}'(n-1)$] and the matrix $\mathbf{X}_{-1}(n-1)$ contains the first $P-1$ columns of the matrix $\mathbf{X}(n-1)$. Consequently, only the first row and the first column of $\mathbf{M}'(n)$ need to be computed. Moreover, using computationally efficient techniques to perform to the matrix inversion operation [10], the overall complexity could be further reduced.

3   Regularization Parameter

Regularization plays a fundamental role in adaptive filtering. An adaptive filter that is not properly regularized will perform very poorly. As shown in Sect. 2, a matrix inversion is required within the MIPAPA. For practical reasons, the matrix needs to be regularized before inversion, i.e., a positive constant is added to the elements of its main diagonal. Usually, this regularization is chosen as $\delta = \beta\sigma_x^2$, where $\sigma_x^2 = E\left[x^2(n)\right]$ is the variance of the zero-mean input signal $x(n)$, with $E[\cdot]$ denoting mathematical expectation, and β is a positive constant (usually referred as the normalized regularization parameter). In practice though, β is more a variable that depends on the level of the additive noise, i.e., the more the noise, the larger is the value of β.

In the case of MIPAPA, we propose to choose the constant regularization parameter based on a condition that intuitively makes sense, i.e., to attenuate the effects of the noise in the adaptive filter estimate. This idea was introduced and explained in detail in [6], in case of the NLMS-based algorithms, including IPNLMS. Moreover, as it was shown in [11,12], the regularization of APA and IPAPA does not depend on the projection order. Thus, following the idea from [6], the regularization parameter of MIPAPA is evaluated as

$$\delta = \frac{1 + \sqrt{1 + \text{SNR}}}{\text{SNR}}\sigma_x^2 = \beta_{\text{SNR}}\sigma_x^2, \quad (12)$$

where $\text{SNR} = \sigma_y^2/\sigma_v^2$, with $\sigma_y^2 = E\left[y^2(n)\right]$ and $\sigma_v^2 = E\left[v^2(n)\right]$ representing the variances of the echo signal $y(n)$ and the near-end background noise $v(n)$, respectively. In (12), the parameter β_{SNR} is the normalized regularization parameter that depends on the SNR (which could be estimated in practice).

4   Simulation Results

Simulations were performed in the context of both network and acoustic echo cancellation. Two echo paths were used, having different sparseness degree, as follows: (i) the first impulse response from G168 Recommendation [13], which can be considered to be very sparse and (ii) a measured acoustic echo path, which is less sparse. Both impulse responses have 512 coefficients, using a sampling rate of 8 kHz. The adaptive filter used in the experiments has the same length ($L = 512$).

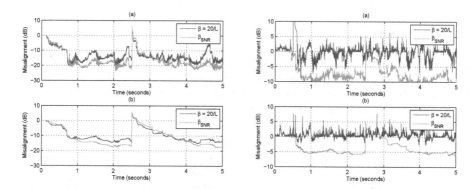

Fig. 1. Misalignment of the MIPAPA using different values of the normalized regularization parameter. (a)–*left*: G168 echo path, SNR = 20 dB; (b)–*left*: acoustic echo path, SNR = 20 dB; (a)–*right*: G168 echo path, SNR = 0 dB; (b)–*right*: acoustic echo path, SNR = 0 dB.

The input signal (i.e., the far-end signal) is a speech sequence. The output of the echo path is corrupted by an independent white Gaussian noise (i.e., the background noise at the near-end) with different SNRs, i.e., 20 dB and 0 dB. In order to evaluate the tracking capabilities of the algorithm, an echo path change scenario is simulated in the experiments, by shifting the impulse response to the right by 12 samples. The performance measure is the normalized misalignment (in dB), which is defined as $20\log_{10}\left[\left\|\mathbf{h} - \widehat{\mathbf{h}}(n)\right\| / \|\mathbf{h}\|\right]$, where $\mathbf{h}$ is the impulse response of the echo path and $\|\cdot\|$ denotes the ℓ_2 norm.

The performance of MIPAPA are compared for two types of regularization. The first one is the "classical" ad-hoc choice $\beta = 20/L$, which was the rule of thumb in many practical scenarios that involved the proportionate-type algorithms [1,2]. The second one is the proposed β_{SNR}. The step-size parameter is set to $\alpha = 0.2$, the projection order is $P = 4$, and the proportionality parameter is chosen as $\kappa = 0$.

The results are presented in Fig. 1. As we can notice from the left side of this figure (where the SNR is set to 20 dB), the performance obtained with the "classical" regularization $\beta = 20/L \approx 0.03$ are very similar to those obtained using β_{SNR}. This is expected, because if we consider $L = 512$ and SNR = 20 dB, we get $\beta_{\mathrm{SNR}} \approx 0.11$, which is quite close to the "classical" value.

The importance of the regularization parameter becomes more apparent in noisy environments. As we can notice from the right side of this figure (where

SNR = 0 dB), the MIPAPA using β_{SNR} outperforms by far the "classical" regularization. In this case, a much higher value of the normalized regularization constant is required; according to (12), for SNR = 0 dB and $L = 512$, we obtain $\beta_{\text{SNR}} \approx 2.41$, which is much higher as compared to the "classical" choice $\beta = 20/L$. Clearly, when using an improper regularization, the misalignment of the adaptive filter fluctuates much and never converges.

5 Conclusions

Adaptive filters with a large number of coefficients are usually involved in echo cancellation. In this context, the MIPAPA represents an appealing choice, since it inherits the good convergence features of the APA and also exploits the sparseness character of the echo paths (specific to the proportionate-type algorithms). However, regularization is an important component of any adaptive filter. It is as much important as the step-size parameter that controls the stability and convergence of the algorithm. In this paper, we have presented a solution to choose the regularization parameter of the MIPAPA as a function of the SNR. The goal was to attenuate the effects of the system noise in the adaptive filter estimate. Simulations performed in the context of both network and acoustic echo cancellation prove the validity of this approach in different noisy environments.

References

1. Benesty, J., Gaensler, T., Morgan, D.R., Sondhi, M.M., Gay, S.L.: Advances in Network and Acoustic Echo Cancellation. Springer, Heidelberg (2001). https://doi.org/10.1007/978-3-662-04437-7
2. Benesty, J., Huang, Y. (eds.): Adaptive Signal Processing-Applications to Real-World Problems. Springer, Heidelberg (2003). https://doi.org/10.1007/978-3-662-11028-7
3. Duttweiler, D.L.: Proportionate normalized least-mean-squares adaptation in echo cancelers. IEEE Trans. Speech Audio Process. **8**, 508–518 (2000)
4. Paleologu, C., Benesty, J., Ciochină, S.: Sparse Adaptive Filters for Echo Cancellation. Morgan & Claypool Publishers, USA (2010)
5. Paleologu, C., Ciochină, S., Benesty, J.: An efficient proportionate affine projection algorithm for echo cancellation. IEEE Signal Process. Lett. **17**, 165–168 (2010)
6. Benesty, J., Paleologu, C., Ciochină, S.: On regularization in adaptive filtering. IEEE Trans. Audio Speech Lang. Process. **19**, 1734–1742 (2011)
7. Hoshuyama, O., Goubran, R.A., Sugiyama, A.: A generalized proportionate variable step-size algorithm for fast changing acoustic environments. In: IEEE International Conference on Acoustics, Speech, and Signal Processing (ICASSP), pp. IV-161–IV-164 (2004)
8. Ozeki, K., Umeda, T.: An adaptive filtering algorithm using an orthogonal projection to an affine subspace and its properties. Electron. Commun. Jpn. **67**(A), 19–27 (1984)
9. Benesty, J., Gay, S. L.: An improved PNLMS algorithm. In: IEEE International Conference on Acoustics, Speech, and Signal Processing (ICASSP), pp. II-1881–II-1884 (2002)

10. Stanciu, C., Anghel, C., Paleologu, C., Benesty, J., Albu, F., Ciochină, S.: A proportionate affine projection algorithm using dichotomous coordinate descent iterations. In: IEEE International Symposium on Signals, Circuits and Systems (ISSCS), pp. 343–346 (2011)
11. Paleologu, C., Benesty, J., Ciochină, S.: Regularization of the affine projection algorithm. IEEE Trans. Circ. Syst. II Express **58**, 366–370 (2011)
12. Paleologu, C., Benesty, J., Albu, F.: Regularization of the improved proportionate affine projection algorithm. In: IEEE International Conference on Acoustics, Speech, and Signal Processing (ICASSP), pp. 169–172 (2012)
13. Digital Network Echo Cancellers. ITU-T Rec. G.168 (2002)

SmartGreeting: A New Smart Home System Which Enables Context-Aware Services

Ana-Maria Claudia Drăgulinescu[(⊠)], Andrei Drăgulinescu,
Ioana Marcu, Simona Halunga, and Octavian Fratu

Telecommunications Department, Electronics,
Telecommunications and Information Technology Faculty,
University "Politehnica" of Bucharest, Bucharest, Romania
amc.dragulinescu@gmail.com

Abstract. Home automation systems are expected to develop a new trend, as they embed new technologies and low-cost devices making them suitable for any budget. Nowadays, the researching efforts are dedicated to designing low-power and low-cost smart home systems that offer personalized services considering multiple scenarios that cover usual daily activities. The main goal of the paper is to analyse the digital output signal of passive infrared sensors used in a configuration of smart home entrance called SmartGreeting. The system can be used to enable personalized services in an entire smart home environment.

Keywords: Persons' counting · Personalized services · Smart home
Passive infrared sensors

1 Introduction

Currently, in home-design systems area, the research is focused on designing low-cost and energy smart home systems [1–5], on finding solutions for solving compatibility issues concerning products under different licences [6, 7] and establishing efficient communication between smart devices [8–10] from the privacy point of view [11], energy consumption [5] and complexity [1, 3]. There is also an increased interest for human usual activities recognition [12, 13], interest motivated by the need to offer context or person-aware services [14]. Moreover, there can be observed the preference for using either low-cost sensors like passive infrared sensors (PIR) [14], either signals or sensors from users' devices instead of increasing the system's infrastructure [15, 16]. Throughout this paper we propose a sensor system that greets a more complex home automation design and enables scenario-aware and person-aware services. The paper is organized as follows: In Sect. 2 we present SmartGreeting system diagram explaining its functioning, including mentions regarding the features that may be extracted and processed. Section 3 presents the methodology of features extraction and analyses the experimental results and, finally, Sect. 4 comprises our conclusions and future intentions.

© ICST Institute for Computer Sciences, Social Informatics and Telecommunications Engineering 2018
O. Fratu et al. (Eds.): FABULOUS 2017, LNICST 241, pp. 158–164, 2018.
https://doi.org/10.1007/978-3-319-92213-3_23

2   SmartGreeting System: PIR-Based Subsystem Analysis

SmartGreeting system consists in 4 sensor nodes types: *PIR* nodes (*PIRx*) based on motion sensors [17] that detect thermal energy of human bodies (presence in the environment); *window sensors (WSx)* nodes consisting in piezoelectric sensors mounted on door and windows responsible for sensing intrusive actions; *light sensors (LSx)* nodes measuring the luminance and adjusting the indoor lighting conditions, temperature and relative humidity sensors (RHT) that monitors environmental conditions and *door sensor (DS)* node with magnetic contact switch and smart lock.

From systems' workflow (Fig. 1a) it can be noticed that the system continuously determines home occupancy and for Presence detection we implement a *Presence Detection* (PD) block using an improved sensors emplacement that, in contrast to previous person's detection and counting system [18], uses data acquired from 2 digital PIR sensors to increase the performance when multiple persons enter simultaneously the residence. The entrance has $l = 100$ cm and $= 208$ cm. Preliminary tests proved that 3 persons can enter simultaneously. This worst scenario represents the main challenge when counting the persons and determining occupancy.

PIR1 and PIR2 sensors were placed at a height $h = 75$ cm on two parallel walls with an offset of 35 cm between them to give information about target detection and direction. We determined 5 detection areas in which the targets may pass. The 100-cm entrance was first divided in 3 equal regions (I–III) and the middles of these regions formed other two regions (IV–V). There are two possible directions: Left-Right or Right-Left. Thus we considered 34 scenarios that cover all possible combinations of these variables and we succeed in extracting features from 28 of them. When PD detects a scenario, *Person Counting* (PC) block increments or decrements the number of persons (PN) which determines one of the following contexts (Fig. 1b):

NOT@Home context: active when $PN = 0$. The system assumes that no occupants are inside and enables *House Breaking Protection* (HBP) which improves residence security. *Presence Simulation* (PS) simulates presence in home by turning on/off the lights and speakers based on an algorithm that follows occupants' habits. PS receives information from Luminosity Sensors through HBP which picks Door and Window vibration sensors signals and turns on alert loudspeaker. *Door lock status* (DLS) is verifies the magnetic contact switch at certain intervals established.

HomeAlone context: active when $PN = 1$ and therefore DLS and HBP are enabled. Unlike NOT@Home scenario PS is no longer required. Still *Physical Activities Monitoring* (PAM) function oversees monitoring daily activities that reflect the status of the person: sleeping, cooking, bathroom using, etc. The main challenge resides in using only PIR sensors to detect these activities. PAM block will control lighting, i.e., dependent on luminosity conditions and the detected tasks; it will turn light on/off.

Smart4Family context: available when the number of persons >1 but <*N* (previously set by the user; it reflects the maximum number of residence occupants). In this case, enabled functions are DLS and *Lighting Control* (LC). The lighting is controlled by luminosity sensor and PIR sensors data. Unlike HomeAlone scenario, PIR sensor data processing is less complex, activities monitoring being disabled.

Oxy+ context is designed to improve residence air quality when environment parameters like temperature, humidity or CO_2 are exceeding comfort thresholds or when a high number of persons is detected. It is stated that a high occupancy rate will determine environmental changes that decrease home comfort. Our system averts such situation through *Person Counting* function and RHT monitoring and activates Oxy+ before persons' number has an impact on air quality.

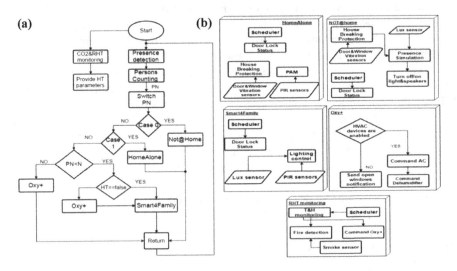

Fig. 1. a. SmartGreeting system diagram **b.** Functional blocks

3   Experimental Results: Extracted Features

To identify the number of persons that enter or exit the residence, we acquired the signals of the two digital sensors of PD subsystem when one (scenarios 17–26), two (scenarios 1–16) and three persons (scenarios 27–28) were walking in all possible directions (L-R/R-L) and regions (I–V). For two persons-scenarios, we provided all the possible combinations of directions and regions. Scenarios 17 to 21 imply L-R walking and regions I–V (in this order), while in scenarios 22 to 26 one person walked from R-L also in regions I–V. In scenarios 1–4 two persons were walking L-R/R-L, L-R/L-R, R-L/R-L, R-L/L-R, in regions I–II. Scenarios 5–8 were dedicated to II–III regions, 9–12 to I–III regions and 13–16 to IV–V regions. In 27 two persons were walking R-L and one R-L, while in 28 all persons were walking R-L. All persons walked with normal speed. Due to technical issues two or three people were asked to pass almost in the same time, in a row (not one after the other). Each scenario was repeated 6 times. We represented digital output of the two PIR sensors when one person passes L-R in regions I and III (Fig. 2) and regions II and IV (Fig. 3).

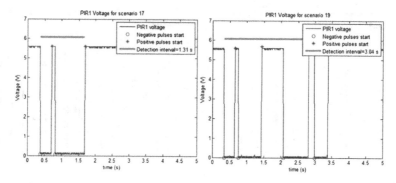

Fig. 2. PIR1 output when one person walks L-R in region I (left) and III (right)

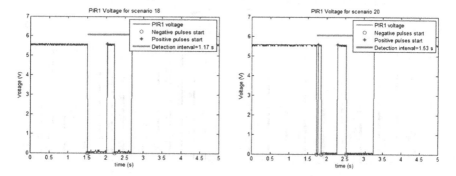

Fig. 3. PIR1 output when one person walks L-R in region II (left) and IV (right)

Digital PIR has two levels: logical 0 (motion is detected) and logical 1 (no detection occurs). Detection start and final are also marked. We observed that features like detection duration (μd), signal variance (Var), number of negative pulses (NPN), pulses width (μPN, μPP), the percentage of negative pulses duration from total duration (μ(X)) for both PIR signals (1 and 2) differentiate the scenarios. Each feature was obtained through averaging sets of values for which we computed the variance to test their reliability. Next, we analyse the importance of two features, detection duration and pulses number, in discriminating between one person and two persons scenarios.

Thresholds are set to identify the scenario. From Fig. 4 it can be seen that through regions I, II and IV L-R has duration of 1.4–1.65 s in the case of single person. New feature can be found to identify more accurately the scenario. Looking to negative pulses number (Fig. 5) we find that only for region I $PN_1 = 1$ (#17) due to the high thermal energy emitted by the very close human body. For one person Region III L-R (#19), duration threshold is irrelevant. If we analyse negative pulses number duration of PIR2 signal, we notice that only #3, #6 and #11 may be confounded with #19, but if we analyse number of negative pulses in Fig. 5, we clearly distinguish #19.

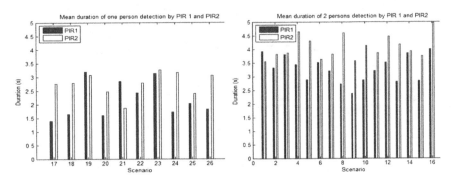

Fig. 4. Mean duration for one (left) and two persons detection (right)

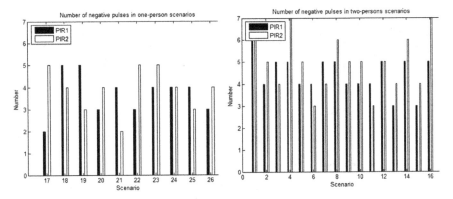

Fig. 5. Number of negative pulses for one (left) and two persons scenarios (right)

When two or more scenarios will be confounded, another feature must be analysed. When two persons walk in the same direction, the PIR that was first triggered will end the first, too. When the persons walk in different directions the PIR that was first triggered will end the last. This helps in achieving more accurately the number of persons that must be incremented or decremented. If our system recognises a scenario in which two persons walk in the same direction, it will decrement/increment with 2.

4   Conclusions and Future Research

The novelty of the system consists in the activation of system tasks according to the continuously updated occupancy detected. Moreover, we succeed in designing a new low-price (under 35€) and low-complexity configuration that gives important information about residence occupancy using two digital PIR sensors output and scenario recognition. In future, we intend to compare other features (pulses durations and signal variation) and their performance in discriminating between all three types of scenarios (one, two and three persons). Future efforts will be dedicated to the walking of the persons one after the other, building and training a classifier for scenario recognition that uses the features extracted. Also, we intend to embed in our system acoustic sensors and test new audio features.

Acknowledgments. This work was supported by a grant of the Ministry of Innovation and Research, UEFISCDI, project number 5 Sol/2017 within PNCDI III.

References

1. Ransing, R.S., Rajput, M.: Smart home for elderly care, based on wireless sensor network. In: 2015 International IEEE Conference on Nascent Technologies in the Engineering Field (ICNTE-2015), Navi Mumbai, pp. 1–5 (2015)
2. Tharishny, S., Umayal, S.S., Nair, P.: Android based smart house control via wireless communication. Int. J. Sci. Eng. Technol. **5**(5), 323–325 (2016)
3. Nayan, N.A., Ikhsan, I.A.M., Takahashi, Y.: Using ZigBee communication technology in a smart home wireless sensor network. In: Proceedings of Second International Conference on Modern Trends in Science, Engineering and Technology (ICMTSET), Dubai, pp. 19–25 (2014)
4. Obaid, T., Rashed, H., Nour, A.A.E., Rehan, M., Saleh, M.M., Tarique, M.: ZigBee based voice controlled wireless smart home system. Int. J. Wirel. Mob. Netw. (IJWMN) **6**(1), 47–59 (2014)
5. Zamora-Martinez, F., Romeu, P., Botella-Rocamora, P., Pardo, J.: On-line learning of indoor temperature forecasting models towards energy efficiency. Energy Build. J. **83**, 162–172 (2014)
6. Bellochio, E., Constante, G., Cascianelli, S., Valigi, P., Ciarfuglia, T.A.: SmartSEAL: a ROS based home automation framework for heterogeneous devices interconnection in smart buildings. In: 2016 IEEE International Smart Cities Conference (ISC2), Trento, pp. 1–6 (2016)
7. Mihaylov, M., Mihovska, A., Kyriazakos, S., Prasad, R.: Interoperable eHealth platform for personalized smart services. In: 2015 IEEE International Conference on Communication Workshop (ICCW), London, pp. 240–245 (2015)
8. Kumar, S., Lee, S.R.: Android based smart home system with control via Bluetooth and internet connectivity. In: 18th IEEE International Symposium on Consumer Electronics (ISCE 2014), Jeju Island, pp. 1–2 (2014)
9. Mihovska, A., Kyriazakos, S. A., Prasad, R., Pejanovic-Djurisic, M., Poulkov, V.: Integration of wireless and data technologies for personalized smart applications. In: 2015 IEEE Wireless Telecommunications Symposium (WTS), New York, pp. 1–8 (2015)
10. Pham, M., Mengistu, Y., Do, H.M., Sheng, W.: Cloud-based smart home environment (CoSHE) for home healthcare. In: 2016 IEEE International Conference on Automation Science and Engineering (CASE), Fort Worth, pp. 483–488 (2016)
11. Kumar, P., Gurtov, A., Iinatti, J., Yliantilla, M., Sain, M.: Lightweight and secure session-key establishment scheme in smart home environment. IEEE Sens. J. **16**(1), 254–263 (2016)
12. Tonchev, K., et al.: Recognition of human daily activities. In: 2015 IEEE International Conference on Communication Workshop (ICCW), London, pp. 290–293 (2015)
13. Kashimoto, Y., et al.: Floor vibration type estimation with piezo sensor toward indoor positioning system. In: 2016 International Conference on Indoor Positioning and Indoor Navigation (IPIN), Alcala de Henares, pp. 1–6 (2016)

14. Al-Naimi, I., Wong, C.B., Moore, P., Chen X.: Advanced approach for indoor identification and tracking using smart floor and pyroelectric infrared sensors. In: 5th International Conference on Information and Communication Systems (ICICS), Irbid, pp. 1–6 (2014)

15. Ma, W., Zhu, X., Huang, J., Shou, G.: Detecting pedestrians behaviour in building based on Wi-Fi signals. In: IEEE International Conference on Smart City/SocialCom/SustainCom (SmartCity), Chengdu, pp. 1–8 (2015)

16. Wannenburg, J., Malekian, R.: Physical activity recognition from smartphone accelerometer data for user context awareness sensing. In: IEEE Trans. Syst. Man Cybern. Syst. **PP**(99), pp. 1–8 (2014)

17. Pololu Robotics and Electronics: PIR Motion sensor. www.pololu.com/product/2731

18. Drăgulinescu, A.M.C, Marcu, I., Halunga, S., Fratu, O.: Persons counting and monitoring system based on passive infrared sensors and ultrasonic sensors (PIRUS). In: 2nd EAI International Conference on Future Access Enablers of Ubiquitous and Intelligent Infrastructures, Belgrad (2016)

Session on Multimedia Security and Forensics

A New Approach in Creating Decision Systems Used for Speaker Authentication

Vlad Andrei Cârstea, Robert Alexandru Dobre,
Claudia Cristina Oprea$^{(\boxtimes)}$, and Radu Ovidiu Preda

Telecommunications Department, Politehnica University of Bucharest,
Iuliu Maniu Blvd. 1-3, 69121 Bucharest, Romania
rdobre@elcom.pub.ro, {cristina, radu}@comm.pub.ro

Abstract. This paper discusses a new approach of a Decision System to be used in Speaker Authentication applications, with particular emphasis on security systems with a small programming data set. This decision system is based on the adjoining of a matched filter response of the two compared signals considering the position of the maximum onto the abscissa of the response graph and afterwards, the use of Kullback – Leibler divergence for comparing the Mel Frequency Cepstral Coefficients' statistical distribution of the password and input speech signal.

Keywords: Speaker authentication · Matched filter
Kullback – Leibler divergence · Mel Frequency Cepstral Coefficients
Security system

1 Introduction

This article aims to provide a new type of decision system for use in the Speaker Authentication domain, itself a subfield of Automatic Speech Recognition. According to [1], Speaker Authentication is the process in which the claimant identifies himself by speech which is recorded as a signal and is tested against the reference model or password (also a speech signal previously created) to verify the claim.

Most of the systems in this field did not use or aimed to create particular methods of analysis of the speech signal but borrowed existing methods from the parent domain of Automatic Speech Recognition. The literature offers algorithms like Gaussian Mixture Models (GMM) [2], Vector Quantization (VQ) [3] or Searching for Digital Watermarking (DW) [4, 5] among mainstay. This paper proposes a new approach. A better understanding of human voice in its biological, phonetic and information carrying aspects yield better methods to be used as decision in an authentication system, namely a matched filter used in conjunction with Kullback – Leibler Divergence.

2 Voice Apparatus

It is known that voice is a sound wave emanating from vibratory parts of our body. We consider voice only that continuous scale of frequencies of the elastic wave that can produce excitation to our auditory apparatus. We consider regular speech that

© ICST Institute for Computer Sciences, Social Informatics and Telecommunications Engineering 2018
O. Fratu et al. (Eds.): FABULOUS 2017, LNICST 241, pp. 167–172, 2018.
https://doi.org/10.1007/978-3-319-92213-3_24

frequency band in which mutually intelligible messages can be sent between humans. The voice apparatus consists of the air pressure system, the vibratory and the resonating system. It creates different parameters of sound (pitch, loudness, tempo) and amplifies or reduces voice harmonics.

It is necessary to study the way voice exits our mouth for information transmission. According to [6], when speaking in any language we produce phonemes which are defined and we distinguish between them by their place of articulation which is the position of the mouth organs (lips, teeth, tongue etc.) at the moment of utterance and the by the manner of articulation which arises from all organs' positions obstructing the airflow column.

From this paragraph, it can be extrapolated that voiced and voiceless phonemes exist. Voiced phonemes are those whose sound wave is quasi-periodic and voiceless are those aperiodic sound waves.

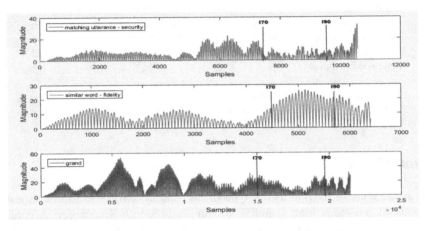

Fig. 1. The position of the maximum in the first case corresponds to a matching utterance of the word *security*. Note that the graph has maximum after the 90th interval. In the case of the second graph, we have a paronym to *security*, namely *fidelity*, so the maximum value is between 70th and 90th intervals. In the case of the different word, *grand*, the maximum is around the beginning of the response, before the 70th interval, thus the word is rejected.

3 Matched Filters

The matched filter implemented in this paper is the first decision test for a speech signal which is compared to the stored password. It acts as a trigger for the more refined statistical Kullback – Leibler divergence method. Of interest is the position of the maxima on the abscissa of the matched filter response for reasons which shall be further detailed.

A matched filter is typically a linear filter that cross-correlates a known signal with a received signal which has noise added to it and finds if in the received signal, the original one is present. Of course, the goal is not to find a signal in a noisy one but to find if a signal is present in another and thus consider the second signal as noise which adds difference in information to the searched signal (any other phonemes/words than the searched one contains is considered added noise).

Based on [7], a filter matched to the signal $s(t)$ will have the impulse response:

$$h(t) = k \cdot s(T - t) , \tag{1}$$

where k and T are arbitrary constants.

As mentioned, it is not of interest if the two utterance signals are perfectly corre-lated between them because this would prove impossible with respect to the complexity of even a short vocal signal. The matched filter is primarily used to analyze the signal in time domain and to detect if the words in the two signals are the same, if they are paronyms or if they are totally different. If the filter response is analyzed, it shall be observed that the autocorrelation of the known signal with itself has on the response graph (here always restricted to the support of the known signal) the maximum value with its abscissa as the last value of the support. Now for two different utterances, it was observed that the value of the maximum is of no use, for example it can happen to be higher for different words than for similar utterances. For this, the system does not analyze quantitatively the matched filter response but qualitatively. We are not inter-ested in the value of the maximum but in its position onto the abscissa and thus the ability of the graph to tend to the autocorrelation one.

For this decision system, it was decided to analyze the position of the maximum by dividing the abscissa of the response in 100 equally spaced intervals and to formulate an answer based on which interval the maximum is situated in. For example, if the maximum is in the first 70 intervals, the filtered signals are majorly different and the system rejects the speech signal. No further decision methods are taken. If the signal is between the intervals 70 to 90, there is a fair possibility that the signals match but decision is taken by a further test. If the maximum is situated in an interval greater than 90 it can be stated that the two utterances match and the divergence test has a great probability of confirming this match. Some situations are illustrated in Fig. 1.

4   Mel Frequency Cepstral Coefficients

Mel Frequency Cepstral Coefficients are the constituents of the Mel Frequency Cep-strum which characterize the power spectrum of a sound wave, over a short time interval. They are linked directly with the sound properties of pitch, loudness and duration. Based on [8] it can be concluded that they are used to extract important linguistic features definitory for each voice in performing automatic speech recogni-tion, in general, and speaker authentication, in particular. They are centered on the information carrying part of the voice disregarding noisy parts and other non-useful signals. Voice is formed and influenced by the vocal tract and the mouth. The shapes of all these organs are represented mathematically as the envelope of the short time power spectrum. Because of the distinctive perception of sound humans have, we need to use the Mel scale, a scale which links our perception of frequency with the real frequency scale in a non-linear manner.

5 Kullback – Leibler Divergence

The Kullback – Leibler Divergence is the second, more refined, test in this decision system. It analyzes the speech and the password subjectively because ultimately this system is used by humans, if we develop powerful objective decision methods we will not be able to obtain a positive system response because our utterances even if we hear them as similar are physically, profoundly different sound waves in terms of frequency, amplitude, duration, envelope of the wave. The Kullback – Leibler divergence is not applied to the signals but to the Mel Frequency Cepstral Coefficients extracted from the vocal waves. The password is formed from five utterances of the same word of which the median one, the third is considered as a reference signal.

5.1 Deriving the Kullback – Leibler Divergence

This divergence is the measurement of discrimination between two probability density functions (PDF). It measures how one PDF diverges from another expected PDF. Regarding information theory, an important measured parameter is entropy which give us an idea of how many units of information are necessary to encode the message. Starting from this, the divergence adds in the logarithmic comparison, another distribution and returning to us the expected logarithmic difference between the first and second distribution.

In terms of information theory, it tells us the number of information units we expect to lose from the first distribution if it is approximated by the second. For two gaussian distributions, P and Q, the Kullback – Leibler divergence is a scalar with:

$$KL(P, Q) = \ln\frac{\sigma_2}{\sigma_1} + \frac{\sigma_1^2 + (\mu_1 - \mu_2)^2}{2\sigma_2^2} - \frac{1}{2} \tag{2}$$

After the Mel Frequency Cepstral Coefficients of each of the five password constituent signals are computed, and of the speech signal to be compared, if we look at the histogram of magnitude versus number of coefficients, they tend to respect a normal distribution. Thus, a Gaussian is fitted for each signal. For the password, the divergence of the four signals versus the reference signal is computed. Finally, the divergence of the speech signal versus the reference signal is computed and we look to see if it is in the range of the password divergences. If the matched filter did not reject the signal and so it arrived up to this point into the algorithm, we have three decision options. If the maximum was above the 90th interval and the divergences correspond, the response is "positive". If the maximum was above the 90th or 70th interval but the divergences did not match the response is "reject". If the maximum was above the 70th interval and the divergences correspond we repeat three times the process, then decide if "positive" or "reject".

6 System Performances

Let us consider some graphs of performance of this decision system which was implemented in a security system such that, from this security perspective we shall look upon them. For each of the graphs below, 20 consecutive utterances were performed and their results were rounded. In the first, the password and the utterances were of the same user, in the second there is a corroboration of the results taken from three different users trying to crack the password in different scenarios. It is worth to mention that these results were obtained from low security passwords, words like *open, password, sharply* and still they yielded good results for a five signal formed password and 20 utterances. It is especially good to see that the passwords with predominant voiceless phonemes (*sharply*) gave a 10% increase in the strength of the password and decision results as it can be seen in Fig. 2.

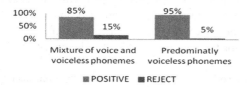

Fig. 2. The results obtained when the authorized user uttered his password.

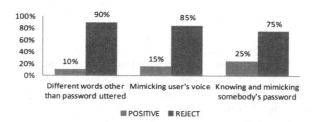

Fig. 3. Here three cases of password breaching by an impostor are presented. Of course the parameter relevant here is the percentage of rejection in each case, which is 75% even if the impostor knows the password yet he still needs to utter it – here lies the strength of the system, as it is not enough to know the password but it also need to be reproduced.

Table 1. Performance comparison between various systems. All results are rounded.

System	Performances [%]	Observations
Ours	85%–95%	Depends on phoneme composition
GMM	80%–87%	Depends on model order 8–16
VQ	57%–95%	Depends on codeblocks (i.e. speakers) 1–8
DW	51%–94%	Depends on test database

Regarding other systems' performances especially with respect to ours in Fig. 2, we analyzed the systems mentioned in sources [2, 3, 5] under tests as much as appropriate to ours namely small input database (5 utterances of 3 s each), small password length, around 3 s, Mel Frequency Cepstral Coefficients when present (Fig. 3 and Table 1).

7   Conclusions

The decision system is versatile, with the "reject" percentage highly influenced by the matched filter interval choice, which can easily be adapted to any language and calibrated after more testing, the choice in this paper was more to explain the concept and so they can be further and further narrowed for better results. Still by knowing both the password and how the user's voice sounds, the ratio of "positive"/"reject" was only 1/4 and this for a low security password, as mentioned. With further tests and more calibration, the performances of a security system with this decision system can be much improved. The authors recommend for this decision system, if used in a security system, as it was the original intent, to use as passwords, speech signals which are profoundly voiceless, for they are more difficult to be breached.

Acknowledgment. This work was supported by a grant of the Romanian National Authority for Scientific Research and Innovation, CNCS/CCCDI - UEFISCDI, project number PN-III-P2-2.1-PED-2016-1465, within PNCDI III.

References

1. Beigi, H.: Speaker recognition. In: Yang, J. (ed.) Biometrics, p. 7. InTech (2011)
2. Reynolds, D.A., Rose, R.C.: Robust text-independent speaker identification using Gaussian mixture speaker models. IEEE Trans. Speech Audio Process. **3**, 72–83 (1995)
3. Hasan, R., Jamil, M., Rabbani, G., Rahman, S.: Speaker identification using Mel Frequency Cepstral Coefficients. In: 3rd International Conference on Electrical and Computer Engineering. ICECE, Dhaka (2004)
4. Faundez-Zanuy, M., Hagmuller, M., Kubin, G.: Speaker verification security improvement by means of speech watermarking. Speech Comun. **48**, 1608–1619 (2006)
5. Nematollahi, M.A., Akhaee, M.A., Al-Haddad, S.A.R., Gamboa-Rosales, H.: Semi-fragile digital speech watermarking for online speaker recognition. EURASIP J. Audio Speech Music Process. (2015). https://doi.org/10.1186/s13636-015-0074-5
6. Ladeforged, P., Johnson, K.: A Course in Phonetics, 6th edn. Cengage Learning. Inc., Boston (2010)
7. Turin, G.L.: An introduction to matched filters. IRE Trans. Inf. Theory **6**, 311–329 (1960)
8. Quatieri, Th.F.: Discrete Time Speech Signal Processing. Prentice-Hall, Upper Saddle River (2002)

Efficient Transform Coefficient Coding
in HEVC

Claudia C. Oprea[✉], Radu O. Preda, Ionut Pirnog,
and Robert Al. Dobre

Telecommunication Department, University Politehnica of Bucharest,
Iuliu Maniu 1-3, 061071 Bucharest, Romania
{cristina, radu, ionut}@comm.pub.ro,
rdobre@elcom.pub.ro

Abstract. This paper presents an efficient coding method of transform coefficients in HEVC video encoding standard. Our approach makes use of spectral characteristics of the transform unit coefficients in inter predicted coding units. Also a coefficient significance assessment algorithm is integrated into the video encoder, for a non-zero coefficients number reduction. It is shown to be a good method from the compression point of view, without quality losses.

Keywords: HEVC · Transform coefficient · Residual coding
Significant coefficients

1 Introduction .

The successor of the video coding standard H.264/AVC, H.265/HEVC, brought innovation into multiple video encoding algorithms and succeeds to outperform the compression efficiency of its predecessor, without any visible loss in visual quality. HEVC includes the regular video coding sections: prediction in space and time, residual transform, and entropy coding.

Frames are split into large coding units (LCUs), which are further partitioned recursively in a quad-tree structure of coding units (CUs). CUs occur in miscellaneous sizes depending on the actual frame content needed to be predicted, starting from 64×64 pixels all the way down to 8×8 pixels. CUs represent the basic unit of prediction in HEVC and they come in two flavors: intra or inter coded. A CU can be divided using one of eight partition modes, depending on the prediction type, so inter CUs are allowed to be as small as 8×4 pixels and 4×8 pixels, indicating there is no 4×4 motion compensation. In inter prediction, like AVC, HEVC has 2 reference lists for single or bi-directional prediction, and can hold up to 16 references each. By limiting the smallest inter block to be one directional predicted, there is less reading from memory and more time and power, so a longer battery life for example.

A residual signal is coded for each coding unit and HEVC supports four transform sizes: 4×4, 8×8, 16×16 and 32×32 pixels. The transform is based on the discrete cosine transform (DCT) and uses basis matrices with approximated integer coefficients, so there is not possible to have a perfect reconstruction after the inverse

© ICST Institute for Computer Sciences, Social Informatics and Telecommunications Engineering 2018
O. Fratu et al. (Eds.): FABULOUS 2017, LNICST 241, pp. 173–178, 2018.
https://doi.org/10.1007/978-3-319-92213-3_25

transform. Non-square CUs are coded using square transform units (TUs). Another quad-tree structure is used to split the residual of a CU into TUs (residual quad-tree - RQT). Supposing a TU has non-zero coefficients, a coded block flag is set to notify it, while the residual coding is signaling the location and the values of those significant coefficients.

This paper focuses on the selection of the significant transform coefficients. Not all non-zero coefficients are actually important for a good frame reconstruction, while the elimination of those considered less important proves to be a favorable solution for bitstream reduction, without perceptual losses in visual quality. The simulations performed on five test videos, concerning only a 4×4 TU size, show minor or no losses in perceptual quality and an improved bitrate value.

2 Residual Coding in HEVC

Four options regarding the residual coding are available in HEVC. First, the difference between the original block and its prediction is transformed, quantized and passed to the entropy coder. Second choice in the standard specification is to skip 4×4 transform and apply the quantization directly to the non-transformed residual signal. Third, transform and quantization can be omitted and the residual is coded directly by CABAC (context adaptive binary arithmetic coding). Last option is to apply pulse-code modulation (PCM) to the original CU, without prediction, transform and everything else.

Our approach concerns the first option, the one most commonly used. The standard specification guide only the inverse transform at the decoder side, leaving the encoder implementation free from regulation. Obviously, the direct transform in the encoder will use the same basis matrices specified for the decoder, while any other method regarding a significant coefficient selection is left at the developer's choice.

There is a single entropy coding method used in HEVC, context adaptive binary arithmetic coding (CABAC), unlike AVC that sustains also context adaptive variable length coding (CAVLC). TUs coefficients are coded in the bitstream differently from AVC: starting with the last position, the coefficients are scanned diagonally, and for each group of 4×4 values, a bit indicates a non-zero value in the 16 coefficients group. Then for each of the non-zero coefficients in a group, the remainder of the level is signaled. Naturally, any residual coefficient decided to be less important by an external algorithm will be omitted from the bitstream, thus conducting to a smaller video bitrate. Such an algorithm should maintain overall visual quality.

Similar attempts were made in the past. An all-zero block detection scheme is proposed in [1], prior to DCT, to reduce the encoding complexity. The aim is the detection of all-zero-quantized blocks, before DCT, so that the following stages of the transform and quantization can be skipped. The drawback of this approach is that it uses the relationship between Hadamard and DCT transform kernels, in a scenario when the encoder performs rate distortion optimization (RDO). RDO is scarcely ever done in real time low-complexity encoders.

More complex research in [2] develop a DCT-based local distortion detection probability (LDDP) model, that can estimate a degree of distortion visibility for any distribution of the transform coefficients regardless the TU size. A perceptual video coding scheme, HEVC compliant, is implemented based on the LDDP model, so that transform coefficients are sufficiently suppressed when possible, in order to obtain a significant bitrate reduction. Another kind of optimization approach is described in [3], which is to early detect zero quantized transform coefficients in 4 × 4 TUs, before implementing transform and quantization. The authors propose two sufficient prediction conditions that are mathematically deduced and relate to DCT, then show the proposed algorithm is able to efficiently predict all-zero 4 × 4 blocks when higher QP (quantization parameter) values are used.

In [4] is presented a method of transcoding of HEVC encoded video. The approach enables a fast transcoding by removing some carefully selected coefficients from the bitstream. The removal of coefficients is done on the bitstream level and provides a bit rate reduction of up to 10%, with the image quality decrease of about 0.2–0.5 dB.

Our approach follows the idea in [4], but is not influenced by the quantization parameter value, nor uses complex algorithms to perceptually assess the transform coefficients' significance. It is inspired by an older algorithm proposed in H.264/AVC reference software, JM [5], and can be used by low-complexity encoders.

3 Transform Coefficient Significance Method

It is quite common in video coding that a substantial number of transform coefficients of the prediction residual are quantized to zero or very small amplitude levels. Considerable bitrate savings can be obtained if these small amplitude levels coefficients, when placed nearby other zero-coefficients, could be reduced to zero as well, without losing quality. This usually orders zeros in the quantized residual coefficient block into long sequential runs that can be encoded efficiently with run-length coding, as previously has been done in JM reference software for H.264/AVC. In the following, the 4 × 4 DCT and the associated quantization functions used by HEVC are briefly presented, which is useful to derive the proposed algorithm for coefficient significance assessment.

Consider the residual 4 x 4 block $r(x, y), 0 \le x, y \le 3$, applied to a 4 × 4 transform in the horizontal and vertical directions, where C is the two-dimensional transform matrix:

$$C = \begin{bmatrix} 64 & 64 & 64 & 64 \\ 83 & 36 & -36 & -83 \\ 64 & -64 & -64 & 64 \\ 36 & -83 & 83 & -36 \end{bmatrix}, \tag{1}$$

In order to achieve more computational efficiency, the standard specifies only multiplication, addition and shift operations in integer arithmetic in the formula of the transform coefficient block, $t(u, v), 0 \le u, v \le 3$:

$$t(u, v) = \left\{ \sum\nolimits_{x=0}^{3} C(u, x) \cdot \left[\left(\sum\nolimits_{y=0}^{3} r(x, y) \cdot C^T(y, v) + 1 \right) \gg 1 \right] + 2^7 \right\} \gg 8, \tag{2}$$

where C^T is the transposed matrix of C, and $\gg$ represents a binary shift to the right.

The quantized transform coefficient, $z(u, v), 0 \leq u, v \leq 3$ is obtained as

$$z(u, v) = sign(t(u, v)) \cdot [(|t(u, v)| \cdot m + e) \gg qbits], \tag{3}$$

where $qbits = 19 + floor(QP/6)$, QP is the quantization parameter, and $e = \vartheta \ll (qbits - 9)$. The offset parameter ϑ is 171 in intra prediction and 85 for inter prediction, while $\ll$ represents a binary shift to the left. The multiplication factor m depends on the quantization parameter and is given in Table 1, as specified by the standard documentation [6].

Table 1. Multiplication factor m.

QP%6	0	1	2	3	4	5
m	26,214	23,302	20,56	18,396	16,384	14,564

At this stage of the encoding process, having the transformed and quantized coefficients in a 4×4 block, the following modified algorithm in [5] is applied. The main purpose is to prevent that single or so-called "expensive" coefficients are coded. Using a TU size of 4×4, there are chances that a single coefficient in a 8×8 CU or 16×16 CU may be non-zero. For example, in JM reference software for H.264/AVC, one single small coefficient (AC level equal to 1) costs at least 3 bits for the coefficient, 4 bits for the EOBs (end of block) for the 4×4 blocks, possible even more bits for the coded block pattern. The total cost for that single small coefficient will then typically be around 10–12 bits.

```
initialize number_zeros = 16;
for(all z(u,v) coefficients) {
if(current_coef_z(u,v) != 0) {
    decrease number_zeros;
    if(current_coef_z(u,v) > amplitude_threshold)    {
        cost(current_coef_z(u,v)) += maximum_cost;
    }
    else {
        cost(current_coef_z(u,v)) += cost_threshold(number_zeros);
    }
    next current_coef_z;
    update number_zeros;
}
}
for(all z(u,v) coefficients) {
    if(cost(current_coef_z(u,v)) > 4) {
        keep coefficient value;
    }
else {
        discard coefficient value;
    }
}
```

The basic idea from H.264/AVC reference software was to keep tracking the number of consecutive zero values in the 4×4 transformed and quantized vector of coefficients. While the consecutive zeros count increases, the cost threshold for a discarded coefficient decreases, thus making the encoding process more efficient. The thresholds in JM have been adapted to the corresponding values needed in HEVC, also the amplitude threshold has been updated: only coefficients having the quantized value smaller than the amplitude threshold can be discarded (set to zero).

4 Implementation and Experimental Results

We simulate the algorithm for coefficient discarding using HEVC reference software provided by ITU-T [7]. The test configuration used a TU size of 4 × 4 pixels independent of the CU size. The algorithm for coefficient elimination run at three QP values, uniformly distributed in the overall QP range (from 0 to 51): $QP \in \{10, 26, 42\}$. Two types of amplitude threshold were taken into consideration: a fix threshold and a content adaptive threshold, computed as the local mean luminance, transformed and quantized according to the current QP value. The fix amplitude threshold is set to a relatively reduced value in order to select only coefficients that have very small values and assign them a low cost of discarding. When the elimination cost is high, the coefficient will remain as it is in the final encoded bitstream, while a lower cost indicates a coefficient to be discarded.

Simulations have been performed for a set of five test videos, all taken at full high definition resolution, 1920 × 1080 p. Objective perceptual visual quality evaluation has been applied to establish the performance of the algorithm presented in this study. We used the structural similarity distortion metric (SSIM) described in [8] for perceptual quality evaluation. In Table 2, the simulations show a distortion metric index that is not implying a decrease in visual quality, since the difference relative to the original sequence can be found at the third and fourth decimal place. There is though a better performance in bitrate in the case of the algorithm with adaptive local amplitude threshold (*ATh*) compared to the fix threshold algorithm (*FTh*), that suggests there is a correlation between the coefficient elimination and the visual contrast sensitivity threshold.

Table 2. BD rate and encoding time of the proposed method with respect to the reference software HM in main profile.

Test sequences	BD rate (*FTh*) Y[%]	Ratio-time (*FTh*) [%]	BD rate (*ATh*) Y[%]	Ratio-time (*ATh*) [%]
CrowdRun	−0.2	−4.3	0.14	−2.7
DucksTakeOff	0.1	−5.0	0.22	−2.1
ParkJoy	−0.1	−3.7	−0.08	−1.7
RiverBed	−3.3	−3.5	−3.5	−2.04
Sunflower	−2.6	−2.4	−2.6	−1.9

The efficiency of the proposed method is measured by the Bjontegaard Distortion Rate (BD-Rate) in Table 2. Also called Bjontegaard delta rate, this parameter corresponds to the average bit rate difference in percent for the same PSNR (Peak Signal to Noise Ratio). The bit rate difference is considered between the proposed algorithm and the original unmodified HM encoder. The percentage ratio-time measure in Table 2 [9] was used to compare the encoding time between the proposed algorithm and the reference software.

5   Conclusions

This paper presents an improved transformed and quantized coefficient elimination system using two types of amplitude thresholding. The bitrate reduction for the proposed algorithm is visible in Table 2 from the BD rate parameter. Further investigations will be done in the future for the following TU sizes, to analyze the same approach for extended depths in the RQT structure.

Acknowledgment. This work was supported by a grant of the Romanian National Authority for Scientific Research and Innovation, CNCS/CCCDI - UEFISCDI, project number PN-III-P2-2.1-PED- 2016-1465, within PNCDI III.

References

1. Bumshik, L., Jaehong, J., Munchurl, K.: An all-zero block detection scheme for low-complexity HEVC encoders. IEEE Trans. Multimedia **18**(7), 1257–1268 (2016)
2. Sung-Ho, B., Jaeil, K., Munchurl, K.: HEVC-based perceptually adaptive video coding using a DCT-based local distortion detection probability model. IEEE Trans. Image Process. **25**(7), 3343–3357 (2016)
3. Hanli, W., Han, D., Weiyao, L., Sam, K., Oscar, C., Jun, W., Zhihua, W.: Early detection of all-zero 4 × 4 blocks in high efficiency video coding. J. Vis. Commun. Image R **25**, 1784–1790 (2014)
4. Wegner, K., Karwowski, D., Klimaszewski, K., Stankowski, J., Stankiewicz, O., Grajek, T.: Homogenous HEVC video transcoding by transform coefficient removal. In: International Conference on Systems, Signals and Image Processing (IWSSIP) (2017). ISBN: 978-1-5090-6344-4
5. H.264/AVC JM Reference Software, August 2008
6. ITU-T, Series H: Audiovisual and Multimedia Systems, H.265. High Efficiency video coding (2015)
7. ITU-T Recommendation H.265.2: Reference software for ITU-T H.265 high efficiency video coding
8. Wang, Z., Bovik, A.C., Sheikh, H.R., Simoncelli, E.P.: Image quality assessment: from error visibility to structural similarity. IEEE Trans. Image Process. **13**(4), 600–612 (2004)
9. Oprea, C.C., Udrea, R.M., Pirnog, I.: HEVC intra partitioning and mode decision using histograms of oriented gradients. In: 12th IEEE International Symposium on Electronics and Telecommunications (ISETC) (2016)

Investigation on a Multimedia Forensic Noise Reduction Method Based on Proportionate Adaptive Algorithms

Robert Alexandru Dobre[(⊠)], Constantin Paleologu,
Cristian Negrescu, and Dumitru Stanomir

Telecommunications Department, Politehnica University of Bucharest,
Iuliu Maniu blvd. 1-3, 69121 Bucharest, Romania
{rdobre, negrescu, dumitru.stanomir}@elcom.pub.ro,
pale@comm.pub.ro

Abstract. In the modern era, audio or video recording is at everyone's disposal any time with very low costs. Technology advances allow cameras and microphones to be installed in the most casual accessories like eyeglasses or clothes. Moreover, multimedia editing is also massively available. Near professional forgeries can be made using free software. Given the aforementioned conditions, it is understandable why multimedia forensics is a topic of great importance nowadays. The paper presents the performances obtained by using proportionate adaptive algorithms in a forensic noise reduction application, i.e., recovering a speech signal drowned in loud music, and argues why these algorithms could be preferred in such application.

Keywords: Adaptive filters · Affine projection algorithm (APA)
Noise reduction · Multimedia forensic

1 Introduction

Considering the scenario in which some people are going to have a conversation which they want to keep secret, what can they do to protect their speech from being recorded by a microphone already placed in the room? It is most likely that they will turn any nearby audio system loud so the music will mask the speech. The microphone will record the very loud music mixed with the speech signal, both affected by the acoustic parameters of the room (reflections will also be recorded) which can be modelled as a finite impulse response (FIR) filter. The progress recorded by the music identification software (Shazam, SoundHound) makes possible the identification of the song. Given the recorded speech drowned in loud music and the studio quality version of the identified song that was played in the room, can the speech be extracted? This situation represents a typical adaptive filtering problem, which is known as system identification [1] (illustrated in Fig. 1), where $s(t)$ is the speech signal, $n(t - \tau)$ is the part of the masking musical signal played in the room, $h(t)$ is the acoustic impulse response of the room, $record(t)$ is the signal recorded by the concealed microphone, $n(t)$ is the identified, full length, studio quality masking melody (found using a music identification software), $h_{est}(t)$ is the impulse response of the adaptive filter (which will estimate the acoustic impulse response of the room), and $n_{hest}(t - \tau)$ is the estimated replica of the masking musical signal. By subtracting $record(t)$ and $n_{hest}(t - \tau)$, a very good estimate of the speech signal will be extracted.

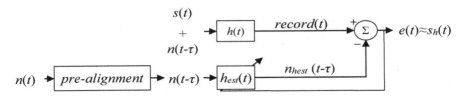

Fig. 1. Graphical illustration of the adaptive system identification configuration in terms of the situation discussed in the paper.

It is almost impossible for the recording to start at the exact time the melody is turned on in the room. A pre-alignment operation (e.g., based on the autocorrelation function between the recorded signal and the studio quality song) is introduced to ease the effort of the adaptive filter. The situation is detailed in [2], which also contains the implementation of the system using the recursive least-squares (RLS) algorithm [1] in Simulink. It was shown in [3] that the basic RLS algorithm, has poor performances if the acoustic properties of the room vary in time, which is the case in a real situation, and an improved version of the system, based on variable forgetting factor RLS (VFF-RLS) algorithm [4] was proposed and provided better results. The disadvantage of the algorithms from the RLS family is the high computational cost. This issue is addressed in this paper in which the affine projection algorithm (APA) [5] and one of its proportionate versions are investigated when used to estimate the impulse response of the room and extract the masked speech signal.

The paper is organized as follows: in Sect. 2 the APA and its proportionate variants are described, Sect. 3 shows the results and Sect. 4 concludes the paper.

2   The Affine Projection Algorithm (APA)

An adaptive filter is synthesized based on an adaptive algorithm that aims to minimize a cost function using two available signals: an input signal [typically denoted with $x(n)$] and a desired signal [typically denoted with $d(n)$]. In the example from the introduction, $record(t)$ is the desired signal, and the pre-aligned $n(t - \tau)$ musical signal is the input signal.

The APA is a very attractive choice being placed (in terms of convergence speed) between the least mean squares (LMS) or the normalized LMS (NLMS) and the RLS, but also from the computational complexity point of view. An adaptive algorithm performance is evaluated in terms of convergence speed and misadjustment. Ideally, in the system identification problem, the adaptive filter will, model the targeted filter after some time. The shorter this time, the faster the convergence speed of the algorithm. In real situations, it is almost impossible for the adaptive filter to perfectly match the filter to be estimated. This remnant difference is called the misadjustment. Obviously, a small misadjustment is desired. The evolution of the adaptive filter over time can be evaluated using the misalignment described in (1):

$$m(n) = \|\mathbf{w}(n) - \mathbf{w}_0(n)\|, \tag{1}$$

where $\|\cdot\|$ is the l_2 norm, $\mathbf{w}(n)$ is a vector containing the coefficients of the adaptive filter, and $\mathbf{w}_0(n)$ is the vector containing the current coefficients of the filter to be estimated. If only real signals are considered, the adaptive filter's coefficients will update after each sampling period using (2):

$$\mathbf{w}(n) = \mathbf{w}(n-1) + \mu \mathbf{A}^{\mathrm{T}}(n) \left[\mathbf{A}(n) \mathbf{A}^{\mathrm{T}}(n) + \delta \mathbf{I} \right]^{-1} \mathbf{e}(n), \tag{2}$$

$$\mathbf{e}(n) = \mathbf{d}(n) - \mathbf{y}(n) = \mathbf{A}(n)\mathbf{w}_0 - \mathbf{A}(n)\mathbf{w}(n-1), \tag{3}$$

$$\mathbf{A}^{\mathrm{T}}(n) = [\mathbf{x}(n), \mathbf{x}(n-1), \ldots, \mathbf{x}(n-M+1)], \tag{4}$$

$$\mathbf{x}(n) = [x(n), x(n-1), \ldots, x(n-L+1)]^{\mathrm{T}}, \tag{5}$$

where $\{\cdot\}^{\mathrm{T}}$ is the transposition operator, L is the length of the adaptive filter, μ is the step size, δ is the regularization parameter, $\mathbf{I}$ is the identity matrix, and M is the projection order, which is a specific parameter of the APA. A larger projection order increases the convergence speed of the algorithm, but also leads to a larger misadjustment.

2.1   The Convergence of the APA

The convergence of APA is an intensively studied subject. Recent research [6] showed that considering:

$$\mathbf{d}(n) = \mathbf{A}(n)\mathbf{w}_0 + \mathbf{v}(n), \tag{6}$$

where $\mathbf{v}(n)$ is a zero-mean white noise (called system noise) which follows the structure in (5), it results the residual misalignment:

$$\lim_{n \to \infty} \mathrm{E}\left\{ m(n)^2 \right\} = \frac{\beta L \sigma_v^2}{(2 - \beta L \sigma_x^2)} + \frac{T_M}{1 - a(\beta, \sigma_x^2, M, L)}, \tag{7}$$

$$T_M \cong 2\beta^2 \left(1 - \beta L \sigma_x^2\right) L \sigma_x^2 \sigma_v^2 \sum_{k=1}^{M-1} (M - k) \left(1 - \beta L \sigma_x^2\right)^{k-1}, \tag{8}$$

$$a\left(\beta, \sigma_x^2, M, L\right) = 1 - 2\beta M \sigma_x^2 + \beta^2 L M \sigma_x^4, \tag{9}$$

$$\beta \triangleq \mu / \left(L \sigma_x^2 + \delta\right). \tag{10}$$

where σ_x^2 is the input signal's variance, σ_v^2 is the variance of the system noise. The above equations help deciding on choosing a projection order M to satisfy convergence speed determined by (9), and misalignment requirements.

2.2   Proportionate Variants of APA

If some properties of the filter to be estimated are known, the adaptive algorithm can be forced to exploit them with the objective to obtain better performance. Acoustic impulse responses, which represent the kind of filters to be estimated in the presented application, are usually sparse (only a small part of coefficients is significant, while the rest are close to zero). Proportionate variants of adaptive algorithms make use of these properties and are tuned to make the largest coefficients be estimated with a higher priority. The update equation for the adaptive filter's coefficients in the case of proportionate APA is:

$$\mathbf{w}(n) = \mathbf{w}(n-1) + \mu \mathbf{G}(n-1)\mathbf{A}^{\mathrm{T}}(n)\left[\mathbf{A}(n)\mathbf{G}(n-1)\mathbf{A}^{\mathrm{T}}(n) + \delta \mathbf{I}\right]^{-1}\mathbf{e}(n), \qquad (11)$$

where $\mathbf{G}(n-1)$ is a $L \times L$ diagonal matrix that contains the information about the aforementioned priorities. The diagonal elements of $\mathbf{G}(n-1)$ are evaluated as in (12) [7]:

$$g_l(n-1) = \frac{1-\alpha}{2L} + (1+\alpha)\frac{|w_l(n-1)|}{2\sum_{k=0}^{L-1}|w_k(n-1)| + \varepsilon}, l = \overline{0, L-1}, \qquad (12)$$

where ε is a small positive constant to avoid division by zero, and $-1 \leq \alpha < 1$. This version is called improved proportionate APA (IPAPA). If $M = 1$, a proportionate NLMS is obtained. A more efficient version was proposed in [8], called memory IPAPA (MIPAPA) for which the update Eq. (11) is written as:

$$\mathbf{w}(n) = \mathbf{w}(n-1) + \mu \mathbf{P}(n)[\mathbf{A}(n)\mathbf{P}(n) + \delta \mathbf{I}]^{-1}\mathbf{e}(n), \qquad (13)$$

$$\mathbf{P}_{1\cdots M}(n) = [\mathbf{g}(n-1) \odot \mathbf{x}(n)\,\mathbf{P}_{2\cdots M}(n-1)], \qquad (14)$$

where $a \cdots b$ subscript denotes the submatrix of $\mathbf{P}$ that contains only the columns from a to b, and $\odot$ is the Hadamard product of two vectors. Equation (14) shows why this variant is called "with memory" prefix. Thanks to recursively computing the $\mathbf{P}$ matrix, MIPAPA is also more computationally efficient than IPAPA.

3   Results

The situation described in the introduction is implemented using Matlab. A speech signal is mixed with a musical signal in -40 dB signal-to-noise ratio (SNR) conditions. The mixture is filtered using an acoustic echo path presented in Fig. 2. The impulse response is changed after 15 s (shifted by 8 samples) in one case. The studio quality melody is used as an input signal for the adaptive filter, and the mixture is used as a desired signal. The performance of the adaptive algorithms is evaluated using the normalized misalignment (in dB) computed as in (15), a lower value indicating a better result. To consider the output signal intelligible, a −10 dB misalignment is enough and obtained also for −20 dB SNR. Figures 3 and 4 reveal that MIPAPA is the most performant. Figure 5 presents the performance improvements with M.

$$m_{normalized}(n) = 20\log_{10}[\|\mathbf{w}(n) - \mathbf{w}_0(n)\| / \|\mathbf{w}_0(n)\|]. \tag{15}$$

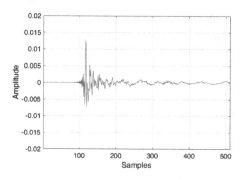

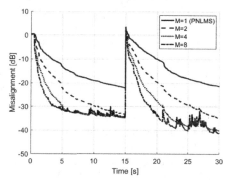

Fig. 2. The variation of the misalignment of various adaptive algorithms when estimating the impulse response illustrated in Fig. 2 with change.

Fig. 3. The variation of the misalignment of various adaptive algorithms when estimating the impulse response illustrated in Fig. 2 without change ($M = 2$, $L = 512$, $\mu = 0.2$).

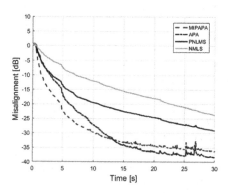

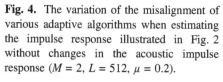

Fig. 4. The variation of the misalignment of various adaptive algorithms when estimating the impulse response illustrated in Fig. 2 without changes in the acoustic impulse response ($M = 2$, $L = 512$, $\mu = 0.2$).

Fig. 5. The variation of the misalignment of MIPAPA when estimating the impulse response illustrated in Fig. 2 for various projection orders and acoustic impulse response change ($L = 512$, $\mu = 0.2$).

4 Conclusions

The paper has proposed and investigated a method for recovering speech masked by loud music using proportionate adaptive algorithms. The situation is described as a system identification problem, and key aspects of the algorithms are briefly presented. The results show that proportionate algorithms improve the functioning of the forensic speech enhancement system compared to the situation in which classical algorithms were used, because usually acoustic impulse responses are sparse.

By studying the convergence of APA presented in Subsect. 2.1 can be concluded that the projection order does not offer a performance gain that always is worth the implied increase in computational complexity. The results in Fig. 5 show that this phenomenon is also present in MIPAPA. In the presented application, the critical performance indicator is the convergence speed and impulse response tracking. The MIPAPA showed the best results in simulations.

Acknowledgment. SES, the world-leading operator of ASTRA satellites, is offering their support for the presentation and the publication of this paper. This work was (partially) supported by UEFISCDI Romania under Grant PN-II-RU-TE-2014-4-1880.

References

1. Haykin, S.: Adaptive Filter Theory, 4th edn. Prentice-Hall, Upper Saddle River (2002)
2. Dobre, R.A., Negrescu, C., Stanomir, D.: Development and testing of an audio forensic software for enhancing speech signals masked by loud music. In: Proceedings of the SPIE 10010, Advanced Topics in Optoelectronics, Microelectronics, and Nanotechnologies VIII, Constanța (2016)
3. Dobre, R.A., Elisei-Iliescu, C., Paleologu, C., Negrescu, C., Stanomir, D.: Robust audio forensic software for recovering speech signals drowned in loud music. In: 22nd IEEE International Symposium for Design and Technology in Electronic Packaging (SIITME), pp. 232–235. IEEE, Oradea (2016)
4. Paleologu, C., Benesty, J., Ciochină, S.: A robust variable forgetting factor recursive least-squares algorithm for system identification. IEEE Sig. Process. Lett. **15**, 597–600 (2008)
5. Ozeki, K., Umeda, T.: An adaptive filtering algorithm using an orthogonal projection to an affine subsapce and its properties. Electron. Commun. Jpn. **67-A**(5), 19–27 (1984)
6. Dobre, R.A., Niță, V.A., Ciochină, S., Paleologu, C.: New insights on the convergence analysis of the affine projection algorithm for system identification. In: International Symposium on Signals, Circuits and Systems (ISSCS), pp. 1–4. IEEE, Iasi (2015)
7. Benesty, J. Gay, S.L.: An improved PNLMS algorithm. In: Proceedings of the IEEE ICASSP, pp. 1881–1884 (2002)
8. Paleologu, C., Ciochină, S., Benesty, J.: An efficient proportionate affine projection algorithm for echo cancellation. IEEE Sig. Process. Lett. **17**(2), 165–168 (2010)

Encrypting Multimedia Data Using Modified Baptista's Chaos-Based Algorithm

Octaviana Datcu$^{(\boxtimes)}$, Radu Hobincu, Mihai Stanciu,
and Radu Alexandru Badea

University "Politehnica" of Bucharest, Bucharest, Romania
od@elcom.pub.ro

Abstract. One of the easiest to implement, yet complex, symmetric key chaos-based ciphers is the one proposed by Baptista in 1998. It has attracted much interest from scholars, who underlined its deficiencies and proposed different methods to enhance it. The present paper proposes an additional step in the encryption procedure - a modulo two sum between the binary representations of Baptista's cryptograms and that of the value of the chaotic logistic map at that very iteration. This results in a flat distribution of the cryptograms. Thus, one of the major drawbacks of Baptista's cryptosystem, the exponential decay of the repartition of the cyphertext values, is surmounted. The original Baptista's algorithm is described, the proposed method is exemplified on a short message and its results are discussed when applied on multimedia files.

Keywords: Multimedia data encryption · Chaos cipher
Baptista-type algorithms

1 Introduction

Since Baptista's proposal of the symmetric key chaos-based cipher in [1] it has attracted much interest from scholars. The cryptosystem has been cryptanalyzed by researchers and several works proposed methods to enhance it. Some algorithms can be found in [2–7], where one can see that Baptista's cipher has also inspired hashing and compression schemes. An overview of existing chaos-based encryption techniques is presented in 2015, by [8].

To overcome one of the major draw-backs of Baptista's cryptosystem, the exponential decay of the repartition of the cyphertext values, the present work proposes an additional step in the encryption procedure. The binary representations of the cryptograms resulted from Baptista's method and those of the corresponding values of the logistic map are added modulo two without carry (bitwise XOR operation). This results in a flat distribution of the cryptograms.

Section 2 briefly describes Baptista's original algorithm. The main contribution of this paper is given in Sect. 3, where the proposed method is exemplified on a short message. Both Baptista's algorithm and the modified one are applied on multimedia files and their results are discussed and analyzed in Sect. 4. Section 5 concludes the paper, underlying the main advantage of the proposed encryption.

© ICST Institute for Computer Sciences, Social Informatics and Telecommunications Engineering 2018
O. Fratu et al. (Eds.): FABULOUS 2017, LNICST 241, pp. 185–190, 2018.
https://doi.org/10.1007/978-3-319-92213-3_27

2 Baptista's Chaos-Based Algorithm

We briefly describe the original algorithm proposed by Baptista [1]:

- The domain of the simplest chaotic discrete-time system, the logistic map (1), is considered for randomness generation. The values of the chaotic map at iteration n, $X(n)$, are in $(0,1)$ and bifurcation parameter b in $(0,4]$.

$$X(n+1) = b \cdot X(n) \cdot [1 - X(n)], \tag{1}$$

Remark. The aperiodic behavior, sensitive to perturbations, the map exhibits for parameters $b > 3.57$ [9], enables a pseudo-random dynamic, described by some probability density functions as the one depicted on the right side in Fig. 1, where the range $[X_{min}; X_{max}] = [0.2; 0.8]$ was divided into 256 equal-length subintervals, and the probability that the values of the logistic map fall within was computed. In Fig. 1 (left), for $b < 3.57$, one can see that the logistic map takes values within four subintervals only.

- Considering the ASCII association, messages such as text, image or sound can be represented as integer numbers. For each of the 256 ASCII characters it is assigned a subinterval of the logistic map range, a site of $\varepsilon = (X_{max} - X_{min})/256$ length.
- The encryption key is chosen to be the parameter b and the initial value of the logistic map, X_1. The parameter b is chosen after an analysis of the distribution it engenders. Figure 1 depicts this repartition for $b = 3.56$ and $b = 3.92$. More results are given on the authors' website[1].
- The chaotic map is iterated 250 times to get it in the stationary regime.
- Starting from the 251-st value of the considered map, the site (subinterval) assigned to the first plain character, I_{m1}, is searched.
- When the amplitude of the logistic map is within I_{m1}, at iteration k_1, the cryptogram for m_1 is generated as the value of that iteration, $C(m_1) = k_1$.
- The logistic map is reinitialized: $X_1 = X(k_1)$ and the assigned site for the next plain character, I_{m2}, is searched, and so on, until the entire plain message is parsed.

We have enciphered a 216255 characters text using the key $(b; X_1) = (4; 0.223860125802667)$. The occurrence of each ASCII character within the plain text is given in Fig. 2. The bifurcation parameter b was chosen to be 4 because the known probability density function of the logistic map for this value [1]. The initial condition X_1 was randomly generated from the range $(0,1)$ and truncated to 15 significant digits equivalent to 64-bits double precision floating point used in the implementation. All digits are relevant, given the high sensitivity of chaotic systems to initial conditions [1]. The length of the plaintext was chosen such that the quantity of encrypted data is sufficient to draw some conclusions regarding the efficiency of the algorithm.

The biased distribution of the cryptograms, as the one obtained in Fig. 2, exposes Baptista's cipher [1] to attacks as the one in [6]. Thus, we propose a method to obtain a uniform distribution for the enciphered versions of the plain messages, such that it

---

[1] http://ham.elcom.pub.ro/~od/cercetare/Fabulous_2017/.

offers no information about the time needed to reach each corresponding subinterval assigned to the characters to be encrypted.

3 Modified Algorithm

For Baptista's algorithm, described in Sect. 2, the iteration k at which the amplitude of the logistic map is within I_{mj}, is the cryptogram of the plain character m_j; the index $j = 1, ..., L$, with L the length of the plain message. Thus, $C = k$.

Prior to sending that value through the communication channel, one more step is implemented, in the modification of Baptista's cipher we propose in this paper. A modulo 2 sum without carry (bitwise XOR) between the value of the iteration k and that of the state of the logistic map, $X(k)$ is added.

For a short example, the plain message '*cipher*', Table 1 gives the ASCII codes, m, the limits of the ε-length subinterval assigned to each ASCII code, the cryptograms which would result from enciphering with Baptista's algorithm [1], C, and the corresponding values of the chaotic system (1) at those iterations, $X(C)$. The values of C are represented on 16 bits, as in Baptista's original algorithm. The proposed step is explained in Table 2, where the 64-bits double precision values $X(C)$ are represented in hexadecimal notation, resulting in four 16-bits words. Further, the results of the bitwise XOR between the cryptograms from Baptista's cipher and the 16-bits words corresponding to the value of the logistic map are shown in the last column of Table 2, in base 10. It can be observed that the most significant bits are not suitable for encryption, as they do not change.

Results are obtained for the key $(b, X_1) = (4, 0.223860125802667)$ and the above mentioned text in Fig. 3. An original and an encrypted image, along with their corresponding histograms are shown in Fig. 4, for the same secret key.

Table 1. Baptista's cipher: message 'cipher' and key $(b, X_1) = (4, 0.223860125802667)$

ASCII code, m	$I_m = [x_{min} + \varepsilon \cdot (m - 1); x_{min} + \varepsilon \cdot m)$	C	$X(C) \in I_m$
99	[0.42968750; 0.43203125)	1123	0.432005039722298
105	[0.44375000; 0.44609375)	1679	0.445796898468479
112	[0.46015625; 0.46250000)	769	0.460193739139050
104	[0.44140625; 0.44375000)	1150	0.441488974614396
101	[0.43437500; 0.43671875)	641	0.434819475135869
114	[0.46484375; 0.46718750)	968	0.465731114802751

Table 2. Proposed encryption: message 'cipher' and key $(b, X_1) = (4, 0.223860125802667)$

C	X(C)	typecast(X(C), 'uint16')				XOR(C, X(C))			
1123	0.432005039722298	1ffd	7754	a5f8	3fdb	7070	29495	41371	15288
1679	0.445796898468479	247a	b6e5	87ef	3fdc	8949	45162	33120	14675
769	0.460193739139050	4675	70db	73d0	3fdd	17780	29658	28881	15580
1150	0.441488974614396	db9a	f8e0	415a	3fdc	57316	64670	17700	15266
641	0.434819475135869	d621	1057	d415	3fdb	54432	4822	54932	15706
968	0.465731114802751	ad0e	e0b3	ce89	3fdd	44742	58235	52545	15381

For an answering machine sound, and the key $(b, X_1) = (4, 0.3)$, one can listen to the encrypted.wav file on authors' website. Also, to test the sensitivity of the proposed cipher to a slight change in the secret key, the encrypted sound was deciphered with $(b, X_1) = (4, 0.3 + 10^{-15})$.

4   Discussion and Analysis

Roughly speaking, the size of the key space is $2^{52} \cdot 2^{52} \approx 2^{108}$, because X_1 and b are represented as 64-bits double precision numbers, with 52-bits mantissa. Nevertheless, more thorough analysis, like the one the bifurcation diagrams in Fig. 5 show, is worth being performed to better approximate the length of the interval parameter b lies in for a good encryption. The distribution of the cryptograms is of great importance. When it is uniform it hides the redundancy of the plain image as it can be observed from the histograms in Figs. 3 and 4. Information entropy is the most important feature of randomness and it has been computed for original and encrypted images in Fig. 5,

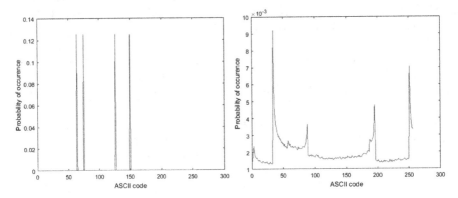

Fig. 1. Probability of occurrence of the cryptograms in the cyphertext for $b = 3.56$ *(left)* and $b = 3.92$ *(right)*; $X_1 = 0.2$ using Baptista's original algorithm.

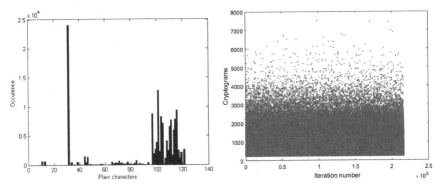

Fig. 2. Histogram for the plain characters and the distribution of their encrypted versions using the original Baptista's algorithm. The plain message is text.

obtaining the values 4.871 and, respectively 7.994bits. The entropy of an image representing noise on 256 gray levels is ideally 8 [10]. If the entropy of the ciphered grayscale image would be less than 8, there exists a certain level of predictability, which indicates a weakness of the cryptosystem. A more detailed analysis of the security level of the proposed cipher is given on the authors' website.

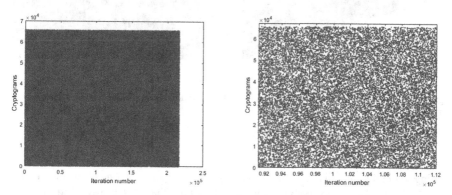

Fig. 3. The distribution of cryptograms using the proposed modified algorithm on text (left) and zoom (right). The secret key: $(b, X_1) = (4, 0.223860125802667)$.

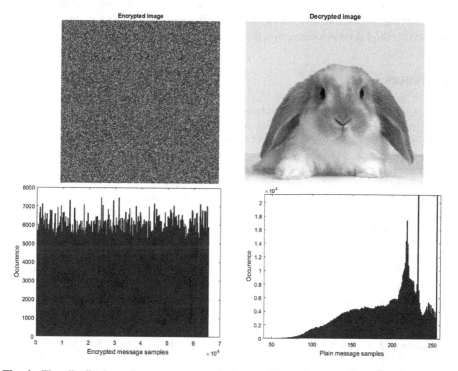

Fig. 4. The distribution of cryptograms with the modified algorithm, applied to an image identical to the decrypted one. The secret key: $(b, X_1) = (4, 0.223860125802667)$.

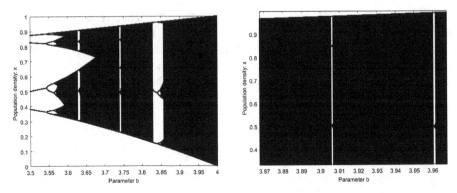

Fig. 5. Bifurcation diagram of the logistic map for parameter b in [3.5; 4] (left) and b in [3.87; 3.97] (right).

5 Conclusions

Aiming to obtain a flat distribution of the cryptograms output by one of the best-known chaos-based enciphering scheme, Baptista's algorithm, the present paper adds a step in the original method. Thus, a bitwise XOR is computed between the value of the 16-bits Baptista's cryptograms and the least significant 16-bits from the binary representation of the double precision floating point values of the corresponding logistic map amplitudes. While solving the exponential decay in the distribution of Baptista's cryptograms, the proposed method does not overcome the increase in the size of the cyphertext.

References

1. Baptista, M.S.: Cryptography with chaos. Phys. Lett. A **240**, 50–54 (1998)
2. Jokimoski, G., Kocarev, L.: Analysis of some recently proposed chaos-based encryption algorithm. Phys. Lett. A **291**, 381–384 (2001)
3. Li, S., Chen, G., Wong, K.W., Mou, X., Cai, Y.: Baptista-type chaotic cryptosystems: problems and countermeasures. Phys. Lett. A **332**, 5–6 (2004)
4. Nitharwal, B., Rani, M., Saini, H.C.: Improving security of the Baptista's cryptosystem using two-step logistic map. Int. J. Comput. Netw. Inf. Secur. **7**(5), 34 (2015)
5. Wong, K.W.: A combined chaotic cryptographic and hashing scheme. Phys. Lett. A **307**, 292–298 (2003)
6. Álvarez, G., Montoya, F., Romera, M., Pastor, G.: Cryptanalysis of dynamic look-up table based chaotic cryptosystems. Phys. Lett. A **326**, 211–218 (2004)
7. Chen, Y., Liao, X.: Cryptanalysis on a modified Baptista-type cryptosystem with chaotic masking algorithm. Phys. Lett. A **342**, 389–396 (2005)
8. Shukla, P.K., Khare, A., Rizvi, M.A., Stalin, S., Kumar, S.: Applied cryptography using chaos function for fast digital logic-based systems in ubiquitous computing. Entropy **17**(3), 1387–1410 (2015)
9. Eckmann, J.-P.: Roads to turbulence in dissipative dynamical systems. Rev. Mod. Phys. **53**, 643 (1981)
10. Gonzalez, R.C., Woods, R.E., Eddins, S.L.: Digital Image Processing Using MATLAB. Prentice Hall, New Jersey (2003). Chap. 11

Session on Optoelectronic Devices and Applications thereof in Communications Domain

Real - Time Spatial Light Modulated Digital Holographic Interferometry Applied in Art Structural Diagnosis

Adrian Sima[1]([✉]), Paul Schiopu[1], Marian Vladescu[1],
Bogdan-Mihai Gavriloaia[1], Florin Garoi[2], and Victor Damian[2]

[1] Faculty of Electronics, Telecommunications and Information Technology,
University "Politehnica" of Bucharest, Bucharest, Romania
adriansima1981@gmail.com
[2] Laser Department, National Institute for Lasers, Plasma and Radiation Physics
(INFLPR), Magurele, Romania

Abstract. In this paper we apply digital holographic interferometry as a structural diagnosis tool to investigate some surface defects in a XIXth century wooden icon. We use a fully digital experimental set-up for real time acquisition and digital optical reconstruction of holographic sequences. The light source is a He-Ne laser, the digital recording component consists of a CCD camera and a spatial light modulator (SLM) works as a digital holographic projector for the optical reconstruction of the interferograms. Both the acquisition set-up and the reconstruction one are functioning simultaneously therefore the changes in the surface structure are visualized in real-time like a digital holographic interferometry "fringe motion picture" with a 20 fps display. Detachment defects of the paint layer are identified using this non-destructive method and the real-time feature has proven to be useful because it gave a very useful dynamicity to the entire investigation process.

Keywords: Digital holography · Interferometry · Art conservation
Lasers · Structural diagnosis

1 Introduction

Because a wave front encodes in itself information about a propagation environment or a reflecting surface, a method for wave front recording can be classified as a remote sensing tool for studying different classes of objects. In most cases light is not a destructive tool when interacts with a high range of objects and, because of this, it can be used to obtain information about their surface, shape, texture, size and their variations in time. Holography and holographic interferometry are methods for recording waves and due to this fact they can be used to obtain information about the environments that generates and reflects waves or support wave propagation [1, 2]. Artworks are a high interest class of objects and in the past years very important research resources are invested in their restoration and conservation. Lasers are widely used in this domain through holography and holographic interferometry as new tools to access invisible information about structural and mechanical properties of artworks. These

O. Fratu et al. (Eds.): FABULOUS 2017, LNICST 241, pp. 193–198, 2018.
https://doi.org/10.1007/978-3-319-92213-3_28

being said holographic interferometry can be regarded as a non-destructive method for structural diagnosis in art [3, 4]. In this paper we intend to improve the speed of data acquisition when applying digital holographic interferometry in art diagnosis by eliminating the numerical reconstruction as a time consuming step and by creating an instant feedback of the method during its appliance by using a spatial light modulator as an instant wave front reconstruction device [5].

2 Theoretical Background

Holographic interferometry is a method through which more than one wave is holographically recorded on the same recording device whether it is a photographic emulsion or a digital pixel area.

Recording the amplitude distribution is a very familiar procedure in classical photography, but more than that, in holography also the phase is recorded by means of interference of an object wave, which carries the object information, with a reference wave, coherent to the object one.

The most of the information regarding a specific object properties like shape, contour, color, texture, etc. can be accessed by recording the wave originated by the object through emission or reflection [6, 7]. Thus being said, because of the phase recording and reconstruction which preserves the 3-dimensionality of the object, holography is a very powerful method for recording and reconstructing waves.

2.1 Digital Holographic Interferometry (DHI)

When an interferogram, which consists of two or more stacked holograms, is illuminated with a coherent light, the reconstructed waves will interfere with one another and the interference fringe pattern translates in itself the modification suffered by the wave between the multiple stacked holographic recordings. The waves corresponding to an initial reference state of the object (A_{o1}) and a consecutive one (A_{o2}) are described by the following equations:

$$A_{o1} = a_0 e^{i\varphi_{o1}}, \quad A_{o2} = a_0 e^{i\varphi_{o2}} \tag{1}$$

The modification suffered by the object between the two consecutive exposures will not affect the wave real amplitude but its phase. The intensity distribution on the sensor for the first and the consecutive holographic frames are:

$$I_{1,2} = \left|A_{o1,o2} + A_R\right|^2 = a_O^2 + a_R^2 + a_O a_R e^{i\left(\varphi_{o1,o2} - \varphi_R\right)} + a_O a_R e^{-i\left(\varphi_{o1,o2} - \varphi_R\right)}. \tag{2}$$

The two waves are numerically added, operation which is equivalent in classical holographic interferometry to a double holographic exposure. The hologram reflectance, R_H, is:

$$
\begin{aligned}
R_H = R_O - K(I_1 + I_2) = T_O &- 2K\left(a_O^2 + a_R^2\right) - Ka_Oa_Re^{i(\varphi_{01}-\varphi_R)} \\
&- Ka_Oa_Re^{-i(\varphi_{01}-\varphi_R)} - Ka_Oa_Re^{i(\varphi_{02}-\varphi_R)}Ka_Oa_Re^{-i(\varphi_{02}-\varphi_R)}
\end{aligned}
\tag{3}
$$

where R_O and K are constants for linear variation of the reflectance. The reconstructed wave, A_R, is modulated by the hologram reflectance, R_H:

$$
\begin{aligned}
A_R R_H = C_Oa_Re^{i\varphi_R} &- Ka_Oa_R^2e^{i\varphi_{01}} - Ka_Oa_R^2e^{-i(\varphi_{01}-2\varphi_R)} \\
&- Ka_Oa_R^2e^{i\varphi_{02}} - Ka_Oa_R^2e^{-i(\varphi_{02}-2\varphi_R)}
\end{aligned}
\tag{4}
$$

The second and the fourth terms describe up to the same real coefficient the two object waves recorded separately [9]. Their phase difference is:

$$
\Delta\varphi(\vec{r}) = \varphi_{02} - \varphi_{01}
\tag{5}
$$

After renaming the coefficients in Eq. (4), the two waves corresponding to the two consecutive states of the object overlap and their superposition gives an amplitude distribution described by:

$$
\Psi = Ca_Oe^{i\varphi_{01}} + Ca_Oe^{i\varphi_{02}} = Ca_Oe^{i\varphi_{01}}\left[1 + e^{i\Delta\varphi}\right]
\tag{6}
$$

The intensity distribution reveals a fringe pattern which encodes the object modifications through the recording steps:

$$
|\Psi|^2 = 2C^2a_O^2[1 + \cos\Delta\varphi(\vec{r})]
\tag{7}
$$

In this paper we opted for an optical reconstruction method of the interference patterns using a SLM and not a numerical one because we tried to keep a specific dynamic feature of the deformation within the reconstructure procedure.

2.2 Optical Reconstruction in DHI Using a Spatial Light Modulator (SLM)

Real time DHI performed in this paper can be described as a sequence display of holographic interferograms generated by successive subtraction (or addition) of consecutive holograms from a reference one. As we pointed out, upwards two holograms stacked on the same recording medium generate a holographic interferogram which can be reconstructed with the help of a reference playback wave.

Choosing an optical reconstruction method we eliminated the time consuming numerical reconstruction process of waves [9] which in facts simulates the diffraction of the playback wave on the holographic amplitude distribution pixel matrix. Using the SLM we practically transform the virtual recorded holograms, consisting in grey levels pixel distributions, into "hard" SLM holograms, which can physically perform instantaneous diffraction and playback wave modulation. The only time consuming process is the subtraction operation of the successive holograms from a reference one.

But this single numerical procedure enables us to display ~15 holographic interferograms/second. This very convenient frame rate leads to a very dynamic investigation method for some structural diagnosis of diffusive objects.

Because of its real time feature one can also use the method for real time monitorisation of object shape variation through a reconstruction or a restoration procedure. The real time DHI ensures an almost instant feedback of a supposed invasive restoration procedure. All this practical advantages makes the method very useful for in situ noninvasive diagnosis and restoring monitorisation.

3   Experimental Set-up

The recording coherent light source was a He-Ne laser working in 632.8 nm wavelength and having a 30 mW output power and the reconstruction one was a green Nd: YAG (532 nm) working in continuous regime. The digital sensor consisted in a CCD monochrome camera with a sensor set at 1280 × 960 pixel resolution which can record at ~30 fps convenient speed. The holographic acquisition was performed through a classical configuration optical set-up (Fig. 1). For the wave optical reconstruction we used a phase only SLM, HEO1080 from HoloEye having a resolution of 1980 × 1080 pixels and a 15.36 × 8.64 mm active area size. Each pixel can display 256 phase levels within 2π phase domain.

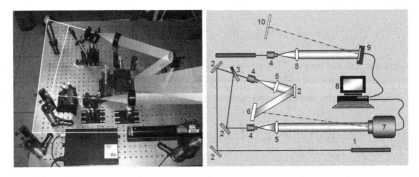

Fig. 1. Experimental set-up for digital recording of holographic sequence in reflexion regime - lab picture (left) and the entire hybrid both acquisition and reconstruction set-up – schematic representation (right). He-Ne laser (1), deflecting mirrors (2), variable beam-splitter (3), spatial filters (4), collimating lens (5), object (6), CCD camera (7), computer (8), phase only SLM (9), projection screen for fringe dynamic pattern real-time visualisation (10). The fringe image is a real one and can be displayed on a projection screen

To the computer unit there are connected the CCD camera sensor, the usual display monitor which shows the holograms in amplitude and also the phase only SLM which converts the virtual amplitude holograms in "hard" phase holograms.

These optical reconstruction procedure enables us to perform "live" diffraction on the SLM and also to instantly display the reconstructed waves at a repetition rate given by the subtraction numerical program ($\sim$15 fps). In the end we practically visualise a live holographic interferometry fringe motion pictures which translates the changes induced in the object surface.

4 Experimental Results

The object used for testing the real time DHI with optical SLM reconstruction was a wooden painted XVIIIth century icon.

There are some consecrated methods to produce interference fringes generated by some changes in the object. Hence, the objects loads can be induced thermally, mechanically or by vibration. We choose the thermal method for noninvasive considerations. So the objects where slightly heated with a hot air flow to induce changes in their surface. The object shape recurrence induces fringes and the structural defects are visible in the fringe patterns discontinuities.

The wave divergence correlated with the light source coherence allowed us to investigate an area with $\sim$30 cm in diameter. Quantitative measurements can be made only for instant intermediate holographic frames (Fig. 2)

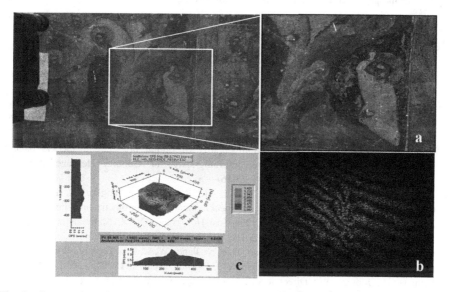

Fig. 2. Structural surface defect in the paint layer of an XVIIIth century wooden icon investigated with real time DHI. In usual visual investigation the defect cannot be noticed (a). In the interferogram one can observe the paint detachment defect (b). The surface profile is generated with OPD (optical path difference) function in IntelliuWave (c).

The fringe orientation and the fringe distance changes constantly as the objects surface returns to its original state before the heat load. This dynamicity of the fringes eases the observation of surface structural defects.

5   Conclusions

Real-time digital holographic interferometry is performed as a noninvasive structural diagnosis tool for defects localization in artworks. The experimental set-up consists in both acquisition and reconstruction configuration working simultaneously. The holographic interferogram sequence reconstruction is done by optical means to eliminate the time consuming numerical method.

Thus being said we may state that, using a hybrid holographic acquisition and reconstruction set-up, we perform both DHI recording and DHI reconstruction in the same time and this detailed description of the experimental set-up can confirm the advantages of optical reconstruction in holography using a SLM pointed in the upper section. Hence, the dynamicity of the process is kept through the reconstruction and the real time fringe visualization and the instant observational feedback confers some very useful features to the optical holograms reconstruction using a SLM.

In the present paper we keep the investigations and the experimental set-up to a demonstrative framework. In the future work we intend to apply the method in more detailed quantitative and qualitative features.

Acknowledgments. SES, the world-leading operator of ASTRA satellites, is offering their support for the presentation and the publication of this paper.

References

1. Osten, W., Baumbach, T., Jüptner, W.: Comparative digital holography. Opt. Lett. **27**, 1764–1766 (2002)
2. Yamaguchi, I., Ida, T., Yokota, M., Yamashita, K.: Surface shape measurement by phase-shifting digital holography with a wavelength shift. Appl. Opt. **45**, 7610–7616 (2006)
3. Tornari, V., Andrianakis, M., Hatzigiannakis, K., Kosma, K., Detalle, V., Bourguignon, E., Giovannacci, D., Brissaud, D.: Complimentarity of digital holographic speckle pattern interferometry and simulated infrared thermography for Cultural Heritage structural diagnostic research. IJOER **2**, 129–141 (2016)
4. Arena, G., Rippa, M., Mormile, P., Grilli, M., Paturzo, M., Fatigati, G., Ferraro, P.: Concurrent studies on artworks by digital speckle pattern interferometry and thermographic analysis. In: Proceedings of the SPIE, Practical Holography XXX: Materials and Applications, vol. 9771, p. 977107, 7 March 2016
5. Collings, N., Christmas, J.L., Masiyano, D., Crossland, W.A.: Real-time phase-only spatial light modulators for 2D holographic display. J. Display Technol. **11**, 278–284 (2015)
6. Schnars, U., Juptner, W.: Direct recording of holograms by a CCD target and numerical reconstruction. Appl. Opt. **33**, 179–181 (1994)
7. Munoz Solis, S., Mendoza Santoyo, F., Socorro Hernandez-Montes, M.: 3D displacemnt measurements of the tympanic membrane with digital holographic interferometry. Opt. Express **20**, 5613–5621 (2012)
8. Ostrovsky, Y.I., Butusov, M.M., Ostrovskaya, G.V.: Interferometry by Holography. Springer, New York (1980). https://doi.org/10.1007/978-3-540-39008-4
9. Abdelhakim, L.: Displacement determination by digital holographic interferometry. In: AIP Conference Proceedings, vol. 1281, no. 1 (2010)

Studies on the Transient, Continuous and Pulsed Regimes of High Power LEDs

Dan Tudor Vuza[1] and Marian Vlădescu[2][(✉)]

[1] Institute of Mathematics of the Romanian Academy, Bucharest, Romania
danvuza@hotmail.com
[2] Optoelectronics Research Center, "Politehnica" University,
Bucharest, Romania
marian.vladescu@upb.ro

Abstract. Monitoring the thermal regime of the high power LEDs used in lighting applications and in optical communications is nowadays a must. The paper presents our studies and experimental results concerning the transient, continuous and pulsed regimes of high power LEDs, based on a method for temperature measurement that makes use of the protection diode embedded in the LED package. The method proved to be consistent with the exponential law describing the transient regime and with the mathematical relation between continuous and pulsed regimes, qualifying thus as a potential monitoring tool for LED-based systems.

Keywords: High power LED · Temperature monitoring · Transient regime
Continuous regime · Pulsed regime

1 Introduction

The increased interest of the industry for applications using IR and also visible light communications called for attention on monitoring the thermal regime of LEDs. Maintaining the LED temperature in the safety area is an essential condition for the reliability of LED-based communication systems. A method for measurement of LED temperature that makes use of the embedded protection diode has been proposed in [1]. In the present paper we apply the method to the study of the variation of the LED temperature under various working conditions. The principles of the method are briefly recalled in Sect. 2. The transient regime, that is the transitions from unpowered to continuously powered and from continuously powered to unpowered, is considered in Sect. 3, where it is shown that a one-exponential law is a reasonable approximation for the temperature variation. Finally in Sect. 4 we study the pulsed regime and we show how it can be used for predicting the steady-state temperature in the continuously powered regime.

2 The Method for Temperature Measurement

The power LEDs we have used in our experiments have embedded in their package a protection diode, reverse connected in relation to the LED anode-cathode, in order to suppress the reverse voltages that may occur accidentally and damage the LED. The

© ICST Institute for Computer Sciences, Social Informatics and Telecommunications Engineering 2018
O. Fratu et al. (Eds.): FABULOUS 2017, LNICST 241, pp. 199–205, 2018.
https://doi.org/10.1007/978-3-319-92213-3_29

method relies on the assumption that we may find the junction temperature of the LED by measuring the junction temperature of the protection diode. For measuring the latter the procedure described in [2] was followed. Namely, the forward voltage V_F of a diode is related to the forward current I_C through the diode via the relation

$$I_C = I_S \left(\exp\left(\frac{V_F}{nV_T}\right) - 1 \right) \tag{1}$$

where I_S is the reverse saturation current, n is the ideality factor and $V_T = kT/q$ is the thermal voltage. Provided that $V_F \gg nV_T$, the product nV_T may be determined by measuring V_{F1} and V_{F2} at two values I_{C1} and I_{C2} of the forward current at the same temperature T and then using the relation

$$nV_T = \frac{V_{F1} - V_{F2}}{\ln\left(\frac{I_{C1}}{I_{C2}}\right)} \tag{2}$$

obtained from (1) by neglecting the term -1. The measurements are done by interrupting the direct current through the LED, sourcing reverse currents through the LED terminals that provide the direct currents I_{C1} and I_{C2} through the protection diode, taking voltage measurements and averaging in order to find V_{F1}, V_{F2}, I_{C1} and I_{C2} and using (2) for determining nV_T. For finding the temperature T a calibration procedure is needed, consisting of recording the value $(nV_T)_{REF}$ of the product nV_T at a known temperature T_{REF} (usually the ambient temperature). Then any other temperature T is determined from the formula

$$T = T_{REF} \frac{nV_T}{(nV_T)_{REF}} \tag{3}$$

in which nV_T has been computed with (2). The procedure is entirely automated and fast enough in order that the momentary interruption of the direct current through the LED has not an observable effect on its temperature. Details of the procedure and the schematic have been given in [1].

3   Transient and Continuous Regimes

In our experiments we have used four power LEDs of type SFH 4232 with embedded protection diodes, of which one mounted on a Bergquist thermal clad square footprint acting as a radiator and the rest unmounted.

The purpose of the experiments of this section was to establish whether a one-exponential law for the temperature evolution of the form

$$T(t) = T_0 + (T_\infty - T_0)(1 - \exp(-t/\tau)) \tag{4}$$

was adequate enough for describing the transient thermal regime of the LEDs. In (4) T_0 is the temperature at $t = 0$ and T_∞ is the limiting temperature as t approaches infinity.

To this purpose the LEDs, initially at ambient temperature, were powered with a current of 0.5 A and allowed to heat for a time Δt, after which the current was interrupted and the LEDs were allowed to cool for the same time Δt. We chose $\Delta t = 10$ min for the unmounted LEDs and $\Delta t = 15$ min for the LED with radiator. During the heating time the current was interrupted every one second and a measurement of the temperature was taken according to the method described in Sect. 2; each current interruption lasted for only 4 ms, meaning that the LED was almost continuously powered. During the cooling time, a measurement of the temperature was taken every 10 ms. The parameters T_0, T_∞ and τ from (4) were determined from the measurements via a best-fit procedure applied separately to the heating and to the cooling processes. Specifically, if T_n was the sequence of measured temperatures, then in a first step the time constant τ was estimated as the inverse of the slope a of the straight line $b - at$ that gave the best fit in the least square sense to the sequence of data $\ln|T_n - T_{n-k}|$ where k is a conveniently chosen constant (large enough in order that the argument of the logarithm is not too small). In a second step, the parameters T_0 and T_∞ were chosen in such way that the right side of (4) in which the already estimated τ has been used gave a best fit to the data T_n in the least square sense.

The estimates from the experimental data are presented below, together with the RMS error between data and estimated laws of the form (4).

Table 1. Heating transient regime

LED	τ (seconds)	T_0 (°C)	T_∞ (°C)	RMS error (°C)
Radiator	132.35	31.4	51.8	0.14
1	34.33	36.6	100.3	0.69
2	32.14	37.5	111.5	0.62
3	28.11	34.9	97.4	0.38

Table 2. Cooling transient regime

LED	τ (seconds)	T_0 (°C)	T_∞ (°C)	RMS error (°C)
Radiator	124.26	52.6	31.9	0.57
1	31.62	97.6	31.9	0.92
2	32.37	109.5	32.1	0.87
3	29.21	95.7	31.9	0.63

In all graphs below the horizontal units are seconds and the vertical units are °C. In Fig. 1 the experimental curves are in blue and the one-exponential curves with estimated parameters are in black; at the scale of the figure they are hardly distinguishable.

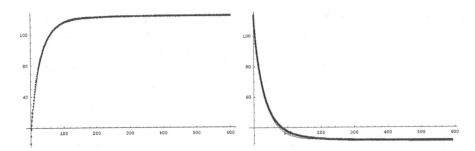

Fig. 1. Heating curve (left) and cooling curve (right) of LED 2 superimposed over one-exponential curves with parameters from Tables 1 and 2.

In Fig. 2 we take magnified views of parts of the heating curve of Fig. 1, which show that the one-exponential is a good approximation at the beginning of the time interval but not so good on the final part on the interval where curve and the data approach their asymptotic values.

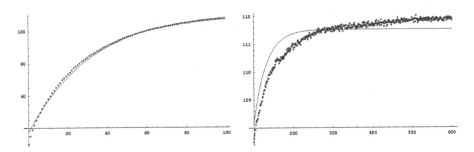

Fig. 2. Heating curve of Fig. 1 restricted to the first 100 s and to the last 500 s.

4 Pulsed Regime

Based on the results of Sect. 3, we shall assume that the one-exponential law (4) is a reasonable approximation of the transient thermal regime of the LED. Let us consider a time interval of length Δt and let T_1 and T_2 be the LED temperatures at the beginning and at the end of the interval. Assume that the LED is turned on at the beginning of the interval and is turned off after a time of $d\Delta t$, with $0 < d < 1$. If T_d is the LED temperature by the time the LED is turned off, then according to (4) T_1 and T_d are related by

$$T_d = T_1 + (T_C - T_1)\left(1 - \exp(-d\Delta t/\tau)\right). \tag{5}$$

where we have replaced T_∞ with T_C, the steady-state temperature of the LED when continuously powered. Also according to (4), T_d and T_2 are related by

$$T_2 = T_d + (T_A - T_d)\left(1 - \exp(-(1-d)\Delta t/\tau)\right). \tag{6}$$

where we have replaced T_∞ with the ambient temperature T_A, the final temperature reached during cooling. Substituting (5) into (6) we find that T_2 is related to T_1 by

$$T_2 = aT_1 + b \tag{7}$$

where

$$
\begin{aligned}
a &= \exp(-\Delta t/\tau), \\
b &= \exp(-(1-d)\Delta t/\tau)\,(1 - \exp(-d\Delta t/\tau))\,T_C + (1 - \exp(-(1-d)\Delta t/\tau))\,T_A.
\end{aligned} \tag{8}
$$

Now assume that at time $t = 0$ we start with the LED at temperature T_0 and we submit it to a pulsed regime so that on every time interval $[(n-1)\Delta t, n\Delta t]$ the LED is turned on at the beginning of the interval and is turned off after a time of $d\Delta t$, d being the duty factor. By repeated application of (7), the temperature T_n at time point $n\Delta t$ equals

$$T_n = a^n T_0 + b \sum_{i=0}^{n-1} a^i = a^n T_0 + b\frac{1 - a^n}{1 - a}. \tag{9}$$

Since $0 < a < 1$ it follows from (9) that the steady-state temperature T_P reached during pulsed regime (that is, the limit of T_n as n grows to infinity) is given by

$$T_P = \frac{b}{1 - a}. \tag{10}$$

Substituting (8) into (10) we arrive at the final expression

$$T_P = \frac{\exp(-(1-d)\Delta t/\tau)\,(1 - \exp(-d\Delta t/\tau))\,T_C + (1 - \exp(-(1-d)\Delta t/\tau))\,T_A}{1 - \exp(-\Delta t/\tau)}. \tag{11}$$

In the case that the switching period Δt is much smaller than the time constant τ we may obtain a simpler form of (11) by approximating $\exp(x)$ with $1 + x$,

$$T_P = (1 - (1-d)\Delta t/\tau)\,dT_C + (1 - d)T_A. \tag{12}$$

Because we have already assumed $\Delta t/\tau \ll 1$ we may omit this number and obtain the final approximation

$$T_P = dT_C + (1 - d)T_A. \tag{13}$$

In the experiments reported in Table 3 the LED was submitted to a pulsed regime with $\Delta t = 1$ ms and a current of 0.5 A. The temperature was measured every second with the method of Sect. 2. The measured steady-state temperature was compared with T_P computed with (13), where we took for T_C the continuous regime temperature of 87.92 °C and for T_A the ambient temperature of 30 °C.

Table 3. Pulsed regime

Duty factor	T_P measured	T_P computed
0.75	73.9	73.4
0.5	57.9	58.9
0.25	44.1	44.5

Table 3 shows a quite satisfactory agreement between the measured and computed temperatures. Based on this, one can propose the following application of formula (13). We have seen from Table 1 that a LED without any special means for heat dissipation may reach temperatures over 100 °C when continuously powered. Therefore it is not always safe to submit the LED to the continuous regime without knowing in advance what steady-state temperature would be reached. Instead, one may submit the LED to the pulsed regime during which lower, hence safer temperatures would be reached. Then, based on the measurements of T_P and of T_A, one can use (13) for predicting the steady-state temperature T_C of the continuous regime without actually submitting the LED to that regime.

5   Conclusions

We have shown that a one-exponential law is a reasonable approximation, although not the most precise, for both the heating curve (transition from unpowered to continuously powered) and the cooling curve (transition from powered to unpowered) of the LED obtained from experimental data. We may conclude that, at least for the purposes of monitoring the thermal regime of the LED, the one-exponential law is a reasonable approximation; according to Tables 1 and 2, it is also reasonable to assume that time constants of the heating and of the cooling curve are the same. The approximation is quite good at the beginning of the time interval and somewhat less precise on the rest of the interval. In Sect. 3 we saw how these conclusions may be used in the study of the pulsed regime. A more precise approximation might use two-exponential laws as proposed in [3].

Another significant conclusion concerns the influence of the radiator on the thermal regime. From Tables 1 and 2 we observe that the radiator reduced in half the maximal temperature reached by the continuously powered LED and at the same time increased the time constant four times.

Finally the method for temperature measurement proved to be consistent with the physical reality and therefore may be used for monitoring the thermal regime of LEDs with embedded protection diodes.

References

1. Vuza, D.T., Vlădescu, M.: Platform for monitoring the temperature of power LED junction by using the embedded protection diode. In: 2016 8th International Conference on Electronics, Computers and Artificial Intelligence (ECAI) Conference Proceedings, pp. 1–6. IEEE Conference Publications (2014)
2. Jones, M.: Accurate temperature sensing with an external P-N junction. Linear Technol. Appl. Note **137** (2012)
3. Han, K., Liu, M., Fan, S., Shen, H.: Improved electrical measurement method for junction temperature of light emitting diodes. Przegląd Elektrotechniczny (Electr. Rev.) **88**(3b), 180–184 (2012)

Performance Improvement of a Multi-head Optical Wireless Communication System

Viorel Manea[1(✉)], Sorin Puşcoci[1], and Dan Alexandru Stoichescu[2]

[1] INSCC Bucharest, Preciziei 6, Bucharest, Romania
{viorel.manea, sorin.puscoci}@inscc.ro
[2] University Politechnica Bucharest, Bucharest, Romania
dan_stoich@yahoo.com

Abstract. Free space optics represents a fast and economical method to transmit digital data at the speed of the order of the Gbps at a distance of a few kilometers. The major limitation is the atmospheric attenuation, especially fog, which can affect the quality of transmission, transfer rate and transmission distance. A useful metric to monitorize the processes is the BER factor. This paper proposes a combination of adaptive optics that use multiple heads of transmission which are focused simultaneously on a single photodetector at the receiver end, in order to provide redundancy and to sustain a minimum data-rate transfer and/or assuring a transmission distance at an acceptable BER. It is assessed, through the simulation, the optimal (technically and economically) number of optical transmitters for which we get a real quality improvement of the transmission for a given bitrate-distance factors.

Keywords: Free space optics · Adaptive optics · Multi-head transceiver

1 Introduction

This paper comes to follow the article "Wireless Optic Last Mile Multi-Gbit/s Communication System" [1]. It doesn't take into account the number and arrangement of the transmitter heads and link availability, the performance of the optical link being evaluated by using eye-diagram that provides information about the overall bit error rate of the system.

Many researchers consider that using multiple-beam optical link could provide a more secure communication from the redundancy point of view. In reference [2] is presented a procedure that compares the multi-beam method with the averaging method, using the structure parameter and the optical intensity variation. The main purpose is to reduce the receiving signal fluctuations in multi-beam FSO setup. Spatial diversity in FSO is analyzed in [3], in which a number of copies of the same signal is launched in atmosphere, using a single or multiple receiver. It was made a deep analysis of the distortion of the signals due to the atmospheric disturbances. The effect of fog on FSO links is analyzed on reference [4]. It was calculated the degree of misalignment between the transmitter and the receiver based on the optical energy that arrive at the receiver end. A WDM approach using multiple beams is made in [5].

© ICST Institute for Computer Sciences, Social Informatics and Telecommunications Engineering 2018
O. Fratu et al. (Eds.): FABULOUS 2017, LNICST 241, pp. 206–211, 2018.
https://doi.org/10.1007/978-3-319-92213-3_30

It is essential to understand how the multiple beams can carry the WDM signals. The paper shows out the BER variations versus optical power and link range. In [6] is proposed a multi-beam hybrid WDM-FSO system model. One single copy of the signal can carry a number of n-distinct signals. Paper [7] proposes a performance evaluation of a multi beam system that uses space-time coding by making an adaptation of a space-time block code from RF systems that are useful for intensity- modulated optical signals.

An analysis of the beam propagation for laser multi-beam FSO for very strong turbulent atmosphere is made in [8, 9]. All the simulations are made for a transmitter with four heads, with a comprehensive discussion about propagation and power budget. A comparison between different numbers of beams based on link distance received optical power and geometrical loss is made in [9]. A comparison between SISO and MIMO techniques for optical field is made in [10]. An investigation on FSO communication with optical amplification based on 4 × 4 T/R combination is made in [11]. Amplification is needed to overcome losses on passive splitters/combiners needed to divide the original signal into n identical copies and to (re)combine the signals at the receiver end. Reference [12] contain ITU recommendation with some prediction methods required for the design of terrestrial free-space optical links related to our subject.

Free space optics domain is currently carefully considered by universities with teaching programs and research projects related to this field [13–15].

2 Description of the Proposed Solution

The starting point is the model for multi-beam FSO BER analysis presented in Fig. 1. Mono and multi-beam measurement conditions are:

- Transmitter: n-CW lasers (n = 1, 2, 4 or 8), f = 1.93 THz, power = 33 dBm, aperture diameter 2.5 cm, beam divergence 0.25 mrad, λ = 1550 nm, transmitter losses 2 dB,
- Type of modulation: L-PPM (L = 8);
- FSO Channel: Range: approx. 1 km, attenuation 30 dB/km (worst case, fog attenuation), minimal BER factor: 10^{-9};
- Receiver: Aperture diameter 20 cm, APD type, gain 3.
- Overall bitrate target: 2.5 Gbit/s

The simulation platform is the OptiSystem suite from Optiwave Corporation. The theoretical assumptions are made in the initial paper [1]. Geometrical attenuation equation is given in [12]:

$$A_{geo} = P_{rec.}/P_{tr.} = 10\log_{10}(S_{tr}/S_{rec}) \tag{1}$$

where $P_{rec.}$ and $P_{tr.}$ are received power and transmitted power respective, $S_{tr.}$ and $S_{rec.}$ surface area of transmit beam at range d and receiver capture surface respective.

$S_{tr.}$ could be approximated by:

$$S_{tr.} = \pi(d\theta)^2/4 \qquad (2)$$

where θ is beam divergence and d is the link distance in km.

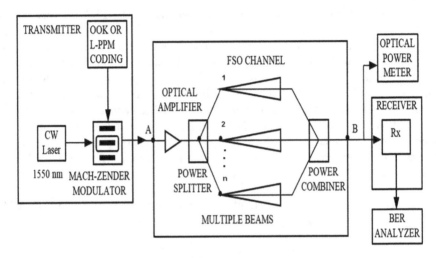

Fig. 1. Model for multi-beam FSO BER analysis

On very short links it is possible for the capture area to be greater than the beam area. In consequence, the value of A_{geo} is mandatory to be set to zero because all of the optical energy is collected by the receiver.

The solution proposed in this paper does not take into account the temporal delays between spatially separated optical beams that arrived at the receiver surface. We assume that all the optical beams arrive at the same time on the receiver surface.

The maximum optical energy for one spot is concentrated into the center of the optical beam and ideally must correspond with the center of the receiver lens. Solution proposed in the scientific literature and industrial realizations use a set of paralleled n-beams (usually n – even number), un-collimated individually on the receiver lens. For this case an optical misalignment is occurred. The calculus for traditional (parallel beams) method include the optical losses and misalignment losses. If the multiple beams are perfectly focused on the receiver lens, we could consider that we have a single centered spot multiplied by n factor. In this case we consider only the optical losses (attenuation introduced by lens) without optical misalignment losses.

3   Results

Figure 2a shows the BER versus link distance for n = 1, 2, 4, and 8 heads with alignment and Fig. 2b BER versus link distance for n = 1, 2, 4, and 8 heads realized in the traditional way. Figure 3 shows out the eye diagram for scenario with four heads with alignment (a) and traditional (b).

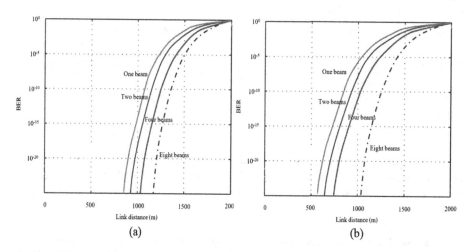

(a) (b)

Fig. 2. BER versus link distance for n = 1, 2, 4, and 8 heads with alignment (a) and traditional (b)

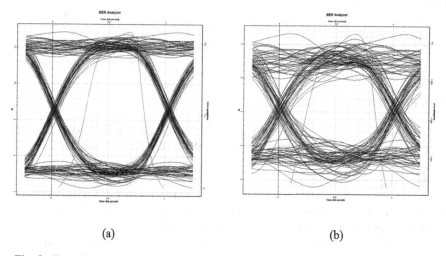

(a) (b)

Fig. 3. Eye diagram for scenario with four heads with alignment (a) and traditional (b)

Table 1 shows out the number of heads, geometrical loss, received optical power and link distance for traditional disposal of the laser heads for un-collimated heads. Collimated head (on the receiver lens area) means that the maximum optical energy for one spot is concentrated into the center of the receiver lens, even if the axis of the head beam does not correspond with the main axis of the transceivers.

Table 1. Number of heads, geometrical loss, received optical power and link distance for traditional disposal of the laser heads.

Head number	Geometrical loss (dB)	Received optical power (dBm)	Achievable link distance (km)
One beam	30.24	−32.2	0.85
Two beams	32.51	−33.1	0.89
Four beams	33.87	−34.6	1.02
Eight beams	34.02	−34.9	1.27

Table 2 shows out the number of heads, geometrical loss, received optical power and link distance for individual focalized laser heads. The geometrical loss decreased and received optical power increased with the consequence of increased link distance.

Table 2. Number of heads, geometrical loss, received optical power and link distance for individual focalized laser heads.

Head number	Geometrical loss (dB)	Received optical power (dBm)	Achievable link distance (km)
One beam	28.02	−34.7	1.21
Two beams	30.24	−35.1	1.29
Four beams	31.76	−35.9	1.42
Eight beams	32.02	−36.7	1.62

4 Conclusions

The proposed solution is suitable only for laser transmitter. It is not recommended to use LED sources due to very high divergence of the optical beam shown in [15], even if we use a beam collimator.

Another problem is represented by saturation of the receiver, for the very small atmospheric attenuation. For foggy atmosphere all the transmitters are used at the full power. For clear atmosphere it's used only one transmitter. It is mandatory to use an automatic gain control system to control the amount of light that arrives at the receiver. Using the concept of "mobility of the heads", it is not important the disposal (position) of the laser heads in the transmitter plane. The main disadvantage is represented by the necessity to (re)align the angle of the laser heads every time when the transmission distance between transmitter and receiver is modified. It is mandatory that every laser head from the transmitter configuration to be focused in the center of the receiver lens in order to assure an optimal signal/noise ratio in fog affected environment.

Future researches will include the calculus of the reliability of the multi-beam optical link using a probabilistic method.

References

1. Viorel, M., Sorin, P., Dan Alexandru, S.: Wireless optic last mile multi-Gbits communication system. In: ICEWC 2015: 17th International Conference on Electronics and Wireless Communication, Istanbul, Turkey, 26–27 October 2015
2. Hovorak, P.: Decreasing of turbulent atmosphere effect by multi beam transmission in FSO. Institute of Radio Electronics Brno University of Technology (2016)
3. Harma, P., Sarangal, H.: Performance evaluation of multiple transceiver FSO for different weather conditions. Int. J. Sig. Process. Image Process. Pattern Recogn. **8**(12), 149–156 (2015)
4. Mahalati, R.N., Kahn, J.M.: Effect of fog on free-space optical links employing imaging receivers. Optical Society of America (2012)
5. Sahu, N., Prajapti, J.C.: Optimization of WDM-FSO link using Multiple Beams under different rain conditions. Int. J. Adv. Res. Electron. Commun. Eng. (IJARECE) **4**(5), 1125–1131 (2015)
6. Robinson, R., Pavithra, R.: Investigation on multi-beam hybrid WDM for free space optical communication system. Int. J. Photonics Opt. Technol. **2**(2), 24–28 (2016)
7. Anguita, J.A., Neifeld, M.A., Vasic, B.V.: Multi-beam free-space optical link using space-time coding. Department of Electrical and Computer Engineering College of Optical Sciences University of Arizona (2016)
8. Kashani, F.D., Hedayati, M.R., Mahzoun, M.R., Ghafary, B.: Beam propagation analysis of a multi beam FSO system with partially flat-topped laser beams in turbulent atmosphere. Optik **123**(2012), 879– 886 (2012)
9. Al-Gailani, S.A., Mohammad, A.B., Shaddad, R.Q.: Enhancement of free space optical link in heavy rain attenuation using multiple beam concept. Optik **124**, 4798–4801 (2013)
10. Kadhim, S., Aldeen, S., Taha, A., Baki, A.Q.: Characterization study and simulation of MIMO free space optical communication under different atmospheric channel. IJISET – Int. J. Innovative Sci. Eng. Technol. **3**(8) (2016)
11. Kaur, H., Sarangal, H.: Simulative investigation on free space optical communication with optical amplification based on 4 × 4 transmitter/receiver combination. IJRECE **3**(1) (2015)
12. Recommendation ITU-R: Prediction methods required for the design of terrestrial free-space optical links. Question ITU-R 228/3, p. 1814 (2007)
13. Marian, V., Paul, S.: Advanced educational program in optoelectronics for undergraduates and graduates in electronics. In: Proceedings of the SPIE, Advanced Topics in Optoelectronics, Microelectronics, and Nanotechnologies VII, vol. 9258, p. 92580B (2015)
14. Marian, V., Dan Tudor, V.: Redundant uplink optical channel for visible light communication systems. In: Proceedings of the SPIE, Advanced Topics in Optoelectronics, Microelectronics, and Nanotechnologies VII, vol. 9258, p. 92581J (2015)
15. Marian, V., Dan Tudor V.: Automated platform for determination of LEDs spatial radiation pattern. In: Proceedings of the SPIE, Advanced Topics in Optoelectronics, Microelectronics, and Nanotechnologies VII, vol. 9258, p. 92581F (2015)

Key Aspects of Infrastructure-to-Vehicle Signaling Using Visible Light Communications

Alina Elena Marcu[1(✉)], Robert Alexandru Dobre[2], and Marian Vlădescu[3]

[1] Center for Technological Electronics and Interconnection Techniques (UPB-CETTI), Politehnica University of Bucharest, Iuliu Maniu blvd. 1-3, 69121 Bucharest, Romania
alina.marcu@cetti.ro
[2] Telecommunications Department, Politehnica University of Bucharest, Iuliu Maniu blvd. 1-3, 69121 Bucharest, Romania
rdobre@elcom.pub.ro
[3] Optoelectronics Research Center (UPB-CCO), Politehnica University of Bucharest, Iuliu Maniu blvd. 1-3, 69121 Bucharest, Romania
marian.vladescu@gmail.com

Abstract. With the appearance of autonomous cars, an infrastructure-to-car communication system can be easily developed by using the visible light communication (VLC). The red and green lights play an important role in the safety of road traffic, being the most significate colors of the traffic light system. The role of the proposed system is to obtain automatic braking if the traffic lights are red and an audio warning in the case of yellow color by modulating the radiation emitted by the traffic light to transmit a code for each of red and yellow lights. A secondary solution is proposed which avoids the modification of the current infrastructure of the traffic light system by adding a supplementary light emission element. The element consists of an infrared emitter used to send either the red color code or the yellow color code depending on the illuminated traffic light.

Keywords: LED · Visible light communication
Infrastructure-to-vehicle system

1 Introduction

In the dawn of the autonomous cars era, the road infrastructure system no longer meets the necessary requirements. A suitable technology that can be used to provide the necessary needs could be the VLC [1, 2].

VLC utilizes a visible light source, i.e. LED, to transmit information. One of the most important situation in which car accidents occur is at crossroads. Forcing the yellow light at crossroads is, unfortunately, a habit which drastically increases the chance of crossing when the red lights switched on.

The next generation, autonomous, cars could be designed to communicate with the signaling infrastructure, reducing the red light crossing to almost zero. This paper

© ICST Institute for Computer Sciences, Social Informatics and Telecommunications Engineering 2018
O. Fratu et al. (Eds.): FABULOUS 2017, LNICST 241, pp. 212–217, 2018.
https://doi.org/10.1007/978-3-319-92213-3_31

investigates the key elements of infrastructure-to-vehicle communication and presents the preliminary results of using VLC to implement such system. Onward, the paper is structured as follows: Sect. 2 describes the proposed communication system, Sect. 3 presents the results, and Sect. 4 concludes the paper.

2 Description of the System

The proposed communication system consists of two subsystems, as shown in Fig. 1. The emission subsystem is mounted on the traffic light and is used to transmit a code for the red light and another code for the yellow light by modulating the voltage applied to the radiating element (usually LEDs) [3]. The code must be chosen in such way to prevent flickering. The second subsystem is mounted on the car and is used to receive the code using an optical receiver and decode it. If the received message corresponds to the red code, the braking of the car will occur. If the message corresponds to the yellow code, an audio warning will alert the car driver that the traffic light is about to turn red. If none of these two codes will be received, then no action will take place.

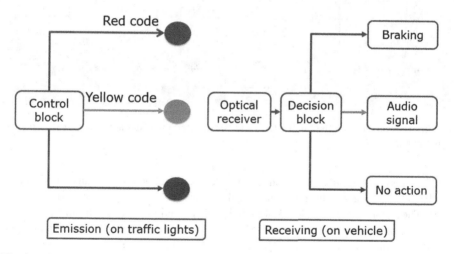

Fig. 1. The block diagram of the infrastructure-to-vehicle signaling system. (Color figure online)

Current signaling system must be modified to permit the modulation of the signal applied to the lamps. A secondary solution which avoids the modification of the current infrastructure of the traffic light system by adding a supplementary emission element to the emission subsystem. The element consists of an infrared emitter used to send either the red color code or the yellow color code depending on the illuminated traffic light. This way the current signaling system must not be modified. Only the information about the light that is on must be extracted, which is a much simpler operation. The receiving subsystem remains the same.

The code consists of synchronization pulses, pulses for logic "0," pulses for logic "1." A word of code is formed by three synchronization pulses and another four pulses representing the four bits carrying the information about the light that is currently on. There were chosen three synchronization pulses for an accurate synchronization (there is a small chance that three synchronization pulses can be obtained by accident. The chances to obtain one synchronization pulse by accident are clearly higher) and four pulses corresponding to the bits to end the code in logic "0". The code would have been ended in logic "0" even if the word would contain only two bits, but four pulses were chosen for possible future expansion of the system. The code is based on the duration between consecutive edges as shown in Fig. 2. The duration between two consecutive edges in case of the synchronization pulse is 50 μs, in case of logic "0" is 200 μs and in case of logic "1" is 100 μs.

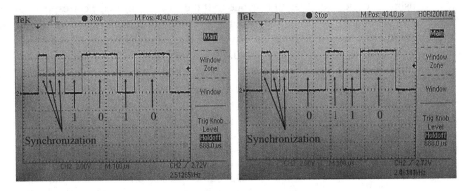

Fig. 2. The waveform of the "1010" (red) and "0110" (yellow) codes at the emitter side. (Color figure online)

On emission, the subsystem consists of a development board that transmits the code "1010" by modulating the red light and the code "0110" by modulating the yellow light. The duration for each word of code is 750 μs and the maximum duration of the code, in case of sending "0000", is 950 μs. In the infrared solution, the development board transmits either the code "1010" or code "0110" through the light emission element depending on the lighted color of the traffic light. Each word is repeated after 775 μs, assuring that flickering will not occur.

The receiving subsystem consists of an optical receiver that captures the light from the traffic lights, transforms it into voltage and, depending on the decoded code, sends the command to brake the car or to transmit an audio warning.

3   Results

The system discussed in the above section was implemented. The emission subsystem consists of a red LED, a yellow LED and a microcontroller. The receiving subsystem consists of an optical receiver (TSL14S), a red LED, a yellow LED, a blue LED and a microcontroller.

In Fig. 3, the microcontroller modulates the voltage applied to the yellow LED with the waveform for the code "0110", therefore, and the TLS14S receives the code from the light emitted by the LED, and if the message was correctly decoded and it corresponded with the code used for the yellow light, the yellow LED who plays the role of the audio warning lights up. A supplementary blue LED is used to determine if the receiving subsystem is powered up.

Fig. 3. The system transmits the code for yellow light ("0110" – right side of the picture) and the receiver successfully decodes it by turning on the yellow LED on its side (upper left side of the picture). (Color figure online)

Fig. 4. The system transmits the code for red light ("1010" – right side of the picture) and the receiver successfully decodes it by turning on the red LED on its side (upper left side of the picture). (Color figure online)

In Fig. 4, the same situation presented above is repeated for the red LED.

In Fig. 5, the infrared solution is implemented and the microcontroller transmits the code "0110", and if the TSL14S received the code corresponding with the yellow light, the yellow LED lightens up.

In Fig. 6, the infrared solution is implemented and the microcontroller transmits the code "1010", and if the TSL14S received the code corresponding with the red light, the red LED lightens up.

Fig. 5. The infrared LED transmits the code for the yellow light and the receiver successfully decodes it (the yellow LED is lit on the receiver side – upper left of the image). (Color figure online)

Fig. 6. The infrared LED transmits the code for the red light and the receiver successfully decodes it (the red LED is lit on the receiver side – upper left of the image). (Color figure online)

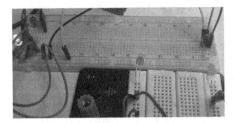
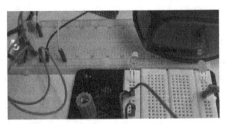

Fig. 7. The system transmits the yellow code, but because of the strong ambient light, the receiver is blinded and unable to decode. (Color figure online)

Fig. 8. An optical filter (Thorlabs LG4) placed in front of the receiver solves the blinding problem, ensuring proper decoding. (Color figure online)

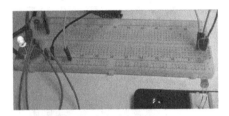
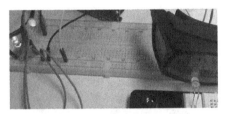

Fig. 9. The system transmits the red code, but because of the strong ambient light, the receiver is blinded and unable to decode. (Color figure online)

Fig. 10. An optical filter (Thorlabs LG10) placed in front of the receiver solves the blinding problem, ensuring proper decoding. (Color figure online)

In real situations, the receiver could be blinded by the ambient light during the day or by flashlights during the night. These situations were investigated in small scale conditions. In Fig. 7, the system transmits the code for the yellow light, but because of the strong ambient light, the receiving subsystem is not able to decode the received message and the yellow LED remains off to indicate this. To solve this problem an optical filter (Thorlabs LG4 glasses [4]) is placed in front of the receiver. In Fig. 8, the system transmits the code and the receiving subsystem is now able to decode the code properly because the ambient light was filtered and the TSL14S receives the incoming message.

In Figs. 9. and 10, the system transmits the code for the red light. In Fig. 9 the system it is not able to decode the received message, and in Fig. 10 an optical filter (Thorlabs LG10 [5]) was placed in front of the receiver to insure the correct decoding of the transmitted message.

The objective of this paper was to present the key elements of infrastructure-to-vehicle signaling. All the experiments in this paper were done using low power LEDs to highlight only the principles. High power LEDs [6] are to be used in real situations to assure a sufficient range.

4 Conclusions

The paper proposes an optical communication system used for the transmission of the messages between vehicles and the automotive infrastructure. The system consists of two subsystems, one for the transmission of the codes for the red and the yellow lights, and another for the receiving and the decoding them. A secondary solution was developed to avoid the modification of the current infrastructure of the traffic light. The supplementary light emission element consists of an infrared emitter used to send either the red color or the yellow color code depending on the illuminated traffic light.

The code consists of synchronization pulses, pulses for logic "0," pulses for logic "1". A word of code is formed by three synchronization pulses and four bits, but any even number of bits can be used to assure the return to zero, for further development. The duration of the pulses must be scaled accordingly to avoid flickering. The code is based on the duration between consecutive edges. The duration for each of the code is 750 μs and the maximum duration of the code is 950 μs.

It was seen that the system could not work in strong lighting condition, therefore an optical filter solution was proposed to filter the ambient light and to ensure the properly decoding of the received message. The next steps of the research includes measuring the optical responsiveness of power LEDs to determine their suitability for visible light communications.

Acknowledgment. SES, the world-leading operator of ASTRA satellites, is offering their support for the presentation and the publication of this paper.

References

1. Pathak, P.H., Feng, X., Hu, P., Mohapatra, P.: Visible light communication, networking and sensing: a survey, potential and challenges. IEEE Commun. Surv. Tutorials **17**, 2047–2077 (2015)
2. George, J.J., Mustafa, M.H., Osman, N.M., Ahmed, N.H., Hamed, D.M.: A survey on visible light communication. Int. J. Eng. Comput. Sci. **3**, 3805–3808 (2014)
3. Ionescu, C., Vasile, A., Codreanu, N., Negroiu, R.: Comparative studies on dimming capabilities of retrofit LED lamps. In: Advanced Topics in Optoelectronics, Microelectronics, and Nanotechnologies, pp. 100102Z–100102Z-10. International Society for Optics and Photonics, Constanţa (2016)
4. Thorlabs LG4 glasses datasheet. https://www.thorlabs.com/drawings/13f86c35c264a5c9-7DC5C175-F09C-1A63-77480014951A8907/LG4-SpecSheet.pdf. Accessed 14 June 2017
5. Thorlabs LG10 glasses datasheet. https://www.thorlabs.com/drawings/13f86c35c264a5c9-7DC5C175-F09C-1A63-77480014951A8907/LG4-SpecSheet.pdf. Accessed 14 June 2017
6. Ionescu, C., Drumea, A., Codreanu, N.D., Vasile, A.: Thermal investigations on high power LEDs. In: Advanced Topics in Optoelectronics, Microelectronics, and Nanotechnologies, pp. 84112Y–84112Y-10. International Society for Optics and Photonics, Constanţa (2012)

Optoelectronic Method for Determining the Aluminium Involved in Symptoms of Attention Deficit Hyperactivity Disorder Children

Elena Truță[1,2], Ana Maria Davițoiu[3], Ana Mihaela Mitu[4],
Alexandra Andrada Bojescu[5], Paul Șchiopu[6], Marian Vlădescu[6],
Genica Caragea[7], Luminița Horhotă[7], Maria Gabriela Neicu[8],
and Mihai Ionică[6,7(✉)]

[1] University for Medicine and Pharmacy "Titu Maiorescu", Bucharest, Romania
[2] Clinical Emergency Hospital, Bucharest, Romania
[3] Clinical Emergency Children Hospital "Victor Gomoiu", Bucharest, Romania
[4] Psychology Cabinet "Ana Mihaela Mitu", Bucharest, Romania
[5] Medical Office "Alexandra Andrada Bojescu", Bucharest, Romania
[6] Optoelectronics Research Center University "Politehnica",
Bucharest, Romania
mihaiionica56@gmail.com
[7] Medico-Military Scientific Research Centre, Bucharest, Romania
[8] University for Medicine and Pharmacy "Carol Davila", Bucharest, Romania

Abstract. Aluminum is a chemical element atomic number 13. It is white-silver, insoluble in water under normal conditions. Despite its natural abundance, aluminum has no known biology function. It is a toxic residue, aluminum sulphate having an LD50 of 6207 mg/kg body, corresponding to 500 g per 80 kg person. Extremely acute toxicity without harm to health is of interest in view of the widespread occurrence of the element in the environment and in trade. Toxicity can be tracked after deposition into the bones and the central nervous system and is particularly high in patients with renal insufficiency. In very high doses, aluminum can cause neuro toxicity associated with altered function of the blood-brain barrier.

Keywords: Optoelectronics · ADHD · Urine · Aluminium · GF-AAS

1 Introduction

Aluminum is a chemical element atomic number 13. Aluminum was noted for being a lightweight metal with a density of 2.7 g/cm3. This quality makes it used in large quantities in the naval and aeronautical industries. High reflectivity is used in the construction of metal mirrors [1]. Aluminum is remarkable for its low metal density and its ability to withstand corrosion. Despite its prevalence in the environment, aluminum salts are not known to be used by any form of life. According to its omnipresence, aluminum is well tolerated by plants and animals [2]. Aluminum alloys

© ICST Institute for Computer Sciences, Social Informatics and Telecommunications Engineering 2018
O. Fratu et al. (Eds.): FABULOUS 2017, LNICST 241, pp. 218–223, 2018.
https://doi.org/10.1007/978-3-319-92213-3_32

have yield strength ranges ranging from 200 MPa to 600 MPa [3]. Aluminum atoms are arranged in a cubic-centered structure. Aluminum has a stacking energy of approximately 200 MJ/m2. Aluminum is capable of being a superconductor with a critical superconductor temperature of 1.2 K and a critical magnetic field of about 100 Gauss (10 mT) [1, 5].

2 Experimental Set-up

The study aims to make a comparison between the concentrations of urine from the batch of children diagnosed with ADHD compared to those in the *"Children's House SOS Children's Villages"* and to analyze the influence of the sex of the children on the urinary concentrations of aluminum. Determination of the urinary concentration of aluminum was done by the atomic absorption spectrometer with atomization in graphite furnace, (GF-AAS) [3, 4].

2.1 Material and Method

The study was conducted between 2013 and 2014 at the "Children's home - SOS Children's Villages" on a 50-child group divided into two groups:

- A group, consisting of 25 children without ADHD, sex repatriation was: 12 boys and 13 girls;
- B group of 25 children with ADHD, broken down by sex SD follows: 14 boys and 11 girls.

The criteria for inclusion of children in A group were:

- age between 7 and 15 years.

The criteria to exclude children in A group:

- the existence of psychiatric diagnosis (mental deficiency, autism, psychosis, etc.);
- the existence of chronic neurological diseases: paresis, infantile brain paralysis.

The criteria for inclusion of children in B group:

- ages 7 to 15;
- ADHD diagnosis: hyperkinetic disorder accompanied by attention deficit, hyperkinetic disorder accompanied by impulsivity;
- duration of pharmacological treatment prior to inclusion in the group, less than or equal to 6 months;
- the possibility of following outpatient treatment.

Sex was not a selection criterion.
The criteria for exclusion of children in B group were:

- children with ADHD who also have other chronic conditions that may influence the quality of life (neurosis, anxiety, dissociation, organic diseases);
- the presence of mild, moderate or severe mental deficiency;

- the presence of neurological deficits of language reception;
- lack of compliance.

From all subjects enrolled in the study, urine was collected from the spot (10 mL).

To determine the concentration of aluminum in urine specimens, it was used a Varian graphite atomizer coupled with atomic absorption spectrometer system:

- Atomic Absorption Spectrometer (AAS 80);
- Programmable sample dispenser, standards, modifiers and thinner (PSD);
- Water Chiller Model Neslab CFT 33;
- Domnick Hunter Nitrogen Generator;
- Argon - gas cylinder under pressure purity 99.9999%;
- Reagents and equipment specific to a laboratory of analytical toxicology.

2.2 Sample Preparation

In 10 ml of urine harvested from each subject in the study lot, 1 ml of 65% HNO_3 was added. The mixture was left in the tube for 20 min and subsequently centrifuged at 2500 rpm for 10 min. The supernatant was the matrix for analysis on GF-AAS.

2.3 Optoelectronic AAS Method for Aluminum

To determine the concentration of aluminum in the injection matrix, the method used for the GF-AAS Varian system shown in Tables 1 and 2.

3 Experimental Results

The average of the urine concentrations of the aluminum was 10.54 µg/L. Sex analysis shows that the average urine concentration in boys was 12.12 µg/L and in girls, the mean was 8.18 µg/L of 1.89. The results are shown in Fig. 1.

Within group B, the mean urine concentrations of aluminum were 10.86 µg/L. Sex analysis shows that the average urine concentration in boys was 12.94 µg/L and in girls, the mean was 8.4 µg/L. The results are shown in Fig. 3. These results show a large distribution of aluminum in urine samples.

These results show a large distribution of urine concentrations of aluminum. The urinary concentration of aluminum allowance for children is in the range 5–30 µg/L [5]. However, the odd Student test shows that the two urinary concentrations of aluminum do not differ significantly statistically for a probability $p > 0.2$. Within group A, the mean urine concentrations of aluminum were 10.2 µg/L. Sex analysis shows that the average urine concentration in boys was 11.16 µg/L and in girls, the mean was 9.24 µg/L The results are shown in Fig. 2. These results show a large distribution of urine concentrations of aluminum.

Sex analysis shows that the value of urine concentrations of aluminum in girls is less than 1.82 µg/L than that of boys. The odd Student Test shows that the two urinary concentrations of aluminum do not differ statistically significantly for a probability $p > 0.6$. Analysis by sex shows that the value of urine concentrations of aluminum in

Table 1. General parameters for AAS.

No.	Parameters	Programming
1.	Type of injection	Auto dilution
2.	Calibration module	Concentration
3.	Type of measurement	Height peak
4.	Standard replicates	2
5.	Sample replicates	2
6.	Smoothing	9
7.	Wavelength	309.3 nm
8.	Slit width	0.2 nm
9.	Lamp current	10 mA
10.	Background correction	Yes
11.	Standard 1	20 µg/l
12.	Standard 2	50 µg/dl
13.	Standard 3	100 µg/dl
14.	Recalibration rate	10
15.	Reslope rate	1
16.	Concentration decimal places	2
17.	Calibration algorithm	New Rational
18.	Replicate % RSD limit	10%
19.	Correlation coefficient limit	0.998
20.	Required detection limit	1 µg/L
21.	Instrument detection limit	0.6 µg/l
22.	Injected volume	15 µl
23.	Sample volume	10 µl
24.	Dilution coefficient	2

Table 2. General parameters for graphite furnace.

Parameter	ST 1	ST 2	ST 3	ST 4	ST 5	ST 6	ST 7
Temp. (^{0}C)	40	85	85	95	120	120	1000
Time (s)	2	5	5	40	40	4	6
Gases	N	N	N	N	N	Ar	Ar
Flow (mL/min)	3	3	3	3	3	3	3
Read	–	–	–	–	–	–	–
Store	–	–	–	–	–	–	–
Parameter	ST 8	ST 9	ST 10	ST 11	ST 12	ST 13	ST 14
Temp. (^{0}C)	1000	2700	2700	3000	3000	40	40
Time (s)	2	2	1	0.1	2	22.3	3
Gases	Ar	Ar	Ar	N	N	N	N
Flow (mL/min)	0	0	0	3.1	3.1	3	0
Read	–	YES	YES	–	–	–	–
Store	YES	YES	YES	–	–	–	–

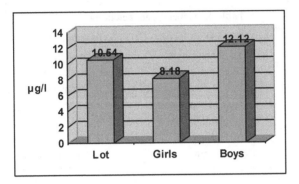

Fig. 1. Distribution of concentrations of aluminum in urine samples.

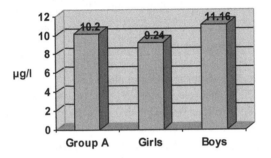

Fig. 2. Distribution of concentrations of aluminum in urine samples of group A.

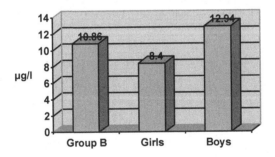

Fig. 3. Distribution of concentrations of aluminum in urine samples of group B.

girls is less than 4.54 µg/L than that of boys. The odd Student test shows that the two media of urinary concentrations of aluminum do not differ statistically significantly for a probability p > 0.3. The results are shown in Fig. 4.

The average of urinary concentrations of aluminum in the two groups do not differ statistically significantly for a probability p > 0.8. The difference between the two media is 0.66 µg/L. The average of urinary concentrations of aluminum in boys in the two groups do not differ statistically significantly for a probability p > 0.6. The difference between the two media is 0.78 µg/L. The average of urinary concentrations of

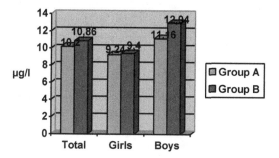

Fig. 4. Distribution of aluminum concentrations of urine samples by groups.

the aluminum of the girls in the two groups do not differ statistically significantly for a probability $p > 0.8$. The difference between the two media is 0.84 μ/L.

4   Conclusions

Analysis of urinary aluminum concentrations in children with ADHD relative to the urinary concentration of aluminum in children without ADHD did not reveal any statistically significant difference.

It can be argued that the occurrence of symptoms characteristic of ADHD can not be correlated with the presence of abnormal values of aluminum in subjects with ADHD.

These results show that aluminum can not be responsible for the presence of ADHD symptoms.

The developed optoelectronic method is relatively simple, reproducible and has a sensitivity that allows analysis of aluminum concentration in urine samples.

No value of urine concentrations of aluminum exceeded the maximum value allowed, which shows that there can be no aluminum contamination of the children in the studied group.

References

1. Helmboldt, O.: Aluminum compounds, inorganic. In: Ullmann's Encyclopedia of Industrial Chemistry. Wiley-VCH (2007)
2. Banks, W.A., Kastin, A.J.: Aluminum-induced neurotoxicity: alterations in membrane function at the blood-brain barrier. Neurosci. Biobehav. Rev. **13**(1), 47–53 (1989)
3. Ionică, M.: Dispozitive şi sisteme optoelectronice pentru măsurarea radiaţiei electromagnetice ultraviolete, vizibile sau infraroşii. Curs. Faculatea de Electronică Telecomunicaţii şi Tehnologia Informaţiei, Universitatea "*Politehnica*" din Bucureşti (2016)
4. Daviţoiu, A.M., Bărcănescu, Ş., Negulescu, V.A., Avram, O., Voicu, V.A., Macovei, R., Tudosie, M., Caragea, G., Forje, M., Mladin, C., Fragkos, A., Ardelean, L., Bumbea, V.: Selenium removal study in patients with chronicrenal disease. In: Therapeutics Pharmacology and Clinical Toxicology, vol. XVII, pp. 167–177 (2013)
5. Shakhashiri B.Z.: Chemical of the week: aluminum. In: *SciFun.org*. University of Wisconsin (2008)

Session on Computational Modeling

Prediction of Coronary Plaque Progression Using Data Driven Approach

Bojana Andjelkovic Cirkovic[1,2(✉)], Velibor Isailovic[1,2],
Dalibor Nikolic[2], Igor Saveljic[1,2], Oberdan Parodi[3],
and Nenad Filipovic[1,2]

[1] Faculty of Engineering, University of Kragujevac, Kragujevac, Serbia
{abojana,velibor,isaveljic,fica}@kg.ac.rs
[2] Research and Development Center for Bioengineering "BioIRC",
Kragujevac, Serbia
markovac85@kg.ac.rs
[3] CNR Clinical Physiology Institute, Pisa, Italy
oberpar@tin.it

Abstract. Coronary artery disease or coronary atherosclerosis (CATS) is the most common type of cardiovascular disease and the number one cause of death worldwide. Early identification of patients who will develop progression of disease is beneficial for treatment planning and adopting the strategy for reduction of risk factors that could cause future cardiac events. In this paper, we propose the data mining model for prediction of CATS progression. We exploit patient's health record by using various machine learning methods. Predictor variables, including heterogenious data from cellular to the whole organism level, are initially preprocessed by feature selection approaches to select only the most informative features as inputs to machine learning algorithms. Results obtained and features selected within this study indicate the high potential of machine learning to be used in clinical practice as well as that specific monocytes are important markers impacting the plaque progression.

Keywords: Coronary artery disease · Atherosclerosis progression
Machine learning · Feature selection

1 Introduction

Coronary artery disease, specifically coronary atherosclerosis, is one of the leading causes of death worldwide. This enduring inflammatory disease of the arterial wall is result of chronic formation of fatty streaks and atheromas, followed by acute thrombotic events. The number of patients with coronary atherosclerosis was rapidly increased over the past decade and the disease has tendency to be an epidemic in the near future [1]. Pharmacological treatment and revascularization are standard treatment modalities used to control and prevent future cardiac events. Several studies [2–4] showed that, although the revascularization of significant hemodynamic stenosis in combination with pharmacological therapy is superior in comparison to medicaments only, not all patients will benefit from revascularization. Understanding of the

© ICST Institute for Computer Sciences, Social Informatics and Telecommunications Engineering 2018
O. Fratu et al. (Eds.): FABULOUS 2017, LNICST 241, pp. 227–233, 2018.
https://doi.org/10.1007/978-3-319-92213-3_33

hemodynamic significance of atherosclerotic lesions via additional assessment is crucial in order to better manage therapy and optimize patient outcomes.

Many artery specific and patient-specific factors are known to contribute to the process of atherosclerosis formation and progression by a complex interaction between biological and mechanical elements. These factors were mostly explored by computing correlations between single features and the angiography outcome. However, several moderate risk factors may, in combination, result in a much higher risk than an impressively raised single factor [5]. For this reason, it is necessary to examine the disease from cellular to the whole organism level and collect the expanded list of factors in order to find the proper combination among them that are the most correlated with the progression of CATS. This will significantly improve strategies for identification of patients with high-risk CATS and early intervention.

The number of computational techniques has been developed in order to understand the mechanisms of CATS progression. On the other side, machine learning methods (ML) provide the framework to learn complex patterns from data. Due to ability to handle the high-dimensionality nature of patients' data [6, 7] and make accurate patient specific predictions in a real time, this approach has become a popular research tool for medical researchers who seek to gain insights and exploit the information in a more effective manner.

In this study, we employ a machine learning approach based on heterogeneous data collected within the SMARTool project [8], which include both imaging data (Coronary Computed Tomography Angiography - CCTA) and clinical, molecular and cellular data, to predict progression of CATS. More specifically, we analyzed information coming from the patients' medical records, biochemical analyzes, adhesion molecules, and monocyte markers with the aim to model the progression of atherosclerosis in coronary vessels. The problem was defined as binary classification problem since we wanted to predict whether the progression of disease will occur or not for a specific patient.

2 Methods

2.1 Patients and Dataset

In this study, we considered medical records of 55 patients obtained within the H2020 SMARTool project. These patients underwent angiographic assessment by coronary computed tomography angiography in order to evaluate the percentage of stenosis. In this study, results were based on the assessment of disease for each patient performed in two time moments, with the average time between two assessment of 10.2 ± 3 months (median time = 11 months). Moreover, wide series of data obtained during the second time-slice were collected, namely, the patient's medical history, relevant risk factors, biochemical markers, therapy and monocyte markers and each patient is described with 72 features (Table 1).

The CCTA metrics adopted to define clinically relevant disease progression at each artery site are the following:

Table 1. List of features in dataset.

Clinical			
Gender (Binary)	Age (Numeric)	BMI (Numeric)	Alcohol consumption (Numeric)
Current Smoking (Binary)	Past Smoking (Binary)	Physical Activity (Binary)	Diet/Vegetable (Binary)
Diabetes Mellitus (Binary)	Dyslipidemia (Binary)	Hypertension (Binary)	Metabolic Sindrome (Binary)
Family History CHD (Binary)	Current Symptoms (Binary)	Infarct (Binary)	CABG (Binary)
PICStenting (Binary)			

Therapy			
ARB (Binary)	Diuretics (Binary)	Statins (Binary)	oral Antidiabetics (Binary)
Aspirin (Binary)	Insulin (Binary)	BETA Blockers (Binary)	ACE Inhibitors (Binary)
DAPT (Binary)	Nitrates (Binary)	Calcium Antagonists (Binary)	Other Drugs (Binary)

Blood Test			
Creatinine (Numeric)	HDL (Numeric)	Leukocytes (Numeric)	Total Cholesterol (Numeric)
Erythrocytes (Numeric)	Hemoglobin (Numeric)	MCH (Numeric)	Triglycerides (Numeric)
Fasting Glucose (Numeric)	INR (Numeric)	MCV (Numeric)	Uric acid (Numeric)
Fibrinogen (Numeric)	LDL (Numeric)	Platelets (Numeric)	aPTT (Numeric)
HCT (Numeric)			

Inflammatory			
ICAM1 (Numeric)	VCAM1 (Numeric)		

Monocytes			
CCR2_% (Numeric)	CD14(++/+)_% (Numeric)	CD163_ RFI (Numeric)	CX3CR1_ RFI (Numeric)
CCR2_RFI (Numeric)	CD14(++/+)_RFI (Numeric)	CD16_% (Numeric)	CXCR4_% (Numeric)
CCR5_% (Numeric)	CD14++/CD16+/CCR2+_% (Numeric)	CD16_ RFI (Numeric)	CXCR4_ RFI (Numeric)
CCR5_ RFI (Numeric)	CD14++/CD16-/CCR2+_% (Numeric)	CD18_% (Numeric)	HLA-DR_% (Numeric)
CD11b_% (Numeric)	CD14+/CD16++/CCR2-_% (Numeric)	CD18_ RFI (Numeric)	HLA-DR_ RFI (Numeric)
CD11b_ RFI (Numeric)	CD163_% (Numeric)	CX3CR1_% (Numeric)	MONOCYTE COUNT_ RFI (Numeric)

Progress (Binary)			

- Plaque progression: further luminal diameter narrowing > 20% at the site of pre-existing stenosis;
- De novo plaque formation: development of a new plaque causing a luminal narrowing >20% in a previously normal segment.

2.2   Feature Selection

In machine learning and data mining, feature selection is the process of selecting a subset of features for use in model construction. There are plenty of studies pointing out that learning algorithms may be adversely affected by the presence of irrelevant and/or redundant features and that feature selection in most of cases improves the classification accuracy [9, 10]. Additionally, feature selection significantly reduces computation complexity, prevents over-fitting and facilitates data understanding as well as data acquiring.

Specifically, in this study we used three state-of-the-art filter algorithms for feature selection: ReliefF [11], mRMR [12] and Gain ratio [13] widely used for extraction of useful features from data.

1. The ReliefF algorithm is based on the idea that useful features should differentiate between instances from different classes and have similar values from instances from the same class. It randomly choses an instance from the dataset, finds its nearest neighbor from the same and opposite class, and updates relevance score for each feature by comparing the values of nearest neighbors to the sampled instance.
2. The mRMR algorithm maintains the features that have high correlation with the class attribute and low inter-correlation among themselves.
3. Gain ratio (GR) normalizes the information gain score of splitting on an attribute by the entropy of this attribute.

2.3   Classification

A set of seven representative supervised machine learning algorithms were used for knowledge extraction and performing of classification [13]: naive Bayes classifier (NB), Bayesian Network (BN), decision tree (DT) based on C4.5 algorithm, Random Forest (RF), Support Vector Machine (SVM), K-Nearest neighbor (K-NN) and artificial neural network (ANN). ANN was constructed as a multi-layer perceptron with one hidden layer, unipolar sigmoid activation function was set in all neurons, and learning algorithm was back propagation with momentum. SVM was run with a polynomial as well as the RBF kernel.

All these algorithms are implemented in WEKA software packet [14] which is used for the resolving of the defined classification problem.

For evaluation of the classifiers, the 10-fold cross validation procedure was used, where, in each repetition, instances belonging to the left-out fold were used for testing purposes (test set), while the remaining observations were used for feature selection and classifier training (training set). In each iteration of the cross validation procedure we applied the classifier's parameter selection algorithm (CVParameterSelection algorithm from the Weka machine learning software) [15] which explores all possible combinations for a set of classifier's parameters by applying nested 10-fold cross validation procedure on the training set. For given classifiers the following parameters were optimized:

- For SVM: $C \in \{10^{-3}, 10^{-2}, ..., 10^3\}$ and degree of kernel $k \in \{1, 2\}$ for polynomial, and gamma $\in \{10^{-2}, 10^{-1}, 0, 10^0, 10^1\}$ for RBF kernel.
- For KNN: $K \in \{1, 3, 5, 7\}$.
- For ANN: number of nodes in hidden layer.

It should be noted that test data were never used for feature selection and training of the classifiers, including the tuning of classifiers.

For measuring the performances of classifiers, we adopted the following metrics: accuracy, sensitivity, specificity, precision and the area under the ROC curve (AUC). Accuracy (AC) is the proportion of the total number of predictions that were correct. Sensitivity (SENS) is defined as the proportion of true positives that are correctly identified by the classifier (e.g., patients with ATS progression), while specificity (SPEC) is a measure of how accurate a test is against false positives (e.g., patients without ATS progression). Precision (PREC) reflects the percentage of patients who actually have the disease among all tested positive. The AUC is an effective and combined measure of sensitivity and specificity that describes ability of model to discriminate between samples that belong to positive and negative classes.

Before the features selection and evaluation of classifiers' results, all data values were normalized to the range [0, 1] by using min-max transformation.

3 Results and Discussion

In this section we present the best results of classifiers' performances obtained by applying the previously described feature selection procedure. The filter algorithms for features selection rank the features from the most important to the less important one according to the statistics they use. We analyzed the results for top ranked k = 5, 10, 20, 30, 40 features. Table 2 clearly shows that MRMR algorithm selection outperformed other algorithms for feature selection. More precisely, the best result was achieved for 20 selected attributes and ANN classifier: **accuracy = 0.891, sensitivity = 0.897, specificity = 0.885, precision = 0.897, AUC = 0.971.**

The most informative selected features are: Diabetes Mellitus, Hypertension, Metabolic Syndrome, Current Symptoms, Aspirin, Oral Antidiabetics, Creatinine, Fibrinogen, INR, MCH, MCV, Total Cholesterol, Triglycerides, CD14(++/+)_RFI, CD14++/CD16-/CCR2+_%, CD163_%, CD16_RFI, CX3CR1_%, CXCR4_%, HLA-DR_%. The study also indicated that among these parameters, CD16_RFI and Hypertension demonstrated the highest correlation with CATS progression. Additionally, a great number of monocytes are selected which in combination with other selected features favors the progression of existing plaque. It is well known that monocytes are directly involved in the process of atherosclerosis formation and a number of other chronic inflammatory conditions. Also, a plenty of studies in literature investigated the monocyte subsets and cardiovascular risk factors. Other selected

Table 2. The best results obtained using classification algorithms in combination with different features selection algorithms.

	Algorithms	ACC	Sens	Spec	Prec	AUC
ReliefF	NB	0.636	0.828	0.423	0.615	0.653
	BN	0.564	0.966	0.115	0.549	0.554
	DT	**0.727**	**0.828**	**0.615**	**0.706**	**0.69**
	RF	0.618	0.552	0.692	0.667	0.64
	SVM	0.618	0.828	0.385	0.6	0.606
	KNN	0.527	0.655	0.385	0.543	0.534
	ANN	0.6	0.793	0.385	0.59	0.612
GainRatio	NB	0.636	0.828	0.423	0.615	0.653
	BN	0.564	0.966	0.115	0.549	0.554
	DT	**0.655**	**0.828**	**0.462**	**0.632**	**0.624**
	RF	0.655	0.759	0.538	0.647	0.664
	SVM	0.618	0.828	0.385	0.6	0.606
	KNN	0.545	0.586	0.5	0.567	0.582
	ANN	0.6	0.655	0.538	0.613	0.553
MRMR	NB	0.745	0.897	0.577	0.703	0.726
	BN	0.564	0.966	0.115	0.549	0.554
	DT	0.727	0.828	0.615	0.706	0.718
	RF	0.673	0.759	0.577	0.667	0.722
	SVM	0.764	0.897	0.615	0.722	0.756
	KNN	0.745	0.724	0.769	0.778	0.827
	ANN	**0.891**	**0.897**	**0.885**	**0.897**	**0.971**

features are already known from the literature as important factors associated to the atherosclerosis disease.

ANN classification algorithm with learning rate set to 0.1 and 6 neurons in hidden layer demonstrated the highest predictive ability. Although our database was relatively limited, results we achieved are encouraging and indicate that ML models can be efficiently developed to predict the prognosis on plaque progression. However, further validation of our results is needed in order to be useful in clinical practice.

4 Conclusion

We presented approach based on medical data analysis aiming to assess the progression of coronary atherosclerosis. Wide series of data obtained from patients' medical records were assembled in order to provide the comprehensive data set able to capture the possible disease manifestations. The results showed that ANN classifier applied on 20 selected features is the most reliable among all tested ML algorithms for prediction whether the patient will be faced with the CATS progression. In the future, we will focus on testing the model on new unseen data and knowledge extraction in order to demonstrate generalization capability and provide explanation of predictions.

Acknowledgments. This work was supported by the Ministry of Education, Science and Technological Development of the Republic of Serbia under grant III41007, and by EU H2020 SMARTool project, project ID: 689068. The authors also thank to SES, the world-leading operator of ASTRA satellites, for their kind support in presentation and publishing of this paper.

References

1. Moran, A.E., Forouzanfar, M.H., Roth, G.A., et al.: Temporal trends in ischemic heart disease mortality in 21 world regions, 1980 to 2010: the Global Burden of Disease 2010 study. Circulation **129**(14), 1483–1492 (2014)
2. Boden, W.E., O'Rourke, R.A., Teo, K.K., et al.: Optimal medical therapy with or without PCI for stable coronary disease. N. Engl. J. Med. **356**(15), 1503–1516 (2007)
3. Tonino, P.A., De Bruyne, B., Pijls, N.H., et al.: Fractional flow reserve versus angiography for guiding percutaneous coronary intervention. N. Engl. J. Med. **360**(3), 213–224 (2009)
4. De Bruyne, B., Pijls, N.H., Kalesan, B., et al.: Fractional flow reserve-guided PCI versus medical therapy in stable coronary disease. N. Engl. J. Med. **367**(11), 991–1001 (2012)
5. Papafaklis, M.I., Mavrogiannis, M.C., Stone, P.H.: Identifying the progression of coronary artery disease: prediction of cardiac events. Continuing Cardiol. Educ. **2**, 105–114 (2016)
6. Bolón-Canedo, V., Remeseiro, B., Alonso-Betanzos, A., Campilho, A.: Machine learning for medical applications. In: ESANN proceedings, European Symposium on Artificial Neural Networks, Computational Intelligence and Machine Learning. Bruges (Belgium), pp. 27–29, April 2016. ISBN 978-287587027
7. Thottakkara, P., Ozrazgat-Baslanti, T., Hupf, B.B., Rashidi, P., Pardalos, P., Momcilovic, P., Bihorac, A.: Application of machine learning techniques to high-dimensional clinical data to forecast postoperative complications. PLOS ONE **11**(5) (2016), https://doi.org/10.1371/journal.pone.0155705
8. EU H2020 project: Simulation Modeling of coronary ARTery disease: a tool for clinical decision support. http://www.smartool.eu/
9. Bolón-Canedo, V., Sánchez-Maroño, N., Alonso-Betanzos, A.: Foundations of feature selection. Feature Selection for High-Dimensional Data. AIFTA, pp. 13–28. Springer, Cham (2015). https://doi.org/10.1007/978-3-319-21858-8_2
10. Saeys, Y., Abeel, T., Van de Peer, Y.: Robust feature selection using ensemble feature selection techniques. In: Daelemans, W., Goethals, B., Morik, K. (eds.) ECML PKDD 2008. LNCS (LNAI), vol. 5212, pp. 313–325. Springer, Heidelberg (2008). https://doi.org/10.1007/978-3-540-87481-2_21
11. Robnik-Sikonja, M., Kononenko, I.: An adaptation of Relief for attribute estimation in regression. In: Fourteenth International Conference on Machine Learning, pp. 296–304 (1997)
12. Peng, H., Long, F., Ding, C.: Feature selection based on mutual information: criteria of max-dependency, max-relevance, and min-redundancy. IEEE Trans. Pattern Anal. Mach. Intell. **27**(8), 1226–1238 (2005)
13. Kononenko, I., Kukar, M.: Machine Learning and Data Mining: Introduction to Principles and Algorithms, Horwood Publ. (2007)
14. Hall, M., Frank, E., Holmes, G., Pfahringer, B., Reutemann, P., Witten, I.H.: The WEKA data mining software: an update. SIGKDD Explor. **11**(1) (2009)
15. Kohavi, R.: Wrappers for Performance Enhancement and Oblivious Decision Graphs. Department of Computer Science, Stanford University (1995)

Optimization of Parameters for Electrochemical Detection: Computer Simulation and Experimental Study

Marko N. Živanović[1]([✉]), Danijela M. Cvetković[1],
and Nenad D. Filipović[2,3]

[1] Faculty of Science, Department for Biology and Ecology,
University of Kragujevac, Kragujevac, Serbia
zivanovicmkg@gmail.com
[2] Faculty of Engineering, Center for Bioengineering, University of Kragujevac,
Kragujevac, Serbia
[3] BioIRC Bioengineering R&D Center, Kragujevac, Serbia

Abstract. It has been shown that for each electrochemical measurement it is necessary first to optimize all the parameters that influence the obtained electrochemical signal. This is a time-consuming process and that is why in this study we focused on the computer simulation of the influence of multiparameters on the electrochemical signal. Herein we used a model system of the electroreduction of ruthenium(III) salt on gold electrode in phosphate buffer solution. Ru^{3+} is often used as redox probe for detection and understanding of nucleic acid hybridization on the electrodes. This study should reveal some new aspects of using the computer simulations in determining the optimal measuring conditions for detection of RNA/PNA hybridoms on the gold surface.

Keywords: Computer simulation · Electrochemistry · Optimization

1 Introduction

Electrochemistry is a discipline widely used in the fields of industry, science, testing of many different small molecules and large biomacromolecules, especially in biosensors [1]. Methods of electrochemical determination are accurate, fast, precise and inexpensive. Defining and establishing of precise and clearly defined parameters of electrochemical determination is of outmost importance. However, practice shows that the establishment and definition of optimal parameters is often very long and the painstaking process which is often far more demanding than later electrochemical analyzes. Determining of individual parameters and their synergy is a time-consuming process. For example, a common electrochemical investigation determines the following parameters: Information about the type of molecule to be tested, type of supporting electrolyte, pH, ionic strength, addition of salts, temperature, type of electrode, voltage range, electrochemical cell geometry, stirring speed, adsorption time and many others. Fortunately, depending on the electrochemical process being monitored and on the applied method of determination, it is often known that a requested electrochemical

© ICST Institute for Computer Sciences, Social Informatics and Telecommunications Engineering 2018
O. Fratu et al. (Eds.): FABULOUS 2017, LNICST 241, pp. 234–238, 2018.
https://doi.org/10.1007/978-3-319-92213-3_34

signal will behave in relation to the change of the given parameters. For example, in monitoring the process of electrocatalytic elution of hydrogen on the mercury electrode in the determination of polyamino acids the definition of the mentioned parameters is of outmost importance [2, 3]. However, as mentioned above, the synergy of change is also very important. It is necessary to estimate how the change of several parameters at the same time will affect the change in the observed electrochemical signal. Therefore, computer simulation methods allow *in silico* predicting the influence of different parameters on the observed electrochemical signal and optimizing the establishment of the determination conditions. In other words, computer simulation enables us to save time and optimize the process of electrochemical determination. If we know the nature of the examined analyte, the methodology and the basic conditions of electrochemical determination, the computer simulation can offer us the most probable optimal conditions for determining. We firstly described experimental setup and numerical model used for computer simulation. Then some initial results for computer simulation and experimental study are compared. Finally, some discussion and conclusions are given.

2   Experimental

2.1   Electrochemical Detection of Ru^{3+} Reduction on Gold Electrode

Case Presentation. It has been known that nucleic acids are electroactive [4]. Using the oscillographic polarography method at controlled AC on dropping mercury electrode changes in the DNA structure were followed. Since then, electrochemistry of DNA and RNA has become booming field in electroanalytics, finally with the production of advanced biosensors. One of many possible methods for electrochemical detection of nucleic acids samples onto gold electrodes is using of Ru^{3+} salt [5]. Investigation of nucleic acid hybridization on gold electrodes can be monitored using redox probes such as hexaamine-ruthenium (III). In this sense, in order to arrive at accurate, precise and reproducible determination, it is necessary to optimize all parameters. In our experiment, we used phosphate buffer of various pHs, ionic strengths, with or without salt addition, in temperature controlled conditions with stirring in various speeds. In this paper, we will try to discuss about fitting of optimal parameters for electrochemical detection of redox probe of Ru^{3+} prior to investigate nucleic acid hybridization.

2.2   Reagents, Solutions and Apparatus

All reagents were purchased from Sigma-Aldrich and were of analytical grade. The measurements were performed with an EmStat-3 potentiostat (PalmSens BV, The Netherlands) operated with the PSTrace v.4.8 software. We used a standard electrochemical cell equipped with three-electrode system. The working electrode was 2 mm diameter gold electrode, the reference electrode was Ag ∣ AgCl ∣ 3 M KCl, with Pt wire as auxiliary electrode.

2.3   Numerical Model

In the modeling of electrochemical deposition on the electrode we used Nernst-Planck definition of species flux through homogeneous media. The flux resulting from the electrochemical potential gradient is typically decoupled into a diffusion term corresponding to activity or concentration gradient driven flow and an electromigration term that accounts for the force of the electric field on charged molecules. The Nernst-Planck flux is defined as:

$$J_i = -\left[D_i \frac{\partial c_i}{\partial x} + u_i c_i \frac{\partial \varphi}{\partial x}\right] \tag{1}$$

where D_i, u_i, c_i and $\frac{\partial \varphi}{\partial x}$ are diffusion coefficient, electrical mobility, concentration and kinetic potential gradient, respectively.

The diffusion coefficient and electric mobility are proportionality constants between flux and the concentration and potential gradients, respectively. They are related by the Nernst-Einstein equation:

$$u_i = \frac{z_i D_i F}{RT} \tag{2}$$

In our study, we are trying to simulate current versus voltage on the specific electrode with diffusion of investigated substance using finite element method [6], against passive diffusion represented by Fick's law:

$$J_i = -D_i \frac{\partial c_i}{\partial x} \tag{3}$$

Mesh model for finite element method analysis consists of 3D finite element elements that result in good convergence [7].

The governing equations are the following:

Nernst-Planck without electroneutrality

$$\delta_{ts} \frac{\delta c}{\delta t} + \nabla \cdot (-D\nabla c - z u_m F c \nabla V) = 0 \tag{4}$$

where δ_{ts} is time scaling coefficient, D is diffusion coefficient, c is drug concentration, z is charge number, u_m is mobility, F is Faraday constant, and V is potential. The Voltage equation which was used is the following:

$$-\nabla \cdot (\sigma \nabla V - J^e) = Q_j \tag{5}$$

where σ is electric conductivity, V is potential, J^e is external current source and Q_j is current source.

3   Results

3.1   Electrochemical Detection

The experimental results of our model obtained with hexaammine-ruthenium(III) in 100 mM phosphate buffer, pH 7.0 are presented in the Fig. 1. Normal pulse voltammograms were obtained at scan rate $250\,mVs^{-1}$ in potential range from -1.0 to

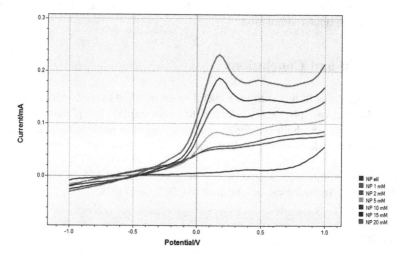

Fig. 1. Normal pulse voltammograms of hexaammine-ruthenium(III) on gold electrode in 100 mM phosphate buffer, pH 7. Scan rate 250 mVs^{-1}.

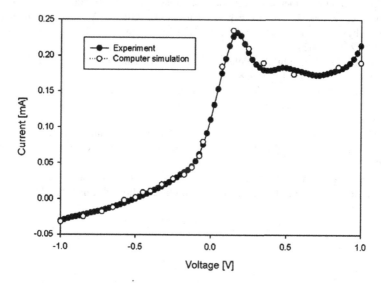

Fig. 2. Comparison of experimental and computer simulation results for normal pulse voltammograms of hexaammine-ruthenium(III) on gold electrode in 100 mM phosphate buffer, pH 7 for NP = 20 mM.

$+1.0 \text{ V}, E_{step} 25 \text{ m V}$, and $t_{pulse} 5$ ms. Under this conditions Ru^{3+} reduction peak was well distinguished from the background discharge in concentration range from 1 to 20 mM at potential around +0.15 V. The peak height gradually increased with increasing the Ru^{3+} concentrations and peak potential, E_p shifted towards more positive potentials.

Comparison of experimental and computer simulation results for concentration of 20 mM at potential around +0.15 V has been presented in the Fig. 2. It can be observed that good agreement was achieved for this specific parameter optimization procedure with computer simulation.

4 Discussion and Conclusions

Computer simulations in this study are useful to do *in-silico* many experiments which cannot be done in real physical world and to better explain the physics behind the process, so it is a high challenge for the future to develop mathematical models that accurately describe effects of electrochemical deposition to the electrode.

Acknowledgments. This study was funded by the grants from the Serbian Ministry of Education, Science and Technological Development III41007, ON174028.

References

1. Wang, J.: Analytical Electrochemistry. John Wiley & Sons VCH, Hoboken (2006)
2. Živanović, M., Aleksić, M., Ostatná, V., Doneux, T., Paleček, E.: Polylysine-catalyzed hydrogen evolution at mercury electrodes. Electroanal. **22**(17–18), 2064–2070 (2010)
3. Vargová, V., Živanović, M., Dorčák, V., Paleček, E., Ostatná, V.: Catalysis of hydrogen evolution by polylysine, polyarginine and polyhistidine at mercury electrodes. Electroanal. **25**(9), 2130–2135 (2013)
4. Palecek, E.: Oszillographische Polarographie der Nucleinsiiuren und ihrer Bestandteile. Naturwissenschaften **45**, 186 (1958)
5. Ahmed, M.U., Nahar, S., Safavieha, M., Zourob, M.: Real-time electrochemical detection of pathogen DNA using electrostatic interaction of a redox probe. Analyst. **138**(3), 907–915 (2013)
6. Filipovic, N., Peulic, A., Zdrakovic, N., Grbovic-Markovic, V., Jurisic-Skevin, A.: Transient finite element modeling of functional electrical stimulation. Gen. Physiol. Biophys. **30**(1), 59–65 (2011)
7. Filipovic, N., Zivanovic, M., Savic, A., Bijelic, G.: Numerical simulation of iontophoresis in the drug delivery system. Comput. Methods Biomech. Biomed. Engin. **19**(11), 1154–1159 (2016)

Assessment of Machine Learning Algorithms for the Purpose of Primary Sjögren's Syndrome Grade Classification from Segmented Ultrasonography Images

Arso Vukicevic[1,2(✉)], Alen Zabotti[3], Salvatore de Vita[3],
and Nenad Filipovic[1,2]

[1] BioIRC, Bioengineering Research and Development Center,
Prvoslava Stojanovica 6, 34000 Kragujevac, Serbia
arso_kg@yahoo.com, fica@kg.ac.rs
[2] Faculty of Engineering, University of Kragujevac, Sestre Janjica 6,
34000 Kragujevac, Serbia
[3] Azienda Ospedaliero Universitaria, Santa Maria Della Misericordia di Udine,
Udine, Italy
zabottialen@gmail.com,
devita.salvatore@aoud.sanita.fvg.it

Abstract. Primary Sjögren's syndrome (pSS) is a chronic autoimmune disease that affects primarily women (9 females/1 male). Recently, a great interest has arisen for salivary gland ultrasonography (SGUS) as a valuable tool for the assessment of major salivary gland involvement in primary Sjögren's syndrome. The aim of this study was to assess accuracy of state of the art machine learning algorithms for the purpose of classifying pSS from SGUS images. The five-step procedure was carried out, including: image pre- processing, feature extraction, data set balancing and feature extraction, classifiers (K-Nearest Neighbour, Decision trees, Naive bayes, Discriminant analysis classifier, Random forest, Multilayer perceptron, Linear logistic regression) learning and their corresponding assessment. The preliminary results on the growing HarmonicSS cohort showed that Naive bayes (72.8% accuracy on training set, and 73.3% accuracy on test set) and Multilayer perceptron (85.0% accuracy in training stage, and 70.1% accuracy at test stage) are the most suitable for the purpose of pSS grade classification.

Keywords: Sjögren's syndrome · Classification · Ultrasonography

1 Introduction

Primary Sjögren's syndrome (pSS) is a chronic autoimmune disease [1]. According to the clinical reports, the annual incidence of pSS among North and South European populations has been estimated at a range from 200 to 3000 per 100.000 individuals [2]. Moreover, among 394,827 affected individuals with systemic autoimmune diseases, pSS was found to be characterized by the most unbalanced gender ratio with almost 10 females affected per 1 male, followed by systemic lupus erythematosus,

© ICST Institute for Computer Sciences, Social Informatics and Telecommunications Engineering 2018
O. Fratu et al. (Eds.): FABULOUS 2017, LNICST 241, pp. 239–245, 2018.
https://doi.org/10.1007/978-3-319-92213-3_35

systemic sclerosis and antiphospholipid syndrome (APS) (ratio of nearly 5:1) [3]. The pSS has a wide range of clinical presentations, from mild disease limited to exocrine glands to severe multi-systemic disorder, and increases the risk of developing a B-cell non-Hodgkin lymphoma, which occurs in about 5% of patients [1].

Currently, the involvement of salivary glands in pSS is assessed by means of complementary tests such as sialometry, sialoscintigraphy and sialography, in accordance with the American European Consensus Group (AECG) classification criteria. Such tests, added to biopsy of the minor salivary gland (MSGB), may provide valuable information on the anatomical and functional damage in these glands; however, their use in clinical practice is limited by its poor specificity for pSS diagnosis. Recently, a great interest has arisen for salivary gland ultrasonography (SGUS) as a valuable tool for the assessment of major salivary gland involvement in primary Sjögren's syndrome. Figure 1 shows an example of manual segmentation of SGUS, adapted from a literature [4]. The aim of this study was to develop tools for classification of pSS using segmented ultrasonography images of salivary gland. The overall workflow is given on Fig. 2 while each of the particular steps is explained in the remainder of this document.

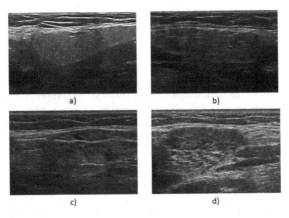

Fig. 1. Ultrasound images of pSS: (a) Grade 0, (b) Grade 1, (c) Grade 2, (d) Grade 3

2   Methods

2.1   Image Pre-processing

The purpose of image pre-processing was to reduce noises and artifact occurred during the image acquisition with a mobile ultrasonography device. Each DICOM image was pre-processed using the procedure sketched on Fig. 3. We first used Wiener filter [5]. Afterwards, we used Matlab's Image processing toolbox implementation of histogram equalizer. Finally, Salt and pepper noise on images war reduced using the two-dimensional median filter.

Fig. 2. Procedure workflow

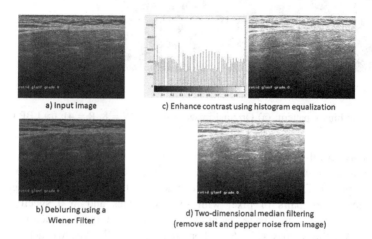

a) Input image   c) Enhance contrast using histogram equalization

b) Debluring using a   d) Two-dimensional median filtering
Wiener Filter   (remove salt and pepper noise from image)

Fig. 3. Image pre-processing.

2.2 Feature Extraction

It is assumed that pSS region is manually segmented, so that only pixels inside the region of interest are further analyzed. The feature extraction represents the process of transformation of selected pixels into the descriptive values suitable for learning classifiers. Since the pSS region is of varying area and shape, we suggested using histogram-based descriptors: Local binary pattern (LBP) and Gray-level co-occurrence matrix (GLCM).

2.2.1 Local Binary Pattern

The example of processed image and the obtained LBP histogram is given on Fig. 4. The LBP feature vector was created in the following manner [6]: (1) Divide the examined window into cells (e.g. 16 x 16 pixels for each cell). (2) For each pixel in a cell, compare the pixel to each of its 8 (in general N) neighbors (on its left-top, left-middle, left-bottom, right-top, etc.). Follow the pixels along a circle (with diameter R), i.e. clockwise or counter-clockwise. (3) Where the center pixel's value is greater than the neighbour's value, write "0". Otherwise, write "1". This gives an 8-digit binary number (which is usually converted to decimal for convenience). (4) Compute the histogram, over the cell, of the frequency of each "number" occurring (i.e., each combination of which pixels are smaller and which are greater than the center). This histogram can be seen as a 256-dimensional feature vector. (5) Optionally normalize the histogram. (6) Concatenate (normalized) histograms of all cells. This gives a feature vector for the entire window. In the present study, we used LPB of N = 8 and R = 4 presented below.

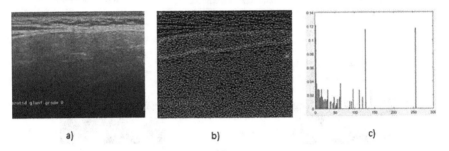

Fig. 4. Local binary pattern: (a) Original image; (b) LBP (N = 8, R = 4); (c) LBP histogram.

2.2.2 Gray-Level Co-occurrence Matrix

GLCM is a statistical method of examining texture that considers the spatial relationship of pixels. The GLCM functions characterize the texture of an image by calculating how often pairs of pixel with specific values and in a specified spatial relationship occur in an image, creating a GLCM, and then extracting statistical measures from this matrix (Fig. 5). After creating the GLCMs, we derived several statistics from them. These statistics provide information about the texture of an image. The list of features extracted for the purpose of the present study was as it follows: Autocorrelation, Contrast, Correlation, Correlation, Cluster Prominence, Cluster Shade, Dissimilarity, Energy, Entropy, Homogeneity, Homogeneity, Maximum probability, Sum of squares: Variance, Sum average, Sum variance, Sum entropy, Difference variance, Difference entropy, Information measure of correlation1, Information measure of correlation2, Inverse difference, Inverse difference normalized, Inverse difference moment normalized.

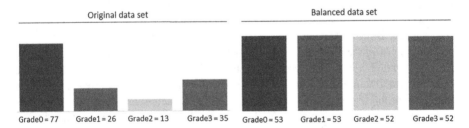

Fig. 5. Classes' distribution. Image left shows original-overall data set. Image left shows the learning data set balanced using the SMOTE algorithm.

2.3 Population Data

For the purpose of the present study we used a dataset of total 153 patients subjected for ultrasonography imaging of pSS. Distribution of each class (Grade 0–3) is shown on Fig. 5. The amount of samples for pSS Grade 4 and 5 was insufficient (2), so they were excluded. Moreover, 100 samples ($\sim$66%) of each class were used for the independent training, while 51 samples ($\sim$33% of each class) were used for independent subsequent testing. As it may be noted, the database had unbalanced distribution of classes – which was solved in training-stage by using the Synthetic Minority Over-sampling Technique (SMOTE) [7].

2.4 Features Selection

The feature selection if performed in order to minimize a number of features, by omitting these that are less correlated with the pSS. Using the wrapper for feature subset selection [8], out of 57 features extracted using LBP and GLCM, 21 features were elected as dominant for the learning process.

2.5 Learning Classifier

Seven different classifiers were considered: K-Nearest Neighbour (KNN), Decision Trees (DT), Naive Bayes (NB), Discriminant analysis classifier (DCA), Random Forest (RF), Multilayer Perceptron (MLP), Linear Logistic Regression Model (LR) implemented in Weka software [9]. Each of classifier was trained using 10-fold cross-validation training and data set described in Sect. 2.3.

3 Results and Discussion

The obtained results are given in Table 1. As it may be noted, the considered algorithms showed variations of the accuracy for learning-derivation data set and independent-test set. In terms of classification accuracy, three top-ranked algorithms on derivation set are: Multilayer perceptron, Random forest and K-nearest neighbour. Considering test set, three top-ranked algorithms on derivation set are: Naive Bayes, Multilayer Perceptron and Linear Logistic Regression. Assuming that, Naive bayes and Multilayer perceptron are suggested as most suitable for the purpose of pSS grade classification. It is worth to mention that the database used in this study represent result of on-going HarmonicSS H2020 EU project, which aims to integrate analysis of regional, national and international cohorts on primary Sjögren's Syndrome towards improved stratification, treatment and health policy making. Since it is well know that performances of machine learning algorithms are varying with database size scaling – presented results could be considered as preliminary indicators that could change as the cohort will growth over time.

Table 1. Classification accuracy of the considered learning algorithms.

Algorithm	Derivation set (Samples: 210)	Test set (Samples: 51)
Decision trees	75.4%	67.7%
Naive Bayes	72.8%	73.3%
Discriminant analysis	76.7%	66.8%
K-Nearest neighbour	83.2%	66.0%
Random forest	84.6%	68.2%
Multilayer perceptron	85.0%	70.1%
Linear logistic regression	82.9%	69.3%

4   Conclusion and Future Work

In the present study we performed assessment of state of the art classification algorithms for the purpose of pSS classification from ultrasound images. The assessment was performed using growing HarmonicSS (H2020 EU project which aims to integrate analysis of regional, national and international cohorts on primary Sjögren's Syndrome) data set. The preliminary results on the growing HarmonicSS cohort showed that Naive bayes (72.8% accuracy on training set, and 73.3% accuracy on test set) and Multilayer perceptron (85.0% accuracy in training stage, and 70.1% accuracy at test stage) are the most suitable for the purpose of pSS grade classification.

Acknowledgments. This study was funded by the grants from the Serbia III41007, ON174028 and EC HORIZON2020 HarmonicSS project.

References

1. Mavragani, C.P., Moutsopoulos, H.M.: Sjögren syndrome. CMAJ **186**(15), E579–E586 (2014). https://doi.org/10.1503/cmaj.122037
2. Shapira, Y., Agmon-Levin, N., Shoenfeld, Y.: Geoepidemiology of autoimmune rheumatic diseases. Nat. Rev. Rheumatol. **6**(8), 468–476 (2010). https://doi.org/10.1038/nrrheum.2010.86
3. Ramos-Casals, M., Brito-Zerón, P., Kostov, B., Sisó-Almirall, A., Bosch, X., Buss, D., Trilla, A., Stone, J.H., Khamashta, M.A., Shoenfeld, Y.: Google-driven search for big data in autoimmune geoepidemiology: analysis of 394,827 patients with systemic autoimmune diseases. Autoimmun. Rev. **14**(8), 670–679 (2015). https://doi.org/10.1016/j.autrev.2015.03.008
4. Baldini, C., Luciano, N., Tarantini, G., Pascale, R., Sernissi, F., Mosca, M., Caramella, D., Bombardieri, S.: Salivary gland ultrasonography: a highly specific tool for the early diagnosis of primary Sjögren's syndrome. Arthritis Res. Ther. **17**(1), 146 (2015). https://doi.org/10.1186/s13075-015-0657-7
5. Wiener, N.: Extrapolation, Interpolation, and Smoothing of Stationary Time Series. Wiley, New York (1949). ISBN 0-262-73005-7
6. Ojala, T., Pietikäinen, M., Harwood, D.: A comparative study of texture measures with classification based on feature distributions. Pattern Recogn. **29**, 51–59 (1996)

7. Chawla, N.V., Bowyer, K.W., Hall, L.O., Kegelmeyer, W.P.: SMOTE: synthetic minority over-sampling technique. J. Artif. Intell. Res. **16**, 321–357 (2002)
8. Kohavi, R., John, G.H.: Wrappers for feature subset selection. Artif. Intell. **97**(1–2), 273–324 (1997)
9. Frank, E., Hall, M.A, Witten, I.H.: The WEKA Workbench. Online Appendix for "Data Mining: Practical Machine Learning Tools and Techniques", 4th edn. Morgan Kaufmann, Massachusetts (2016)

Autonomous System for Performing Dexterous, Human-Level Manipulation Tasks as Response to External Stimuli in Real Time

Ana Neacşu[(✉)], Corneliu Burileanu, and Horia Cucu

Speech and Dialogue Research Laboratory, University Politehnica of Bucharest, Bucharest, Romania
{ana.neacsu, corneliu.burileanu, horia.cucu}@speed.pub.ro

Abstract. The system solves a complex puzzle, namely a Pyraminx (Rubik's pyramid), demonstrating the degree of movement complexity that the Kinova robotic arm can achieve. The system is composed of three important parts: the first one's main purpose is to capture real time images from the Kinect sensor and to process them into input data for the second module. The second part, the core of the system, performs all necessary computations in order to make a movement decision based on the available data. The third part represents an interface with the robotic arm, transposing the decision from the second block into pure movement data, passed to the Kinova's controller.

Keywords: Image recognition · Shape recognition · Color detection
Kinect · Robotic arm · Clustering · Autonomous system

1 Introduction

Nowadays, society tries to accept and integrate persons with various disabilities. They comprise an estimated population of one billion people globally, of whom eighty percent live in developing countries and are overrepresented among those living in absolute poverty.

The core of this project is the robotic arm created by Kinova robotics to aid people battling disabilities. For someone with severe motion disability some trivial tasks, such as picking up a glass of water may represent a challenge [15]. In this context, it is imposed to find an efficient solution to give these people some independence. Hence, the need to develop a system capable of performing human level motions.

The paper is organized as follows: Sect. 1 presents the motivation, the objectives and the outline of this thesis, along with some technical details about the hardware used to develop this project. Chapter 3 is the first chapter that illustrates contributions of the author of the thesis. It describes the data acquisition process and the image processing methods that were approached. Chapter 4 deals with the development of an algorithm that solves the Pyraminx puzzle. Chapter 5 focuses on the implementation the actual moves of the robotic arm. Finally, Chapter 6 summarizes the main conclusions of the thesis.

© ICST Institute for Computer Sciences, Social Informatics and Telecommunications Engineering 2018
O. Fratu et al. (Eds.): FABULOUS 2017, LNICST 241, pp. 246–252, 2018.
https://doi.org/10.1007/978-3-319-92213-3_36

1.1 Objectives

In this context, this thesis aims to present a system capable of performing a given task without any kind of human intervention. We want to achieve human-like dexterity – the Kinova robotic arm is equipped with six degrees of freedom, having the capacity to accomplish manipulation tasks that require high dexterity. In order to prove this point, we will use the robotic arm to solve a Pyraminx, as response to external stimuli, represented by images captured with a Kinect module in real time.

1.2 Hardware Technologies

In this paper, we use the Jaco 3 model, produced by Kinova Robotics. Launched in 2010, JACO is a six-axis robotic manipulator arm with a three-fingered hand. This device significantly improves the lives of persons with reduced mobility by assisting anyone with an upper body mobility impairment to perform complex actions. This robot has a total of six degrees of freedom, it is made of carbon fibre structure, it is light weighted and it can reach the floor with standard installation on wheelchair. The gripper offers the option of using two or three fingers. Each finger is covered with high friction rubber pads, making grasping objects easy [1, 2].

2 Modeling the Initial Setup of the Pyraminx

Pyraminx is a puzzle in the shape of a tetrahedron working on the same principle as a Rubik's cube. It consists in 4 axial pieces, that have octahedral shape, and they can only rotate around the axis they are attached to, 6 edges, that can be permuted in any direction and 4 trivial tips, that can be twisted independently. To permute its pieces, the Pyraminx must be twisted around its cuts [4].

2.1 Shape Recognition and Color Detection – Method I

The purpose of this module is to create a matrix of colors that describes the initial state of the puzzle that will serve as input for the solving algorithm. Figure 1 illustrates how the system works:

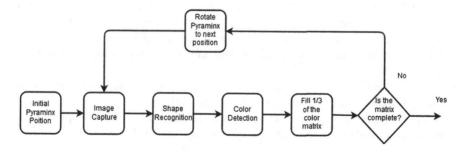

Fig. 1. Modeling initial setup

A. **Image Capture**

To be able to create a matrix that contains all the colors from the pyramid, is not enough to have only one image of the puzzle. As our objective is to create an autonomous system, we didn't consider the option of moving the Kinect sensor manually to take pictures from different angles. The solution that we've implemented consists in rotating the stand that is holding the pyramid using a servo-motor and a Hall sensor connected to an Arduino board, as seen in Fig. 2 [14].

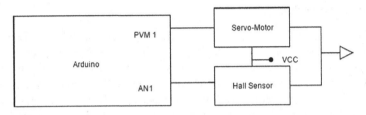

Fig. 2. Servo-motor configuration

The system works as follows: the Kinect sensor takes a picture, the servo motor rotates the pyramid at 2.09 rad, then a second photo is taken. To be able to obtain all the colors from the puzzle, three photos are needed, one for every lateral face (the top face appears in all of them).

B. **Shape Recognition**

Object detection and segmentation is the most important and challenging fundamental task of computer vision. It is a critical part in many applications such as image search, scene understanding, etc. However, it is still an open problem due to the variety and complexity of object classes and backgrounds [13].

The images obtained at the previous step must be processed, to extract the color of every triangle. In order to do that, we used a shape recognition algorithm that detects the vertexes of all the triangles from the image. The shape recognition is implemented using OpenCV library and consists of:

- HSV conversion – the image we capture using the Kinect is in RGB. We transposed it to HSV, because in this domain it is easier to perform color detection. The biggest problem was to detect the yellow color, because it was very close to the white edge. We obtained the best results using the Hue component [10].
- Canny edge detection - it is a multi-stage algorithm to detect a wide range of edges in the image [1].
- Triangle detection – we filter the edges found on the previous step and keep only the forms that can be approximated with a triangle [13].
- Filter out duplicate triangles – there is the possibility to have some duplicate vertexes, so we filter them to obtain the number of triangles that we need.

C. Color detection

After the previous step is performed, color detection becomes a simple task: using the coordinates of the three vertexes of all the triangles, we can find the middle point of each of them. We perform color detection on a small area around the middle of each triangle, using the HSV conversion [7]. Finally, after all the processing the program will return a 5×12 color matrix. Each row of the matrix represents a row of colors on the pyramid, and each 3 rows form a face of the puzzle.

Remark 1. Using this method, we have obtained good results only in certain conditions: natural light and white background. Because the colors of the puzzle are not matte, if there is too much light, it will be reflected; in this case the recognition task becomes much more difficult and the error rate increases significantly.

From the experimental point of view, we have observed that this algorithm does not distinguish between the yellow color of the triangle and the white contour of the Pyraminx, which lead to frequent and significant errors in the recognition task, even in optimal light conditions. Hence, we decided to try another method, presented in the following sub-chapter.

2.2 Shape Recognition and Color Detection – Method II

To overcome the disadvantages from the previous method, we tried a totally different approach, based on machine learning techniques, starting from the observation that, depending on the light and angle, the colors of the pieces have very different properties, covering a wide range of shades. So, for each color we defined several classes, to cover all the possibilities. Figure 3 shows how we obtained the color model. The idea is to train a system that can separate the colors form the Pyraminx, considering the colors to be discrete random variables. The separation is done based on two parameters of the image: the mean and the standard deviation [11]. In this method, the whole image is analyzed. Afterwards, the color detection is performed and the last step consists in shape recognition.

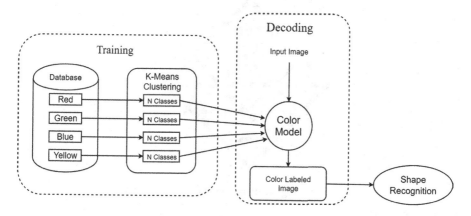

Fig. 3. Color detection algorithm

2.3   Data Acquisition and Clustering

To apply such an algorithm, we needed a database consisting in different images with the Pyraminx, which we created using the Kinect Module. The database contains 100 pictures of the puzzle, taken in different light setup (natural light and different neon light). Next, we have separated all the pieces from all the images based on their colors, using Paint.net, resulting in four images (one for each color) containing all the useful information from the database. These images were used for training a system that discriminates colors, based on two parameters: Mean and Standard Deviation [5].

We used K-means algorithm as a clustering method to separate each color in different classes. This vector quantization process derived from the signal processing domain. In data mining the method is very popular for cluster analysis. Parsing n observations into K groups named "clusters" is made based on the proximity of the observation to the prototype of the array [6].

Remark 2. Using this method, we have obtained better results than with the previous one, but still there were problems regarding the recognition of the yellow color, because it reflected most of the light. Hence, we decided to replace the shiny stickers from the Pyraminx with matte ones and use a unicolored background when the Kinect module takes the pictures. This way, the color recognition works perfectly, regardless the light conditions.

3   Solving Algorithm

In order to permute all the pieces, using a single arm and having the pyramid fixed on a stand, we developed an algorithm that will solve the puzzle using only 4 main moves, as showed in Fig. 4. We defined the moves in only one direction (clock-wise for move 1 and 2 and counter-clockwise for move 3); the reverse move is equivalent with two successive moves.

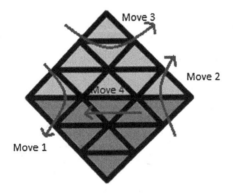

Fig. 4. Pyraminx moves

Using only these moves in different combinations, one can solve the Pyraminx in all situations. The algorithm we developed works as follows:

- *Align the Centers and Corners* - The first step in solving the Pyraminx is to know, even if the pieces are scrambled, what color corresponds to each face. There are two easy ways to figure out what is the color of one face: if one can match three center pieces having the same color on one face, that is the color of the face. The other solution is concentrating on the corner pieces. All three corner pieces from a face can be positioned to match color, and that is the color of the face. The next problem is to correctly position the center pieces, and that is done using a simple function. The verification must be done over just one face. If the centers are correctly positioned on one face, all the other center pieces will be in place. The same principle is applying to corners [3, 12].
- *Solve the Top Face* - After all the centers and corners are in place, the next step is to completely solve one face. This is done by placing the 3 edges corresponding to the color of the face we want to solve on their correct position. There are 12 different possible solution for each piece. The first possibility that we are considering in this algorithm is the one in which the desired side is placed on the top face, but not in the right position. In this case, the piece must be lowered on the second layer, and later positioned correctly on the first Layer. Depending on its position, a different combination of moves is required to lower a certain piece. After all the sides are placed somewhere on the second layer, we defined some fundamental sets of moves, that used to move a certain side into the right position [8].
- *Placing the Lower Edges* - After the top piece is solved, there are only three lower edges that can be out of place. Depending on their position, four different cases can occur, and for each a specific algorithm will be applied:
  - Case A: In the most fortunate case, after solving the top face, all the lower edge pieces are in the right place and the pyramid is solved.
  - Case B: one edge piece is in the correct and the other two need to be flipped
  - Case C: one edge pieces is wrong and the other two have one color that lines up with the adjoining side.
  - Case D: All three edge pieces are completely wrong but when you turn the top corner, they will line up with the bottom perfectly [9].

4 Performing the Moves

This part represents the interface with the robotic arm, transposing the set of movements computed by the algorithm into pure movement data, passed to the Kinova's controller. The input will consist in a string of numbers, each number being correlated with one of the four moves.

Since all the moves are complex and require high precision, the position of all the actuators are updated during a move, so the action is smooth and as natural as possible.

Controlling the robotic arm requires two steps: manipulate the arm using the joystick and then program the hand to automatically perform the action, using functions from the *.dll* file provided by Kinova, which receives as parameter an angle (how many degrees the actuator rotates from its previous position).

For the movement to look natural and coherent, the actuators are updated at different moments of time, synchronization representing one of the greatest challenges of this project. For each move, the arm starts from a default position, called home position and the final position of the actuators was experimentally found, using the joystick and the monitor function of Kinova Development Center API. By subtracting this new coordinates of each actuator from the values from home position, we deduced how many degrees each actuator must rotate, which is the parameter we need in our code.

5   Conclusion and Further Development

Our project represents just a small example of what one can do using a robotic arm as complex and efficient as the one from Kinova.

In the future, we want to develop a system that reacts to different types of real time stimuli: control the arm with vocal command.

Another improvement we would like to implement in the future implies equipping the arm with various sensors to improve furthermore its precision and autonomy. Interconnecting two or more such robotic arms, one can create a robot capable of performing almost all the moves that a human being can do.

References

1. Kinova robotics website. http://www.kinovarobotics.com
2. Kinova robotic Jaco User Guide. http://www.kinovarobotics.com
3. Pyraminx Puzzle. http://www.nerdparadise.com/puzzles/pyraminx
4. Rubik's Triangle. http://www.ruwix.com/twisty-puzzles/pyraminx
5. Hartigan, J.A., Wong, M.A.: Algorithm AS 136: a k-means clustering algorithm. J. Roy. Stat. Soc.: Ser. C (Appl. Stat.) 28(1), 100–108 (1979)
6. Kanungo, T., Mount, D.M., Netanyahu, N.S., Piatko, C.D., Silverman, R., Wu, A.Y.: An efficient k-means clustering algorithm: Analysis and implementation. IEEE Trans. Pattern Anal. Mach. Intell. 24(7), 881–892 (2002)
7. Sural, S., Qian, G., Pramanik, S.: Segmentation and histogram generation using the HSV color space for image retrieval. In: Proceedings of the 2002 International Conference on Image Processing, vol. 2, pp. II–II. IEEE (2002)
8. Frey, A., Singmaster, D.: Handbook of Cubic Math. Lutterworth Press (2004). ISBN 9780718825551
9. Beasley, J.: The Mathematics of Games. Dover Publications (2006). ISBN 0486449769
10. Bear, J.H.: What is the HSV. https://www.thoughtco.com/what-is-hsv-in-design-1078068
11. Li, F.-F.: Machine learning in computer vision. http://www.cs.princeton.edu/courses/archive/spr07/cos424/lectures/li-guest-lecture.pdf
12. Joyner, D.: Adventures in Group Theory: Rubik's Cube, Merlin's Machine, and Other Mathematical Toys, 322 p. Johns Hopkins University Press (2008)
13. Forsyth, D., Ponce, J.: Computer Vision: A Modern Approach. Prentice Hall, Upper Saddle River (2011)
14. Han, J., Shao, L., Xu, D., Shotton, J.: Enhanced computer vision with Microsoft kinect sensor: a review. IEEE Trans. Cybern. 43(5), 1318–1334 (2013)
15. Hendrich, N., Bistry, H., Zhang, J.: Architecture and software design for a service robot in an elderly-care scenario. Engineering 1(1), 027–035 (2015)

Recent Experiments and Findings in Baby Cry Classification

Elena-Diana Şandru$^{(\boxtimes)}$, Andi Buzo, Horia Cucu,
and Corneliu Burileanu

Speech and Dialogue Research Laboratory, University Politehnica of Bucharest,
Bucharest, Romania
{diana.sandru,andi.buzo,horia.cucu,
corneliu.burileanu}@upb.ro

Abstract. Studies have shown that newborns are crying differently depending on their need. Medical experts state that the need behind a newborn cry can be identified by listening to the cry – an easy task for specialists but extremely hard for unskilled parents, who want to act as fast as possible to comfort their baby. In this paper, we propose various experiments on a previously developed fully automatic system that attempts to discriminate between different types of cries, based on Gaussian Mixture Models. The experiments show promising results despite the difficulty of the task.

Keywords: Baby cry · Automatic newborn cry recognition · GMM-UBM
K-Fold cross validation

1 Introduction

Newborns are fully dependent on adults and they are able to communicate only by crying. In this manner, the newborns express their physical and emotional state; there are several reasons for a newborn to cry, but the list can be synthesized in: hunger, tiredness, pain, discomfort, colic, eructation. As a parent it can sometimes be hard to work out which need the newborn wants you to take care of, making the process of fast need satisfaction really difficult.

Specialists (neonatologists and pediatricians) have the necessary experience to distinguish between different types of cries and identify the newborn's need. Nonetheless, medical experts consider that determining the need behind the cry is more accurate if the expert also looks at the expression of the face or the position of the body; the experience level of the listener is also essential. In addition, the newborn's cry can be used to determine whether he/she suffers from pathological diseases, thus problems can be early discovered and attended, this being vital for the newborn. Cries which have an unusual sound, duration, intensity or height can show that the newborn is suffering from a specific disease [1].

The newborns' cry represents in fact a special case of human speech, being considered a short-term stationary signal (as the speech). However, the cry signal is a more random signal than a periodic one, since newborns do not have full control of the vocal tract. From functional point of view, a newborn cry is composed of four parts, in this

© ICST Institute for Computer Sciences, Social Informatics and Telecommunications Engineering 2018
O. Fratu et al. (Eds.): FABULOUS 2017, LNICST 241, pp. 253–260, 2018.
https://doi.org/10.1007/978-3-319-92213-3_37

order: a sound coming from the expiration phase, a brief pause, a sound coming from the inspiration, phase followed by another pause. Obviously, there are elements that can be individualized for each child, such as sound, pause duration or even repetitions [2]. Compared to adult speech, a cry represents a complex neurophysiological act, being the outcome of an intense expulsion of air pressure in the lungs, causing oscillations of the vocal cords and leading to the formation of sound waves [3].

Abou-Abbas et al. [4] determined important audible cry component boundaries of continuous recordings collected noisy environment, in order to build a cry database, thus contributing to developing different cry based applications.

The clear advantages of identifying the need behind a newborn's cry determined several researchers to build automated systems for recognizing newborn needs using the acoustic signals of cries. However, so far most of the studies have been focused on recognizing only one need, leading to detection systems. The current paper represents recent experiments conducted within the SPLANN[1] research project, which aims to build an automatic recognition system of the newborn cries – an identification system – for five key needs: colic, discomfort, eructation, hunger and pain.

The work is based on research performed a priori, representing a continuity of the following papers: development of a fully automatic system that attempts to discriminate between different types of cries using a database created and labeled based on the Dunstan Baby Language (DBL) baby-cry classification video tutorial [5] and using the SPLANN infant crying database [6].

Both databases are labeled at expiration level, therefore the previous detection [5, 6] was in terms of expiration. The novelty of this paper emerges from a new approach – the detection for SPLANN database is performed also at cry level, namely a succession of expirations (variable), instead of a single one. In order to obtain results at cry level, a score fusion technique was used. For automatic classification, we employed a method that was successful in speaker and language recognition: the GMM-UBM (Gaussian Mixture Model - Universal Background Model). At the same time, a series of experiments have been carried out to determine to what extent the signal bandwidth and derivatives of MFCC (Mel Frequency Cepstral Coefficients) features contain discriminative information between needs, in other words, have an impact in the accuracy of recognition.

The rest of the paper is structured as follows. Section 2 describes in detail the classification methods used in the experiments. Section 3 presents the recent experiments conducted in the baby cry classification area and finally Sect. 4 is dedicated to conclusions.

2 Baby Cry Classification Methods

The classification of a baby cry based only on the audio signal represents a task similar to the classification of phonemes, closed-set speaker identification and audio-based closed-set language identification. This study addresses the problem of newborn cry

---

[1] SPLANN research project: http://www.softwinresearch.ro/index.php/en/research-projects/splann.

recognition by classification algorithm based on GMM, successful in speaker recognition [7]. GMMs are trained with cry recordings from different categories, labeled in advance, as seen in Fig. 1.

The training is done in two stages; in the first stage, a universal model is trained using all the recordings from all categories – the algorithm for UBM training is EM (Expectation Maximization). In the second stage, UBM model is adapted using all the recordings of a specific type of cry – the algorithm used for this adaptation is MAP (Maximum A Posteriori Probability).

The process of recognition itself is simple: each test recording is evaluated with each GMM and is scored against that particular GMM. The model for which the highest score was obtained is the winner, being used to decide which need was causing the baby to cry – namely, the cry class attached to GMM will label the given recording.

As mentioned in Sect. 1, the aim of the study was to obtain results *at cry level*, namely a succession of expirations, instead of a single one. Thus, a score fusion technique was used (as illustrated in Fig. 2). This method involves three steps: (i) obtaining a score for each need (cry class) for each expiration, (ii) summing the need scores over a sequence of N expirations and (iii) comparing the scores obtained for each need. The need with the highest score is declared to be the need for the whole sequence of expirations (for the baby cry).

An important aspect regarding this approach is deciding whether the first expirations of a cry are more discriminatory than the rest. This question arises from the fact that if the newborn's need is not satisfied quickly, he/she begins to cry hysterically and the complaints of different needs begin to resemble. To test this hypothesis we filtered the first N expirations (by varying N) of each cry and trained and evaluated the system each time with N changed.

Driven by the small dimension of Dunstan database [5], K-Fold cross validation method was implemented as validation method, such that the results to be statistically significant. K-Fold means dividing the database as follows:

- all recordings of a need are randomly sorted;
- the database per need is split into 10 equal divisions;
- during 10 experiments with the same purpose, each division will be once a test database and 9 times part of the training database;
- steps 1–3 are repeated 10 times resulting 100 datasets;
- to compute the accuracy, the averages of each iteration with 10 folds is taken. From these, the final average and standard deviation are computed and reported in the experimental test sections.

The same approach was used for SPLANN database, but since K-Fold is an exhaustive method, an arbitrary database was used to vary the way of extracting the signal features (sampling frequency, derived features) – once the most appropriate features were chosen, experiments are conducted with K-Fold to take into account their statistical significance.

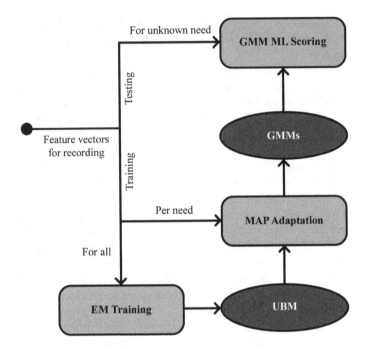

Fig. 1. GMM-based recognition scheme

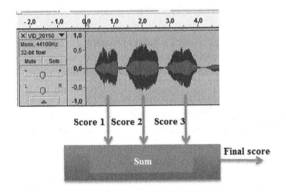

Fig. 2. Score fusion technique working principle

3   Baby Cry Classification Experiments

3.1   Baby Cry Databases and Audio Features

For the experiments presented in this paper, two databases are used. The first one –
Dunstan Baby Language Database [5] has been used to prove that information about
need is found in the spectrum of the signal; it contains cries for five needs: "EAIRH" –
flatulence, "EH" – eructation, "HEH" – discomfort, "NEH" – hunger, "OWH" –

tiredness. The second database used was SPLANN Infant Crying Database [6], seven times bigger than the Dunstan database; the recordings of the cries were collected in the hospital with the help of a mobile phone application.

The application allowed neonatal experts to easily label the need for crying after they diagnosed it (having the possibility to look at the face expression and body position of the newborn); the data labeling validation consisted in comforting the newborn. This database contains five types of cries (eructation, discomfort, hunger, pain, colic).

To characterize the cry type we used 13 MFCC extracted from overlapped windows (a similar setup as for speech and speaker recognition); moreover, we also used their derivatives and accelerations in order to determine to what extent the signal band and MFCC derivative features contain discriminative information between needs, in other words, have a role in the accuracy of recognition. For the validation we used K-Fold permutations. The metric used to compare different scenarios was recognition accuracy: the percentage of correct classifications among all classifications performed.

3.2 Experimental Results

A. Dunstan Database – Signal Bandwidth and MFCC Features Derivatives

The experiment aimed to determine to what extent the signal bandwidth and derivatives of MFCC features contain discriminative information between needs; the experiment was conducted at expiration level, using K-Fold permutations.

Table 1 illustrates the results obtained on recognition tasks; first column highlights the sampling frequency (implicitly indicating the signal bandwidth) and numbers 13 or 39 suggest that only MFCC (the 13 coefficients) or derivatives and accelerations (a total of 39 coefficients) were used. The values presented are average values, with the confidence interval of 95% being ± 6%. Columns 2 to 6 illustrate the results obtained starting with a simple GMM-UBM (4 Gaussian densities) up to a relatively complex model (with 128 Gaussian densities).

The results presented as recognition accuracy (percentage of correctly identified needs for the tested cries) are presented in Table 1. We can observe that when the signal band is larger, the recognition accuracy is also higher – this means that there is information about need at high frequencies. Also, MFCC derivatives and accelerations contribute to the discrimination of needs.

Table 1. Recognition results on Dunstan database (in percent)

Features/#densities	4	8	32	64	128
MFCC_8kHz_13	57.5	71.0	65.9	63.3	62.4
MFCC_8kHz_39	59.1	73.5	73.4	71.1	72.8
MFCC_16kHz_13	68.9	68.8	61.5	61.4	60.4
MFCC_16kHz_39	61.1	77.5	77.4	72.6	69.5
MFCC_32kHz_13	76.8	70.1	68.3	61.5	59.4
MFCC_32kHz_39	65.3	79.5	79.1	75.5	72.3

B. SPLANN Database – Signal Bandwidth and MFCC Features Derivatives

We replicated the same experiment presented in Sect. 3.2(A) for SPLANN database, but using the arbitrary database. Table 2 shows the obtained results at expiration level and Table 3 illustrates the recognition accuracy for the entire succession of expirations for a cry, using score fusion technique. Again, when the signal bandwidth is higher, the accuracy of the recognition is also higher – this means that there is information about need at high frequencies. At expiration level, MFCC derivatives and accelerations contribute to the discrimination of needs; however, the same behavior cannot be observed at cry level. It is possible the expirations recovered due to MFCC derivatives and accelerations may not affect the decision already taken based on other expiration.

Table 2. Recognition accuracy vs features and number of Gaussian densities at expiration level

Features/#densities	4	8	32	64	128	256	512
MFCC_8kHz_13	29.7	28.4	33.4	32.4	33.8	35.5	36.2
MFCC_8kHz_39	27.7	29.1	32.4	31.7	33.4	35.4	35.8
MFCC_16kHz_13	34.0	33.1	34.9	36.1	37.8	39.2	39.1
MFCC_16kHz_39	32.1	34.7	38.0	37.7	41.7	42.6	39.9
MFCC_32kHz_13	34.3	37.8	40.4	40.0	38.7	38.2	42.2
MFCC_32kHz_39	37,8	39.5	42.7	44.1	45.3	47.2	47.3

Table 3. Recognition accuracy vs features and number of Gaussian densities at cry level

Features/#densities	4	8	32	64	128	256	512
MFCC_8kHz_13	31.3	32.8	34.3	34.3	34.3	35.8	40.3
MFCC_8kHz_39	29.9	32.8	35.8	31.3	35.8	35.8	34.3
MFCC_16kHz_13	44.8	38.8	40.3	37.3	40.3	41.8	38.8
MFCC_16kHz_39	38.8	37.3	37.3	37.3	38.8	41.8	38.8
MFCC_32kHz_13	44.8	50.7	52.2	50.7	49.3	46.3	49.3
MFCC_32kHz_39	49.3	50.7	50.7	50.7	52.2	50.7	52.2

C. SPLANN Database – First N Expirations vs Entire Cry

Motivated to find how much useful information contains the entire succession of expirations in a cry, we performed this experiment to find if the first expirations of a cry are more discriminatory than the rest. This question arises from the fact that if the newborn is not satisfied with his/her need, he/she begins to cry hysterically and the cries due to different needs begin to resemble.

We filtered the first N expirations (by varying N) of each cry and we trained and evaluated the system every time N was changed. Because we expected the difference in results to depend strongly on the choice of the test database and given the fact that using this method the database has been compressed, we used K-Fold permutations to compute a confidence interval. It should be noted that not all the cries had N expirations; in these cases, all the expirations available from the cry were taken.

Figure 3 illustrates the recognition accuracy at expiration level – it shows a slightly decreasing trend with N. This trend is not observed in the results at cry level presented in Fig. 4. A possible explanation may be the following: the end-of-cry expirations that have a lower score fail during the fusion to overturn the score with the first exhalations. But with these results, we can neither accept the hypothesis nor reject it. The experiment should be repeated when a larger database is available.

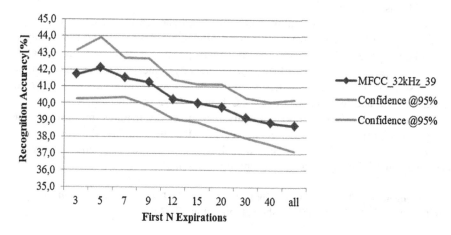

Fig. 3. Recognition accuracy at expiration level with the first N expirations

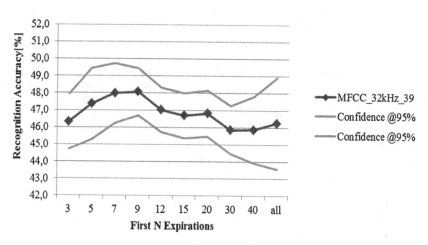

Fig. 4. Recognition accuracy at cry level with the first N expirations

4 Discussion and Conclusions

Motivated by our previous results on infant cry classification, we've extended our research on refining the previously developed automatic system that attempts to discriminate between different types of cries. The first important conclusion is that there are discriminatory elements in the signal spectrum captured in the MFCC features – confirmed by the experimental results where the accuracy much higher than the random threshold was obtained.

However, the level of discrimination is not good enough for satisfactory accuracy of the recognition system. Therefore, other features, e.g. features from time analysis, should be included in the analysis. The cry signal spectrum contains information about the need at frequencies up to 16 kHz. The features dynamics (their change over time) has a discriminatory role, as evidenced by the higher recognition accuracy when the derivatives and accelerations of the MFCC features have been used.

Future work involves an in-depth analysis of other cry features, but also of other recognition algorithms (such as Support Vector Machine). Finally, the crying recognition system must be integrated into a multimodal recognition system. This system may also contain image or video recognition elements.

Acknowledgement. This work was supported in part by the PN II Programme "Partnerships in priority areas" of MEN - UEFISCDI, through project no. 25/2014.

References

1. Reyes-Galaviz, O.F., Reyes-Garcia, C.A.: A system for the processing of infant cry to recognize pathologies in recently born babies with neural networks. In: Proceedings of the 9th Conference Speech and Computer SPECOM 2004, pp. 552–557, St. Petersburg, Russia (2004)
2. Zeskind, P.S., et al.: Development of translational methods in spectral analysis of human infant crying and rat pup ultrasonic vocalizations for early neurobehavioral assessment. Front. Psychiatry 2(Art. 56), 1–16 (2011)
3. Zeskind, P.S., Lester, B.M.: Analysis of infant crying, chapter 8 in biobehavioral assessment of the infant. In: Singer, L.T., Zeskind, P.S. (eds.), pp. 149–166. Guilford Publications Inc., New York (2001)
4. Abou-Abbas, L., Tadj, C., Fersaie, H.A.: A fully automated approach for baby cry signal segmentation and boundary detection of expiratory and inspiratory episodes. J. Acoust. Soc. Am. **142**, 1318–1331 (2017)
5. Bănică, I.-A., Cucu, H., Buzo, A., Burileanu, D., Burileanu, C.: Automatic methods for infant cry classification. In: Proceedings of International Conference on Communications COMM 2016, Bucharest, Romania (2016)
6. Bănică, I.-A., Cucu, H., Buzo, A., Burileanu, D., Burileanu, C.: Baby cry recognition in real-world conditions. In: Proceedings of International Conference on Telecommunications and Signal Processing, TSP 2016, Vienna, Austria (2016)
7. Togneri, R., Pullella, D.: An overview of speaker identification: accuracy and robustness issues. IEEE Circuits Syst. Mag. **11**(2), 23–61 (2011)

Author Index

Printed in the United States
By Bookmasters